HOLDING THE LINE

PRESERVING THE KENT AND EAST SUSSEX RAILWAY

HOLDING THE LINE

PRESERVING THE KENT AND EAST SUSSEX RAILWAY

N. PALLANT

ALAN SUTTON

First published in the United Kingdom in 1993 by
Alan Sutton Publishing Limited
Phoenix Mill · Far Thrupp · Stroud · Gloucestershire

First published in the United States of America in 1993 by
Alan Sutton Publishing Inc · 83 Washington Street · Dover · NH 03820

British Library Cataloguing in Publication Data

A catalogue record for this book is available from the British Library

ISBN 0–7509–0548–4

Typeset in 11/12 Times.
Typesetting and origination by
Alan Sutton Publishing Limited.
Printed and bound in Great Britain by
The Bath Press Ltd, Bath, Avon.

To Angela,
for everything else worthwhile

'Let not Ambition Mock their useful toil'

Elegy, written in a country churchyard,
THOMAS GRAY

Contents

Preface

'Of course, the old K&ESR Association never got anywhere . . .' The scene was Tenterden Town station some time in the 1970s and the speaker was someone who seemed to have only known the line after it had re-opened. Frankly, his words annoyed me, but, as I was not an active volunteer by then, it was neither the time nor the place to make an issue of the matter. I felt I knew differently. Even if my own contribution had been all too modest, I had been there at least some of the time. I knew just how much had been achieved and how much of themselves others had put into trying to re-open the line.

I have long had an ambition to set down the story of the Kent and East Sussex Railway Preservation Society (later the Association) and have been glad of the opportunity, which first presented itself in January 1991, to do just that. It is possible to tell this tale from either the 'volunteers' viewpoint' or as a 'company history'. Either perspective has its contribution to make and I have attempted to strike a balance between the two.

This book is in no way intended to be autobiographical, but some personal references are appropriate. Around these I have been able to build the course of events as seen by the volunteers. Personal impressions have also been a useful starting point for describing such intangibles as atmosphere and mood. This perception predominates in the first half of the story and arises naturally from the more intimate scale of the earlier days. Some might argue that such an approach should be excluded from a railway history, but the struggle to save the K&ESR involved real people, often driven by that most suspect thing – emotion. During the writing of the later chapters of the book, company history started to become more apparent, and it was not until I reread the text that I realized this reflected the growth, in all senses of the word, attained by the organization.

The K&ESR is said to have a unique heritage; a weak link is said to be a chain's strongest point. If the railway's history is viewed as a succession of linked episodes, then perhaps the strength of that heritage may be judged by the events which took place during that most critical of times, the ten years from 1961 to 1971.

Author's Note: A work of this kind must, of necessity, seek to reconcile differing opinions and recollections about the course of events. The right of individuals to dissent from opinions stated in this book is recognized. In instances where it has not proved possible to reconcile conflicting accounts, alternative versions are given.

Acknowledgements

Thanks are due to the following (mentioned here in no particular order) for their time, help and patience during the writing of this book: Andrew Webb, Richard Halton, Robin Doust, Derek Dunlavey, Philip Shaw, John Miller (particularly for access to the Tenterden Railway Company archives), Peter Carey, Derek Reader, Colin Edwards, Malcolm Dunstan, Ron Cann, Peter Benge-Abbott, Peter Davis, G.W. Pickin, George Jones, Ray Marlow, Dennis Ovenden, Dave Sinclair, Terry Heaslip, Cathy Roberts, Leonard Heath Humphrys, Chris Lowry and, for general encouragement and other assistance, David Stratton, Mark Toynbee and Donald Wilson.

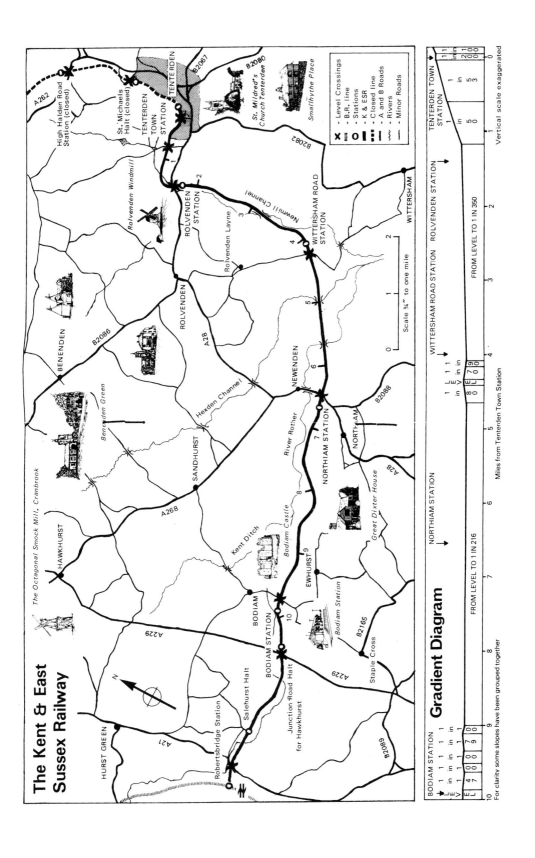

The Kent & East Sussex Railway

Legend:
- X – Level Crossings
- ▬ – B.R. line
- O – Stations
- ⋮⋮ – K & ESR
- ‖ – Closed line
- ═ – A and B Roads
- ∿ – Rivers
- — – Minor Roads

Scale ¾" to one mile

St. Mildred's Church Tenterden

Smallhythe Place

Rolvenden Windmill

Beneden Green

The Octagonal Smock Mill, Cranbrook

Bodiam Station

Bodiam Castle

Great Dixter House

N

Gradient Diagram

BODIAM STATION						
L in	in	in	in	in	in	in
E	L	1	1	1	1	1
V	4	0	0	9	0	0
L	7	0	0	0	0	0

NORTHIAM STATION	WITTERSHAM ROAD STATION	ROLVENDEN STATION		TENTERDEN TOWN STATION

FROM LEVEL TO 1 IN 216

FROM LEVEL TO 1 IN 350

Miles from Tenterden Town Station

Vertical scale exaggerated

For clarity some slopes have been grouped together

The Kent & East Sussex Railway

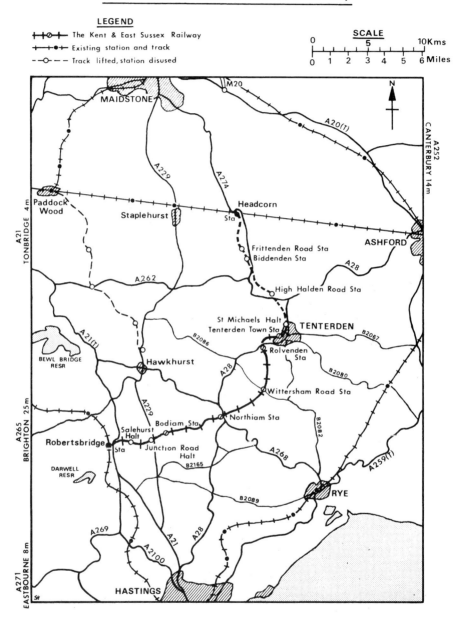

SCALE

0   5   10Kms

0   1   2   3   4   5   6 Miles

N

M20

MAIDSTONE

A20(T)

A252 CANTERBURY 14m

A229

A274

A21 TONBRIDGE 4m

Paddock Wood

Staplehurst

Headcorn Sta

ASHFORD

Frittenden Road Sta
Biddenden Sta

A28

A262

High Halden Road Sta

St Michaels Halt
Tenterden Town Sta

TENTERDEN

B2067

A21(T)

B2086

Rolvenden Sta

BEWL BRIDGE RESR

Hawkhurst

A28

B2080

Wittersham Road Sta

B2082

A265 BRIGHTON 25m

A229

Bodiam Sta

Northiam Sta

Salehurst Halt

Robertsbridge Sta

Junction Road Halt

A268

DARWELL RESR

B2165

A259(T)

B2089

RYE

A269

A28

A21

A2100

A271 EASTBOURNE 8m

HASTINGS

PART ONE
The Preservation Society

I

Sometime during 1951 my parents took me to the Festival of Britain, which was being held on London's South Bank. Various items of railway interest were on display, including the then new locomotive *William Shakespeare*. It was not, however, that mighty Pacific which was to remain among the fading memories of the occasion but the satirical and surrealistic railway created by the cartoonist Roland Emmett. It would never have occurred to me, a small boy fascinated by a collection of wispy, collapsing carriages and locomotives

Tenterden Town station during the 1960s (Chris Lowry)

with kettles, that this might have any basis in reality. It is possible, however, that this railway owed something to a cartoon border Emmett had completed for *Punch* which had appeared in that magazine's issue for 3 June 1946. His illustration accompanied a poem by C. Hugh Bevan about the Kent and East Sussex Railway.

That such a relatively obscure minor line should have achieved this much hold on the imagination of even a minority is, in itself, remarkable. The K&ESR was not old as railways go; it dated from 1900, was single track throughout its length and, when opened from the South Eastern and Chatham Railway at Robertsbridge, had initially been known as the Rother Valley Railway. The first terminus was at the present day Rolvenden station (then called Tenterden) and an extension to Tenterden Town came into use in 1903. A second, and much longer, extension to Headcorn on the Tonbridge–Ashford main line was opened in 1905. The first sixty-one years of the line's history have been carefully chronicled,[1] but it should be remembered that the K&ESR formed part of the light railway empire, or unofficial fifth 'Group', which was managed from offices in Salford Terrace, Tonbridge by Lt. Col. Holman F. Stephens.

'Light railways' (on which subject the Colonel was an acknowledged expert) were built in accordance with Light Railway Orders granted under the provision of the Light Railways Act of 1896. The Act encouraged railway building in areas where traffic was not expected to be heavy by easing various regulations, including those relating to gradients, line curvature, fencing, level crossings and station facilities. In exchange for these relaxations, restrictions were imposed on maximum speed and axle loadings.

The Colonel had very singular ideas about how railways should be run and kept most of his enterprises out of the railway amalgamations of 1923. The results of this were that by the 1930s the K&ESR had an alluring, eccentric atmosphere which owed much to its run-down rolling stock (a good part of which was second- or even third-hand) and not a little to the landscape through which it ran. The railway during this period has been described as a resort for railway enthusiasts and it certainly attracted the attention of the middle-class young men who would, in the postwar years, become the elders of a vastly expanded railway hobby. The K&ESR managed to survive Col. Stephens' death, the Depression and the Second World War, only to be nationalized in 1948, which in reality meant it was absorbed by its larger neighbour, the Southern Railway. Passenger services ceased in January 1954 and the section from Headcorn to Tenterden was closed altogether, although hop-pickers' specials continued on the southerly part of the railway until 1958.

But to return to 1954. On 7 January, only four days after the passenger service ceased, the following letter was sent to the Southern Region by a Mr S.J. Baker:

Dear Sir,

re: late Kent and East Sussex Branch

This line, so near London, is such a really rural museum piece that before the lines are uprooted is it not possible to consider preserving it as such? It does seem to be in a different category . . . from other branch lines . . .

What about the suggestion of a year's trial of the following: run a single coach steam train with just a driver and conductor who would collect the fares, and without any station staff. Surely in these days one could install an automatically fired oil burner to raise the steam, which would not require the services of a fireman.

The unit, if operated must be steam, not a diesel, in order to preserve the Victorian [*sic*] atmosphere; a similar sort of outfit used to operate between Oxted and East Grinstead . . .[2]

I appreciate that this line between Headcorn and Robertsbridge has been operating at a dead loss for many years, but as it is such an 'out of this world' section [it] ought to be preserved for that reason. Probably if the service suggested really connected with goods trains at each end, the numbers of passengers could be increased a lot.

Furthermore the character of the line and area are such that some income could perhaps be earned from Film Companies. Please give it consideration.

Mr Baker received the sort of curt and routine reply one would expect. An interesting thing about the letter was that, whereas Mr Baker had referred to the line as a branch, the official who replied to him referred to it as 'the Kent and East Sussex Railway' – almost as if he couldn't bring himself to think of it as part of BR! Otherwise, preservation might exist in far-off Wales, but the Weald was not then ready for such notions.

Growing affluence and leisure time for hobbies kept the K&ESR in the public eye, and enthusiasts' specials sometimes appeared. In particular, these included the 'Rother Valley Limited' railtour, organized by the Locomotive Club of Great Britain on 19 October 1958, and a Ramblers' excursion on 18 October 1959. It has been claimed that these trains did much to prepare the way for the story which is related in this book.

Phase two of the Kent Coast Electrification Scheme provided an opportunity for the Southern Region to tidy up its system in the South-east. Flood damage occurred on the K&ESR, in November 1960 and a 5 mph speed limit was imposed. Taking the opportunity, the Southern Region, through the British Transport Commission, which then had responsibility for the rail system, sought to close the line. It came as no surprise to some people when, in early 1961, Tenterden Town station was repainted – this was a common method of tipping a line's accounts into the red. The Transport User's Consultative Committee held the usual inquiry but there were only three objectors, one from Tenterden, one from Northiam and Tom Dadswell, the proprietor of Hodson's Mill at Robertsbridge. These protests were, of course, to no effect and in a further announcement it was made known that the line would close with effect from 12 June.

This left Tom Dadswell with a considerable problem. Hodson's Mill was slightly less than a mile from Robertsbridge station but relied on rail transport to bring in the grain which was its raw material. The SR had told Hodson's Mill (in a wonderful example of how not to conduct customer relations) that the final part of the journey would have to be made by road. This brought forth the reply that if the Southern would let him have an engine he would move the wagons himself. Nobody was more surprised than Mr Dadswell when he was offered a suitable locomotive then out of use at Brighton! This turned out to be P class No. 31556. The locomotive was inspected, a price agreed and No. 31556 arrived at Robertsbridge two days later on Friday 30 June. The BR crew gave the mill staff minimal instruction but help came from the local policeman, PC Young, who had previously been a BR fireman. No. 31556 went into use the next day and was named *Pride of Sussex* after one of the flours produced at the mill.

BR ran its final freight service on Saturday 10 June 1961 and the final passenger working was another LCGB special the following day. The nearby, and also much-loved, Hawkhurst branch closed the same day, and only Westerham, in the north of the county, was left to represent a railway scene that was fast disappearing. That line succumbed too in October, immediately producing a preservation project. But by then the history of the K&ESR had also taken a new turn.

The news that the K&ESR was to close became known to three of the senior pupils at Maidstone Grammar School – Tony Hocking, Gardner Crawley and Neil Rose. They discussed among themselves the possibility of establishing a preservation scheme for the railway. At that time railway preservation was coming to the end of what, in retrospect, was the first period of its history. The Talyllyn and Festiniog railways were reasonably well established and the Ravenglass and Eskdale was just emerging. To many people this was the preservation movement. On the standard gauge the Middleton Railway had come under the management of a Trust in 1959 and, while wishing neither to underestimate the achievements of that line, nor to ignore the existence of the Midland and Great Northern scheme (now the North Norfolk), it was the Bluebell Railway which was to show the rest of the standard gauge movement the way. Re-opened the previous year, the Bluebell had shown that it was possible to prise lines away from BR and successfully operate a service. Railway history in general was in the latter part of the phase which stretched from the modernization plan of 1955 to the Beeching Report of 1963. The result of this in preservation terms was that the focus was moving away from individual items of rolling stock (a trend which for practical purposes started with the purchase of the ex-LB&SCR 0–4–2 locomotive *Gladstone* by the Stephenson Locomotive Society before the Second World War) to the maintenance of the overall scene as a working museum.

Tony Hocking emerged as the most prominent of the grammar school trio and, following an item in the *Kent Messenger*, he was contacted by the equally youthful Robin Doust, who at that time lived in Tunbridge Wells but had spent part of his boyhood close to the line in the village of Bodiam. Tony and Robin met at Tenterden on what is remembered as a warm Saturday afternoon in March and laid their plans. One result of these was further media coverage by the now defunct Southern Television. This in turn gave publicity to a well-attended public meeting (some library books had to be borrowed on how to conduct this) which was arranged at the Rother Valley Hotel on the windswept marshes at 3.00 p.m. on 15 April 1961. The chair was taken by M. Lawson Finch, the first historian of the K&ESR, and in a mood of optimism among the 125 or so people present, a steering committee was appointed. Optimism had, however, been momentarily checked when somebody, speaking from the floor, bluntly told the meeting that no bank was going to loan them £50,000, but then cheered everyone up again by wishing the scheme good luck. A further awkward moment was also provided by someone on the platform (who it was is not recorded) who, having said that the Bluebell Railway was a success, then added, 'We have seen what Sussex can do. Let's see what Kent can achieve.' He was sharply reminded he was still in Sussex!

The aims were, at that stage, to run full passenger and freight services, winter and summer, with voluntary labour assisting a small full-time workforce. It was a scheme to run, on the standard gauge, a functioning railway and not merely a demonstration line. Steam was envisaged as the principal form of traction but mention was also made of obtaining an ex-GWR railcar. By the end of the meeting the Kent and East Sussex Railway Preservation Society had been formed. The first members were signed up, by Robin Doust, immediately afterwards.

That inaugural meeting was similar to many held, both at that time and over the following years, as the pace of rail closures increased. The K&ESR scheme had, however, some essential differences: the length of the line involved and the proposal to run freight and local services. With the exception of the Middleton Railway (which had had a particularly singular history and background), none of the then existing schemes had any notion of carrying freight. Their purpose was to keep their line (and steam-hauled stock) running by means of tapping the tourist and enthusiast market. If they picked up any local passenger traffic that was a bonus. The approach taken by the K&ESR project was in part a recognition of the line's past and possible potential and also, it has to be said, part of a reaction which was building up against the Bluebell Railway's early management style. That line's very title and the slogan 'Preserving the Puffer for Posterity' was not popular with everybody. None of this is intended as a criticism of the Bluebell Railway which was dipping its toe in the murky but lucrative pool of a commercial approach. The underlying arguments of commercialism and development versus authenticity are still part of the steam railway movement's ongoing, and increasingly sophisticated, debate about what it should be doing.

Robin Doust has written vividly of the appearance of the K&ESR during that period:

I recall with feeling my first ride on the line after its closure together with Tony Hocking. On a scorching hot summer day after 12 June 1961, we were making a very unofficial inspection of the rather doubtful collection of assets which was all that was left of the railway, when we came across a long disused and very rusty SE&CR pattern platelayer's trolley in a ditch at Rolvenden, and were unable to resist the temptation to go for a ride on it. We rolled along quite merrily down the slight gradient towards Wittersham Road, along track already sporting long grass, yellow in the summer sun, and shedding clouds of seed at our passage. However, coming back was another matter, and we arrived back at Rolvenden later in the afternoon pouring sweat and footsore after a long, hard push – I'm sure Tony was slimmer after that occasion than ever again since! That day was also the day I opened the railway telephone box at Rolvenden, and picked up the earpiece of the ancient wooden cased Ericsson telephone to examine it, to be shocked into speechlessness when a voice actually answered from Robertsbridge demanding to know who the hell was playing with it – those were the days before the copper wire thieves got to work, and it may have been the last time the through link was ever used, since by the time of our visit a few days later, the line was dead.

The K&ESRPS was not without its critics and one letter which appeared in *Railway Magazine* stands out in memory. This said that if it had been possible to turn the clock back to the 1930s and preserve the Colonel Stephens engines, the ramshackle rolling-stock and the old yard at Rolvenden, nobody would have contributed more willingly than the correspondent. He went on to add, however, that the K&ESR was just another British Railways goods branch and one rather less interesting than most!

To describe the K&ESR, at any point in its existence, as 'uninteresting' would seem to miss the point, while to wish to preserve the 'ramshackle' aspects of the railway begged various questions about what might happen over the ten years that followed, let alone later decades.

The fledgling Society's early approaches to the Southern Region had been interpreted as favourable (the early correspondence was, indeed, not discouraging), but progress seems to have slowed somewhat by the time of the first Annual General Meeting on 15 July 1961. This was held in Tenterden Town Hall, a delightful Georgian building straight out of *The Mayor of Casterbridge*. The Town Hall had a large central meeting room which was used for local functions of all kinds, and a stage at one end eminently suitable for speakers addressing a gathering. Members would come to know the Town Hall meeting room well over the years.

The AGM itself is worth relating in some detail. Robin Doust (who by this stage was K&ESRPS Secretary) opened the meeting and then proposed that Mr Lawson Finch once again take the chair. After some initial remarks he handed back to Robin who explained that difficulty had been experienced in getting information out of BR. He had dealt with this in a manner which those who came to know him would soon recognize as typical of his characteristic tenacity. He had visited Waterloo and seen the Deputy General Manager of the Southern Region, Mr McKenna. This direct approach led to Robin being informed that there was a legal difficulty over the running of trains by anyone other than BR over the line's level crossings. The matter was being considered by the Ministry of Transport and until a decision had been reached no further progress could be made. This, in retrospect, has something of the 'fob-off' about it but the Deputy General Manager added that there was no intention of removing the track until the future of the line had been decided. He saw no reason why the Society should not be allowed to establish a light railway museum at Tenterden and would contact the Rating and Estates Department so that arrangements for the Society to rent the building could be made as quickly as possible.

Tony Hocking then told the sixty people present that the Society had just over £80 in the bank and about a hundred members, before there was a more general discussion which included the appearance of Dennis Pope, a well-known figure in railway preservation at the time and notable for his large black moustache and a motorcycle-sidecar combination named *Hesperus*. The latter part of the meeting saw the election of a formal Committee, which was: Mr M. Lawson Finch, Chairman; Mr W. Morris; Mr B. Sharp (a former employee on the line), Track Maintenance Adviser; Mr Doust, Secretary; Mrs Sykes, Rolvenden Representative; Mr C.J. Mills, Tenterden Representative;

Mr R.A. Harman, Treasurer; Mr Cross; Mr W.H. Austen, Engineering Adviser; Mr L. Heath Humphrys. The last two names are interesting: Mr Austen was the son of the line's former manager, who had taken over after Col. Stephens' death. Bill Austen junior had also worked for the K&ESR (as well as for the East Kent Railway) and had been responsible for civil engineering. Leonard Heath Humphrys was an important figure during the revival of the Festiniog Railway, in the days when that famous narrow-gauge line was being brought back from limbo. The list is, incidentally, almost exactly as published, and with its use of the titles 'Mr' and 'Mrs' is an interesting social comment on the period. Such things are, of course, far less rigorously used now (even in similar lists issued by the Tenterden Railway Company).

An account of the AGM was carried in the second edition of the K&ESRPS newsletter, *The Farmers' Line*, a typical duplicated club magazine of the days before desktop publishing and cheap photocopies. The newsletter was mainly written by Robin Doust and there were two other items which pointed to future developments. The first of these was that the Society had been offered 'at least one locomotive', while the second announced that representatives of the K&ESRPS and BR had met at Tenterden on 8 August to discuss the use of the station by the Society. The keys were received on the morning of Saturday 30 September. TheK&ESR had a headquarters.

II

It was during a Sunday afternoon in October 1961, and as a result of an exchange of letters with Robin Doust, that I first arrived in Tenterden and found where, between the fire station (now demolished) and the Vine Inn, Station Road led downhill from the broad, tree-lined High Street. In a like manner to Mr Baker in his letter to BR, many who know the K&ESR would recognize the existence of a special, almost tangible sense of presence in the area served by the railway, whether the countryside be marshland or Weald. This feeling is particularly intense in the town, and can almost amount to 'a sense of something else' or place-memory of all the centuries which have linked Saxon 'Tenet-wara-den' with modern Tenterden. Whatever the reason, the K&ESR has undoubtedly drawn on, and perhaps contributed to this. It was immediately apparent on that October afternoon and awareness of it has been renewed with each subsequent visit.

Tenterden Town station was simplicity itself. The building was brick-built but functional without being unattractive. Some modern point levers were to be seen (all ground frames, there was no signal-box) but others owed more to the nineteenth than the twentieth century. The most striking thing was the sea of long, waving grass which covered the whole station area and fanned out from the ungated level crossing towards the cutting at the far end of the yard.

The work in hand included cleaning up outside the station building, scrubbing the booking office, which was remarkably filthy, and weeding the platform loop, which for the K&ESR was surprisingly well ballasted. Shortly after arrival a cultured and slightly built young man introduced himself. This was Robin Doust and he immediately impressed me by remembering our brief correspondence. By the end of the afternoon the Society had acquired another member.

Tenterden was the traditional headquarters of the railway and there were good practical reasons (the standard of the building, transport links, facilities in the town) why the station should continue in this role. It nevertheless, and together with the magnetic appeal of the town, made the project Tenterden-centred, when even the earliest preservation proposals gave emphasis to the line in its entirety. This has continued down to the present, sometimes against the intentions of those managing the project and on occasion because events have conspired to that end.

Initially, one's personal contact with the K&ESR was confined to discovering the remainder of the line. Up to Bodiam, with its romantic and famous castle, the railway ran through fairly typical East Sussex countryside. This carried on to Northiam, where the scenery changed as the broad valley of the Rother met the long arm of Romney Marsh which came up from the sea. The land was flat and the railway ran across the natural rises and falls in what had, in times past, been the sea bed.

It was in the valley more than anywhere else that the railway appeared to have grown out of the ground. Salehurst Halt had disappeared altogether and Junction Road stood in grassy loneliness by the highway. Bodiam appeared to be decaying fast, although a coal merchant still operated from the yard. Despite the ever-present grass and undergrowth, Northiam was perhaps a little better and the coal trade reasonably brisk. Wittersham Road had also vanished except for its siding, but the most startling sense of desolation was at Rolvenden, once the site of the locomotive shed and workshops. All that remained above rail level was the water tower (said to incorporate the frame of the four-wheel railbus of 1905), the water crane and the platform mound. This last item, although topped by a corrugated-iron hut, resembled a Bronze Age barrow in the bleakness of Hardy's Egdon Heath.

Around this time another permanent way inspection trolley came to light in the trolley hut at Tenterden. This was of the 'row-boat' rather than 'pump' type, a design in which the crew sat on the floor and operated the top bar of a propelling frame with their hands and the bottom with their feet. Being the Society's nearest approach to rolling stock, the trolley was repainted and lined out in Col. Stephens' Oxford blue locomotive livery, and, in a modest way, looked quite impressive. The trolley, mounted on a float and complete with crew in Edwardian costume, was entered for Tenterden Carnival in March 1962, where it won the Society a second prize.

The Southern Region had thrown the Society a crumb of comfort at the end of January when it had offered to sell the Tenterden–Rolvenden section. As this in no way met the aspirations of the K&ESRPS, the Society's position was made clear to the Estates and Rating Department during a meeting at Victoria. After some weeks' further thought the Southern Region agreed to

Valuation Inspection party at Tenterden on 7 June 1962. The first four men from the left are BR officials, followed by Leonard Heath Humphrys, Robin Doust and George Jones (George Jones collection)

sell the entire line, and although no price was given this represented something of a victory. Both parties subsequently met on site on 7 June to discuss the exact boundaries of the property to be sold to the Society.

Also during this period, BR made another offer to the Society which might have completely changed the course of events. On two occasions, and during the course of discussions with Southern Region officers, it was suggested to the K&ESRPS that it move its activities to the Hawkhurst branch. For all its attractive qualities, and its somewhat higher standard of construction, the Hawkhurst line was not seen as having that additional individuality which was part and parcel of the K&ESR.

Activity, which mainly consisted of attacks on the sea of weeds and other undergrowth, was at first confined to the Tenterden station area but soon began to spread down the bank towards Cranbrook Road. Despite the recent repainting of Tenterden Town station, some further attention was discovered to be necessary and the Southern Region on hearing of this wrote to complain that the painting of windows exceeded the terms of the tenancy agreement. Robin Doust, in inimitable fashion, exercised his creativity and replied that it was not windows which had been repainted but window frames. Despite this minor hitch, BR had no general objection to the Society carrying out maintenance on the railway as it helped to prevent the line becoming too much of an overgrown eyesore. The museum, which had been part of the *raison d'être* for renting the station, was established in the parcels office, the Society HQ being in the booking office. The museum collection included tickets, handbills, photographs and other small relics, while Eddie Bye from

Norwood built, at his own expense, a 4 mm scale layout which represented Rolvenden and Tenterden during the interwar years. Eddie also built a smaller, portable layout of Wittersham Road for use at exhibitions.

The volunteer force, although not large, was beginning to grow. Robin Doust and Len Heath Humphrys were frequently around, as were three lads from the town, Alan Crotty (who was to pick up an interest in photography from Robin), Dave Webber and Colin Beaumont. Another local boy, who at about twelve years of age must have been one of the youngest volunteers, was Ricky Lawrie. Colin Beaumont's parents owned a greengrocer's shop in the High Street and it was here that the spare key to the station was kept. In those more trusting times it was possible to gain access to the premises, on reasonable proof of identity, simply by going and asking Mrs Beaumont for the key. Later on, when Robin Doust was in need of 'digs' and wished to be near the railway, he lodged with the Beaumonts in the flat above their shop.

Micky Sargeant, a BR employee and friend of Dennis Pope, began to put in an appearance, having worked with him on the Bluebell line. Today, the two railways enjoy a special relationship. It was not always so and in the early 1960s there was a steady trickle of ex-Bluebell volunteers arriving at Tenterden, following their disenchantment with the regime at Sheffield Park. One Sunday afternoon two young men arrived at the station on a motorbike. Their names were Dick Beckett and Derek Dunlavey and both were BR engineering apprentices who had at first joined the Bluebell Railway to gain some additional professional experience. They had, however, found themselves washing up. Deciding that enough was enough, they had abandoned the dirty dishes and headed for Tenterden. Their appearance was fortuitous as the talked of arrival of 'at least one locomotive' was developing into some definite news.

Len Heath Humphrys told the 1962 AGM about these motive power developments. The locomotives in question were to be donated by the Standard Brick and Sand Company of Holmethorpe, near Redhill, Surrey, and were named *Dom* and *Gervase*. Both were of Sentinel design (at least nominally in one case) with vertical boilers and four-wheel geared drive. Len had handled the negotiations with Standard Brick and Sand.

Gervase had originally been built by Manning Wardle in 1900 as a conventional 0–4–0 saddle tank for J.S. Peters of Merstham. By 1928 she was completely worn out and was rebuilt by Sentinel at Shrewsbury to an approximation of one of their designs which retained only the frames and running plates. Even the wheels, which continued to be coupled by rods, were of Peckett origin. *Gervase* moved to Holmethorpe in November 1949.

Dom was a more conventional Sentinel but had had, if anything, an even more bizarre history. She had been built in 1927 as the engine portion of a railcar on the Jersey Eastern Railway. *Dom* came to the mainland in 1929 and worked in Chatham Dockyard before sale to Peters at Merstham in 1935, where the gearing was altered to make it suitable for shunting. She preceded *Gervase* to Holmethorpe, going there in 1946. While with Standard Brick and Sand, the original bodywork was replaced with an adequate but rather crudely finished structure.

Gervase was delivered to Tenterden on a low-loader, twenty-four hours late, on 14 June 1962 and after a certain amount of dashing up and down the A28 in members' cars. She became K&ESR No. 10 and *Dom* No. 11 after her arrival the following day. As delivered, both were in a faded green livery. On arrival, *Gervase* proved to be the better of the two and work on her began immediately, parts being cannibalized from *Dom*. Robin Doust sent out a press release about the arrival of the locomotives and as a result was asked to meet a reporter from a local paper at Tenterden. The journalist looked at one of the rather battered new arrivals and remarked, 'Is it a diesel?'

It had been decided as early as 1961 to form a Locomotive Trust to raise money to buy the motive power and own the locomotives separately from the railway and the risks attendant to running it. Transport costs for *Dom* and *Gervase* were supposed to be £30 and to be met by the Society. It was planned to form the Locomotive Trust when the bill arrived but it never did. For the moment, the formation of the Trust was postponed.

These events did, however, lead to the establishment of the Loco Department, led by Dick Beckett and Derek Dunlavey. These two were firm friends despite the fact that, in many ways, they could not have been more different. Dick, the motorcyclist, came from Surrey and, despite the grammar school background he shared with Derek, had a touch of the 'Rocker' about him. He possessed an acerbic (and then fashionable) wit and was mercurial of temper, which left no one in any doubt should they have upset him. He was also a skilled engineer and an entertaining companion. Derek by contrast was a Geordie, although his family home was by that time in Bexhill. Outwardly he appeared the southerner's image of the Tyneside working man and he certainly possessed all the skills traditionally associated with the North-east. His considerable abilities enabled him to talk on anything from the Theory of Relativity (he also had a keen interest in science fiction) to the plays of Shakespeare, a number of which he seemed to know intimately. He also had a calm and tolerant personality which marked him out at an early stage for the leadership he soon assumed among the volunteers.

The Loco Department, whose early secondments included Alan Crotty and Dave Webber, established itself in the corrugated signals hut at the end of Tenterden yard and conveniently close to the short siding where the locos were stabled. To start with the hut was a model of tidy working, every item of equipment being stored in racks along the walls. Unfortunately this admirable system soon degenerated into a heap of permanently missing tools and numerous arguments.

The boost to morale provided by the presence of *Dom* and *Gervase* led to a perceptible increase in the tempo of activity. Volunteers began to find it necessary to stay in Tenterden overnight and people began camping out in the booking office. This was the only accommodation available (the booking office had both a stove and a small gas cooker) and greasy volunteers, together with their piles of blankets and baked bean tins, began an uneasy co-existence with the secretarial side of the Society.

The Loco Department got used to being the centre of attraction and being asked silly questions by the camera-and-duffel-bag brigade (fluorescent anoraks had not been invented then). *Gervase* required a complete overhaul, a major task being the removal of the firebox from the boiler. This really required a pit but no such thing had been available on the Kent and East Sussex since the demolition of Rolvenden shed in the mid-1950s. Such challenges are the stuff of which railway preservation is made and this problem was overcome by the simple expedient of digging a large hole between the rails. Unfortunately, when the volunteers returned to Tenterden the following Saturday, and thanks to the high local water table, they found they had a viable well and no pump to drain it. Much heaving of buckets later, work resumed. Eventually, and after an impeding inch of scale had been removed at the bottom, the firebox was dropped out using an improvised hoist.

By the end of the year the magazine was reporting that the Society's insurers had passed the boiler, subject to a few areas of corrosion being welded, and that hydraulic and steam tests were awaited. All boiler mountings were removed and repaired, while the axle-box bearings were checked and found to be in much better condition than expected. The springs were in a poor state (one had seven leaves broken) but they were repaired. The original feed-water pump was missing and was replaced with conventional injectors.

One of the first attempts to partially move the focus of attention away from Tenterden was under way during the latter part of the year. Work was begun at Northiam and a large contingent of volunteers from King's College, Wimbledon, under the leadership of Alan Dixon, spent their autumn half-term holiday there. They succeeded in clearing the station up to a noticeable extent and the Committee started issuing pleas for volunteers to report to the new scene of activity.

Some time during this early period the Society was told that the body of the four-wheel Royal Saloon which, in Col. Stephens' time, had become K&ESR carriage No. 10 still existed as a summerhouse at Plaistow in Sussex. Recovering the saloon would have been a major coup for the Society and immediate efforts were made to trace it. Regretfully these were too late; the bodywork had been broken up a few months earlier and only the base remained.

By late 1962 the magazine had evolved from the duplicated *Farmers' Line* into the printed *Rother Valley Railway*. The Commitee had agreed to the change of format on 7 October and to the new name on the 28th of that month, although the title was still being discussed as late as 1 December! In the Christmas edition, the regular progress report (written by Robin Doust) stated that the Society's valuer thought the line was worth about £37,000 and that negotiations were continuing for a loan amounting to around 70 per cent of this figure. It was proposed to raise the remaining 30 per cent of this, together with working capital, by a share issue. A Tenterden resident who was a member of the Society (later revealed as being a Mr Davis) had shown an interest in taking up 51 per cent of this and possibly the whole amount. He also indicated he would do this on much more favourable terms than those which would have been available from a City source. A Special General Meeting was to be called when further information was available.

On the locomotive front a fund had been established to purchase Terrier No. 32670 (formerly K&ESR No. 3, and the last surviving example of the old railway's rolling stock) and three coaches, but further donations were earnestly requested. Captain Howey of the Romney, Hythe and Dymchurch Railway had offered the Society his 0–4–4 tank locomotive *Dunrobin,* together with its accompanying saloon coach for £1,100 and that these purchases would be pursued as soon as negotiations for the line had been completed. Sadly, *Dunrobin* was one of the first of a list of locomotives which did not make it to the railway – she eventually went to Canada. More hopefully for the future, the Western Region had stated it was prepared to sell a diesel railcar to the K&ESR for £600, although this was rather more than the Society could afford and the idea was temporarily dropped.

In the previous September it had become known that the Committee had considered the possibility of purchasing a tramcar from the then recently closed Glasgow system for use as a refreshment and bookstall facility at Tenterden. This proposal had led to 'considerable controversy' and resulted in a questionnaire being sent to members to ask whether or not they wanted the tramcar. In the event the answer was 'No' (eleven for, fifty-four against) but the subject gave rise to a series of letters in the *Rother Valley Railway* which were notable both for their 'Disgusted of Tunbridge Wells' tone and for contemporary attitudes towards railway preservation.

One in particular, which was published in the Christmas 1962 edition, was among the most interesting and typical. The writer of this letter argued that, although the proposed facilities were obviously desirable, a tramcar would be an incongruous sight which would offend any real supporter of the K&ESR, and that if the Society turned the railway into a fairground for visitors local people would not be prepared to take it seriously. The correspondent then became prophetic and suggested buying a motor lorry instead and moving the museum away from the station building (both achieved many years later). He further suggested that if private individuals wanted to buy a tramcar they keep it at the 'other place' (i.e. the Bluebell Railway), and invited further correspondence by stating that it would be interesting to learn what other members thought constituted 'Preservation'.

The replies rumbled on for a few months, one including the first appearance of sentiments which will be familiar to anyone with even a quite recent knowledge of the railway: 'Come to think of it, Col. Stephens would quite certainly have introduced [ex-GWR] railcars on his lines, so perhaps [they are] not so out of the way after all.'

III

In the world beyond the K&ESR, 1963 was regarded as having been one of the most significant years of the twentieth century. It began with one of the worst winters in living memory and by New Year's Day southern England had disappeared beneath a blanket of snow. On the K&ESR work became virtually impossible, although a few of the most determined continued to arrive in

Tenterden at weekends. The Locomotive Department were among those who struggled on and Derek Dunlavey later recalled digging a component from *Gervase* out of a snowdrift.

During January Southern Region representatives had met Society officers in the frozen depths of Robertsbridge to discuss extra land which the Society hoped to purchase (including the section to Hodson's Mill), use of the SR's water facilities and sidings which K&ESR trains would use. These would have to be extended to form a run-round loop and a separate platform built. A document, addressed to the Southern Region authorities, dated 13 February 1963 and signed by Leonard Heath Humphrys, indicates that the locomotive release line would have to be long enough to accommodate an ex-SE&CR 01 class 0–6–0 or, most intriguingly, an ex-GWR 'Dukedog' 4–4–0. It was hoped that access to the bay platform would eventually be regained.

Other locomotive types previously considered (during the inaugural meeting in 1961) included the ex-L&SWR Adams radial 4–4–2Ts and the Beattie 2–4–0 well tanks. Consideration was later given to the Manning Wardle 0–4–0 saddle tank which had been Wantage Tramway No.7. She was in poor condition, however, available for only £80 and ultimately was not preserved. In addition, Robin Doust had sent one of the Society's then numerous begging letters to the owners of an unusual Peckett 0–4–0 side tank. This locomotive belonged to Hardman and Holden Ltd of Manchester and, much to everyones' surprise, they were prepared to donate her to the K&ESR. Her name was *Marcia*.

The *Rother Valley Railway* for January/February announced that the Society had taken over Bodiam station. This brought the number of work sites on the line to three. Fortunately, thought had been given to the need to do something about improving the volunteers' ability to move themselves, as well as equipment and materials, around the railway. The solution was found in a very strange conveyance that somehow had about it the ethos of the K&ESR of old – a 1934 Morris 20 motorcar. This vehicle was loaned by Brian Blackwell, an ebullient, striped blazer-wearing, travelling ticket inspector from Essex who was also interested in non-vintage 1930–40 cars and subsequently did much to establish a proper historical regard for them. The dark blue and black Morris was particularly suitable because its wheels were 4 ft 8½ in. apart and conversion to rail use was easily achieved by substituting inspection trolley wheels for the ones with rubber tyres (with Coke cans for hub caps) and locking the steering. Many years later, and after he had sampled travel in a number of countries across two continents, Robin Doust was to write that the Morris provided the most comfortable journey he had ever made on rails. Apart from Brian Blackwell, the railcar's two most regular drivers were Andrew and Malcolm Webb, twin brothers from Crayford in north-west Kent. They were entrusted with this task partly because they were among the first of the younger volunteers to pass the (road) driving test and because they were seen as two of the steadier personalities among the same group! The Webbs both worked for Post Office Telephones and consequently had skills, quite apart from driving, which were of use to the Society. The complement of crew is said to have never looked less than twelve!

The Morris railcar was quite adequate on an outward journey from Tenterden but was quite unsuitable for driving long distances in reverse. Not only was the maximum speed reduced from 40 mph to 5 but rapid overheating occurred. This was the cause of blown core plugs on two occasions (as well as incurring the wrath of Brian Blackwell) and it was realized that some means had to be found of turning the car. This was achieved by unlocking the steering, getting the car off the rails, carrying out a three-point turn and reversing the process. This was alright if a level crossing was handy (not one on a public highway of course – perish the thought!) but otherwise turning involved manhandling the vehicle, which weighed about a ton, off the track. It was on one of these latter occasions that a wheel ran over Kevin Blakiston's foot. Fortunately Kevin, who worked for the CEGB, was wearing the 'Toetector' steel-capped boots supplied by his employers and he got away with bruising. 'Toetector' boots became quite popular among the volunteers after that. The railcar could also haul a loaded flat trolley, which allowed a reasonable load to be carried.

It is worth pausing in the narrative for a moment to relate the atmosphere on the K&ESR two years into the preservation project. On arrival in Tenterden the town's special presence, which was described earlier, was, as ever, readily apparent. For a Londoner, even one from the suburbs, the air was at once both cleaner and richer, although, Tenterden not being a smokeless zone, Station Road often produced a curious though not unpleasant blend of fresh air, domestic coal smoke and vegetation. By the level crossing beyond the station a rural landscape opened up and fell away back towards Rolvenden. The railway was below the level of the High Street but its elevation was above much of the countryside lying to the south-west of the town. Some lines of my own free verse describe this scene towards the end of winter:

> ... the chasing
> Clouds somewhere over the valley. Behind
> The filters of the distance the hills shade
> Down, even in this colder air, through greys,
> Past blues. Mid distant the trees crack bare,
> Long fingers across the paler, whitening
> Edge of a sky that climbs towards the
> Deeper blue of the zenith. Foreground rough
> Grassland seems frost-burnt brown by winter.

For the summer scene one's own words are inadequate and it is necessary to turn to Thomas Hardy's description of Blackmoor Vale: 'The atmosphere beneath is langerous ... the prospect is a broad rich mass of grass and trees, mantling minor hills and dales ...'

It has often been noted that this broad vista once extended further, but immediately opposite the station has, since the 1940s, been obscured by several buildings of a design midway between a Nissen hut and a blister hangar. These had originally been built to house a government 'buffer depot', where emergency food supplies were stored. In the early 1960s the depot contained sugar, a substance which appeared to have attracted every wasp in south-west Kent. At one time the insects were a positive menace on that side of the yard. Eventually the relevant ministry cleared the resulting infested mess out of one of the buildings and with it the ammunition boxes the sugar had been stored in. Ammunition boxes were afterwards to be found the length of the K&ESR containing track parts, loco parts and a host of other items. Some may still be in use.

The station scene was in that condition preservation sites have often had part way between the departure of BR and the achievement of their full independence. Grass still appeared in numerous places where it should not have been, the flower beds were overgrown (with indications of some efforts to tidy up) and in the yard occasional piles of sticky yellow clay were to be found where holes had been dug. A ten-speed racing cycle against the station wall indicated that Robin Doust was around. Robin could often be found in the booking office, which was where he tackled the Society's paperwork. The office, like the station itself, had its own distinctive musty smell, but no one seemed to suspect the dry rot which, many years later, led to the whole floor having to be replaced. In the middle of the room was a typical railway stove, its iron pipe chimney going straight up through the ceiling. The shelves next to the ticket hatch contained a large collection of the *Railway Magazine* stretching back to the pre-war years. In one corner was a pile of blankets, while in another was the small table which served as Robin's desk and on which his portable typewriter (a vital piece of equipment for the Society) could usually be found. Nearby was the telephone. STD had not yet reached the town, and its number, Tenterden 43, had been in use for some years. The reconnection of the phone line after the volunteers' arrival had brought an entry reading 'K&ESR' (with 'Preservation Society' added) back to the directory.

Out in the yard one might perhaps look up on hearing the chimes of the clock in the fifteenth-century tower of St Mildred's Church and notice trees which had appeared in photographs of the railway for decades. Coal staithes still held their black diamonds but the coal merchant had become reliant on delivery by road. Beyond the platform end and across the running line and the sidings were the personnel and assets of the Loco Department. *Gervase* was being slowly re-assembled and her shabby green paintwork was disappearing beneath a new coat of Oxford blue. Dick and Derek would usually be hard at work assisted by a growing band of able lieutenants, which included Alan Crotty, Dave Webber, Kevin Blakiston and Alan Castle. The Loco Department would usually greet their fellow members cheerfully enough, providing you did not stop them for too long. Whether he stopped for a moment or not, Derek Dunlavey would be constantly relighting his well-known trademark – a hand-rolled cigarette. On occasions when he was working on some grubby part of a locomotive this would take on the appearance of an emaciated cigar. Other volunteers would be involved in clearing the weeds and undergrowth and, in the museum, Eddie Bye was to be found at work on the model railway, often aided by John Smallwood.

But in these early times it was *Gervase* that tended to be the centre of attraction. This even took on a charmingly rural dimension – quite in line with caricatures of the K&ESR – when a pair of robins (yes, there were lots of jokes at the Secretary's expense about this) nested in one of the front buffers, entering through a hole in the middle of the face. On the mechanical front the first steaming gradually drew nearer. Eventually the work reached the stage where *Gervase* could actually be lit up and, according to one witness, there were at least six people on the footplate as the pressure gauge reached the boiler's operating figure of 280 lb per sq. in. *Gervase* being vertical-boilered, the 'pop' type safety valves were mounted in the cab. Everyone appeared to have forgotten this and, while they were looking for leaky pipes, at the water level and so on, the safety valves lifted with a tremendous boom. This was quite normal, but in the circumstances led to a hurried mass evacuation. They thought the boiler had exploded!

Gervase proved to be a reliable, very powerful but rather slow locomotive. She performed well despite sundry clunks, jerks, the noise of the transmission chain, and the strange waddle which characterized her movement. The injectors played up from time to time and could sometimes, but, as we shall see, not always, be cured with a swift blow. At this distance in time it is probably safe to admit that her early use was unauthorized – by BR – although the boiler was insured. She was steamed on a number of occasions and it was during one of these that her crew ventured out of the yard and down the bank. On approaching Cranbrook Road a car was noticed parked near the level crossing. It quickly became apparent that this belonged to the Kent Police, then just beginning to earn their fearsome reputation in transport matters. Apprehension immediately set in and a rapid retreat was made back to Tenterden station. This was probably quite unnecessary as the policemen in

Gervase, as restored, in the summer of 1963. The lad in a peaked cap is Ricky Lawrie. Ricky tragically died some years later while still a young man (Tenterden Railway Company)

the car may well have been curious, taking a break or parked by Cranbrook Road for some other reason. *Gervase* was often accompanied by the unpowered *Dom* and it was said more than once that No. 11 would never run under her own steam again. This proved to be accurate but she was at least beginning a humble if useful career as a brake van.

In contrast to these heartening developments the general progress of the project had slowed down again. The Society had submitted a counter offer to BR based on the amount of money the backer (as the *Rother Valley Railway* still referred to him) was prepared to put up.

King's Wimbledon were continuing work at Northiam and were making progress clearing the track. They always seemed detached from the main volunteer group, but if one visited the station while working in the area the building would be found in good order with working electricity and a small stove available for cooking.

It was stated in the Preface that some personal references are relevant. One such is in connection with the museum, as it was in the spring of 1963 that I started to assist Eddie Bye, particularly with the model railway. This, at times, earned me a certain amount of comment from other volunteers, much of it regarding the usefulness of these activities. Although maintaining the railway's heritage was (and is) vital and there were some publicity spin-offs, after nearly thirty years it has to be said they were probably right!

In my defence, I must state that I was then part way through the transformation from 'spotty Herbert' with number-filled notebook to serious railway enthusiast and presented a very fair approximation of that later creation, Private Pike of *Dad's Army*. As such, the museum work fulfilled a need to be one of the lads (at least in my own estimation) and useful among so many of my volunteer contemporaries who were already acquiring skills. All this had positive effects in the end and I was, not too long afterwards, to be found in work parties on the line. Railway preservation has done as much for many other unassertive young people, as was once noted by *New Society* (a now vanished weekly magazine) in relation to evidence it had found, appropriately enough, on the K&ESR.

On 22 June 1963, the Annual General Meeting was held and the membership again gathered in Tenterden Town Hall. Robin Doust stated that the Society had got BR's price for the line down to £38,500 and much of the remainder of the meeting was concerned with fairly routine business. There was, however, some dissent when it came to the election of the Committee. Half its members were, in accordance with the constitution, to resign, three out of the six people involved being prepared to stand again. Rightly or wrongly, the Chairman, Mr Mills, proposed that these three be elected *en bloc* and this was seconded by Henry Frampton-Jones. An objection was then raised by a Mr Pickin (who at that time was unknown to most ordinary members) and who wished three members of the Committee to be elected individually rather than *en bloc*. After this matter had caused some delay to the proceedings, he was persuaded to withdraw his proposal, no seconder being forthcoming. This was the first time Mr Pickin had appeared at a General Meeting, although he was to become a prominent figure in the early years of the project. He had also been writing to various Committee members for some months previously.

Mr Pickin states that at this AGM he presented various proposals regarding ideas he had formulated for the revival of the railway. He has told me that among these was the idea of buying the line by 'hire-purchase' (i.e. by instalment payment or via a mortgage), BR having told him this would be possible. The minutes make no mention of this, although a contemporary newspaper account says that he accused the Committee of making 'wrong policy'. The wording was broad enough to have possibly included the hire-purchase issue. The idea was significant, however, and would arise again on the long road to re-opening the railway.

Before the meeting was closed there was one other interesting little incident. Tony Hocking reported that the K&ESRPS membership of the Railway Preservation Association (not to be confused with the Association of Railway Preservation Societies) had been a waste of time. He had been invited to attend only one meeting and found on arrival that the K&ESRPS was the only Society represented. He had not heard from the RPA for over six months and, not surprisingly, the meeting agreed not to renew the Society's membership.

At the station a sudden flood of members leaving the meeting found what was to become one of the most enduring memories of that day – *Gervase* trundling about under the watchful eye of a BR inspector. The Society was running a locomotive with official blessing, but not very far. There was no running down to Cranbrook Road on this occasion and the inspector objected when *Gervase* got too near the level crossing at the end of the station.

The arrival of the Society's third locomotive, the 1923-built Peckett, *Marcia*, was the next major event. Following Hardman and Holden's offer to donate this diminutive 0–4–0T, provided the K&ESRPS paid the transport costs, Derek and Dick visited Manchester to assess *Marcia*'s condition and found that not only did she look like a conventional steam locomotive but that she was in reasonably good condition. Being an industrial locomotive, *Marcia* had no vacuum brake but her size hardly indicated that she would be used on passenger trains. Seventy pounds was required to pay for transport costs and this amount was to be raised by six members, this exercise being intended to bring about the formation of the proposed Locomotive Trust. But again the bill didn't turn up and, again, the formation of the Trust was postponed.

Marcia arrived by low-loader at Tenterden on 18 July. Her nameplates had been removed at the request of one of the donor's directors. The loco bore the name of his wife and he did not wish its use to continue. But names have a habit of sticking, even if on the K&ESR the little Peckett officially became No. 12. Her very small size, which made a Terrier look large by comparison, and tiny driving wheels seemed to belong to a smaller gauge and she arrived wearing the same shade of weathered green which *Dom* and *Gervase* had first carried. She was, at least nominally, a runner, and her boiler certificate was not due to expire for a fortnight. The temptation to steam her was irresistible, so much so that she was first lit up one weekday summer evening with a view to a run down the line. In the cab, the pressure gauge rose to the magic 160 lb per sq. in. and the regulator was opened. *Marcia*, however, gave a loud hiss and refused to move. It was evident that the locomotive would not start without some persuasion. The effective solution to the problem was to insert a pinch bar between the wheels and rail and lever accordingly. After some runs up and down the platform road it was time for the 'off'.

Despite these events taking place midweek, about fifteen volunteers were present and it was decided to take *Dom* along to accommodate everybody and to act as a brake van. All went well on the downhill run to Rolvenden, *Marcia*'s small wheels revolving at what seemed a furious rate. Once at Rolvenden the decision was taken to carry on towards Wittersham Road. Soon afterwards the guard, Robin Doust, seeing that the track was heavily overgrown and knowing that the permanent way was in doubtful condition, thought it best to try and slow the train by the time-honoured method of applying the handbrake in the van (i.e. *Dom*). This proved all too effective as the train came to a halt amid some giant gorse bushes. (The reaction of the footplate crew was unprintable.) Attempts to restart only led to ferocious wheel slip on *Marcia*'s part, which gradually made an already slimy mess of crushed vegetation on the track even worse. The prickly undergrowth was even making it difficult to leave the train, but two of the braver souls eventually descended to the track armed with pinch bars and handfuls of sand. Their efforts were successful and *Marcia* was persuaded to move forward.

Some distance on another stop was made, this time by the Newmill Channel Bridge. (Throughout the remainder of this book the then existing bridge will be referred to as 1029[3] to distinguish it from the present-day structure.) The stop was made to check 1029 before proceeding. The bridge was in appalling condition, the abutments having been undermined both by flooding and one of the numerous springs in the area. It had been a critical factor in the closure of the line and had a distinct dip in the middle. Crossing 1029 produced mild anxiety, rather like the feelings experienced taking off in an aeroplane, but continued to do its job at a minimal level until the new bridge was built by the Tenterden Railway Company.

Although the volunteers decided to press on along the line, *Marcia* appeared to think otherwise and showed even greater reluctance to get under way. The train stopped again near Wittersham Road, where the track had been distorted by heat, and there the little locomotive gave up altogether. The valve gear was now in such a condition that the left-hand cylinder was trying to drive *Marcia* in one direction while the right-hand cylinder was intent on driving her in the other.

The sun was beginning to set as Robin Doust and another volunteer set off towards Wittersham Road in search of help. The Rother Levels area was a lonely place and it soon appeared that the Society's efforts at publicity had not reached an isolated farmhouse which possessed the only telephone line visible. Once the sight of smoke rising above the trees had convinced the farmer that his unexpected visitors were neither mad (well, possibly not) nor about to rob him, the use of the telephone was obtained. There then followed a lunatic sequence of events, lasting some twenty minutes, while Robin persuaded the operator of the manual exchange that Sheffield Park was not in Yorkshire and before the Sussex dialect of Charlie Kentsley of the Bluebell Railway could be heard at the other end. Although Charlie had a wealth of knowledge on locomotive matters and was only too anxious to help (he was planning to move to the K&ESR at that time), *Marcia*'s ailments were beyond even his expertise. The sad end to this night's work was the dropping of *Marcia*'s fire and the abandonment of two-thirds of the K&ESR rolling stock (excluding the Morris 20) in one of the most remote spots in south-east England. The final act was played out by the farmer who drove one batch of volunteers back to Tenterden and by Dave Couchman who returned to Wittersham Road in his Morris Minor to collect the remainder.

An anxious few days followed before a rescue could be attempted. *Marcia*'s tanks had been rapidly emptying when the fire was dropped and the nearest water was a mile away. A swift discussion on the following Saturday morning (this included Charlie Kentsley who had come over for the day) led to the conclusion that, taking everything into consideration, the best hope was to steam *Gervase* and retrieve the other two locomotives. *Gervase* had, however, not been steamed since the AGM and this had been enough time for mischief to set in. Tenterden station boasted precisely one tap in the late summer of 1963, and this had to serve for mixing cement, brewing tea, cleaning volunteers and (via a long and leaky hose) filling the tanks of locomotives. It had taken an hour to fill *Gervase*'s 400 gallon tank but, by a commendable 10.30 a.m., steam had been raised. No sooner had Dick Beckett opened the regulator than the bottom of the tank cracked, the water gushed out and another fire had to be dropped. Undaunted, the resourceful Loco Department rushed off to Webb's in the High Street to buy a quantity of rapid-drying waterproof cement. An hour later the whole process started all over again and this time everybody had crowded onto the footplate when, guess what? The cement cracked and a further 400 gallons of water descended onto the track.

Success was achieved after a layer of polythene sheeting had been laid over the bottom of the tank, although a persistent leak was evident. *Gervase* and working party headed off to Rolvenden, and the last remaining water crane on the line, before running unsteadily through the overgrown section near 1029. Here, further water was taken on by means of a bucket chain, the filling-up only just keeping ahead of the leak. It was early evening before *Marcia* and *Dom* were sighted. There was a rapid coupling up and a hurried return to 1029 where the buckets went back into action again.

Gervase's right-hand injector was already out of action, and no sooner was an attempt made to top up the boiler than the left-hand injector failed as well. It was a moonless night (even today the area can attain a medieval darkness beyond the villages and small towns) and there was no alternative but to dismantle the left-hand injector by the flickering light of a flare lamp. While this was being done a small brass component was dropped irretrievably into the undergrowth and the prospect of an even more ignominious abandonment loomed. In desperation the right-hand injector was tried and it worked. One final, and in the darkness dangerous, topping up of the tank and *Gervase* restarted, only to slow again half a mile from Rolvenden through lack of coal! Fortunately the volunteers had brought a number of bow saws with them and, by rapidly pillaging the abundant supply of wood growing by the line plus a telegraph pole, the situation was retrieved.

The train stopped again for *Gervase* to replenish her tanks at the water crane but nearly ran out of steam 300 yd up Tenterden Bank. Events thus far had contained more than an echo of *The Titfield Thunderbolt* and the parallel was about to become even more pronounced. Undaunted by the one-in-fifty gradient, twenty volunteers climbed down to the track and started to push, while Charlie Kentsley stared intently at the rapidly disappearing water level in the gauge glass. The combined weight of the train was over 35 tons which, while not much by most railway standards, was enough on a steepening gradient at the end of a tiring day. At Cranbrook Road steam pressure was allowed to build up again before the level crossing and the last section into Tenterden was attempted. The remaining climb up to the station was taken at 7 mph, with everyone back on the footplate, a full head of steam and the chimney roaring and emitting wood sparks in a most spectacular fashion. As in the previously mentioned film, and despite the late hour, the doors of houses near the line flew open and the populace came out to see what 'that lot at the railway' were doing.

It has to be admitted that much in this episode hardly sounds promising for a Society intending to run a full public service, and would probably not be acceptable today. Other problematical runs will be related in subsequent chapters but it is accurate to say that, during the first ten years of preservation, the K&ESR never had another day quite like that one. Laughable and amateurish these efforts may seem, but it would be a mistake to dismiss them lightly. They revealed much of the tenacity and ingenuity which, in the years up to 1971, were to serve the K&ESR very well indeed.

Peckett 0–4–0T Marcia *(No. 12) and Terrier No. 3 in front of the Rolvenden water tower in 1966.* Marcia *is in her first, Oxford blue, K&ESR livery, while the Terrier still has her final BR livery. Note the obliterated decals and numbers (Dennis Ovenden)*

IV

Early in September 1963 members received the following letter signed by Robin Doust in his capacity as Secretary:

> Enclosed . . . you will find a copy of the Society's detailed prospectus relating to the re-opening of the line. The prospectus is designed to serve a dual purpose. Firstly, it has been inserted in every copy of the September edition of the magazine *Railway World* with the principal object of obtaining nationwide publicity. Secondly, it is intended to give all members of the Society the opportunity to invest in the Railway, an opportunity, the possibility of which has been the subject of many enquiries by members for several months.
>
> In order to complete the outright purchase of the line, a sum amounting to £11,000 is required, and it is essential that we should know whether this amount will be forthcoming by 1 October this year, by which date we are required to give the Southern Region a definite answer as to whether we wish to proceed with the purchase.
>
> There has been an amazing amount of publicity attached to our project, particularly since we have set ourselves to run a commercial enterprise and public service of a nature which certain quarters have deemed as impossible. Our railway constitutes an opportunity, possibly the last ever to be presented in this country, for private enterprise to be allowed to run a standard gauge public railway service, as opposed to a mobile museum, and it provides a last opportunity for those many people who feel the wholesale closure of branch and secondary lines will mean the draining away of the life blood of the main lines to demonstrate their interest in a practical way.
>
> However, whether you would like to give a last branch line a last opportunity to operate on an economic basis, or whether you feel that branch lines should be retained on the grounds that they provide a public service, or whether you are fed up with the state of the country's roads or whether you feel that branch lines are an integral part of the structure of English country life and should be preserved like Ancient Monuments – whatever your reasons for wanting to see branch lines in general remain open, and the Kent and East Sussex in particular to re-open – now is the opportunity to demonstrate your feelings in a practical way by helping in however small or large a way . . .

The sum of £11,000 quoted was the amount required over and above that which it was hoped would be supplied by the backer plus the initial operating capital.

The prospectus itself gave the information that the purchase price had now been reduced to £36,000 and that the offer of £27,000 by the local backer was on the basis of the railway being 'leased back' to the Society for 'an agreed period of years'. There was no indication of what might happen after the lease expired. Other offers were, however, invited. Bridge 1029 was seen as 'requiring attention' and it was hoped to re-open the line in two sections: Robertsbridge–Northiam and Northiam–Tenterden Town. The intention of running both freight and passenger services was restated. It was hoped to carry 90,000 railway enthusiasts and make an operating surplus annually. BR had advised that it intended to put the permanent way up for tender by scrap merchants if the Society was not in a position to complete arrangements by 31 October.

The prospectus envisaged a threefold organisation for the railway: a Limited Company to operate and own, or lease, the line; the Preservation Society (which would become a Company Limited by Guarantee and supply volunteer labour); and 'The Kent and East Sussex Historical Trust', which was much the same idea as the Locomotive Trust but was to concern itself with those 'items of historical interest which no longer play any part in the day to day operation of the railway'. This aspect of the proposals was never proceeded with and the care of such items came under the general organization of the Society and its successors.

The back page of the prospectus consisted of a form which enabled members and others to contribute financially to the scheme by way of donations, provide bank guarantees or state if they wished to purchase shares in the event of a public company being floated. Any money received would, in the meanwhile, be held by the Kent and East Sussex Appeal Trust. The Trust, which was separate from the Society, had been established the previous year to take advantage of the provisions of the trust fund laws. All Appeal Trust officers were members of the Society.

The Special General Meeting to discuss the prospectus and the issues associated with it was held in Tenterden Town Hall on 7 September 1963. The Chairman, Mr Mills, was unwell and the meeting was opened by Leonard Heath Humphrys, his opening remarks reiterating much of what was said in the prospectus. The local backer required the payment of 8 per cent interest on capital or Bank Rate (now Minimum Lending Rate) plus 4 per cent. He added that an alternative, albeit an expensive alternative, to the backer's offer was to float a public company and that the meeting had been called to decide on a course of action.

Mr Heath Humphrys then opened the meeting to the floor and various general points were raised. These were typified by Mr Penny's questions about the valuation of the land and the movable assets. (Arthur Penny specialized in asking uncomfortable questions at General Meetings, while stopping just short of actually making then abrasive. He later became a Committee member.) A Mr Wethers suggested establishing warehouse accommodation at the station sites, and was told that the possibility was being actively investigated. This reads very oddly in the 1990s, when warehouses have sprouted along Kent's main roads to a chorus of disapproval, and probably no one would dare suggest building one in the Rother Valley. I have been told that this, and later similar ideas, were derived from the Derwent Valley Railway's success with such schemes. The Derwent Valley line, a freight-only standard-gauge enterprise of similar size to the K&ESR, had escaped nationalization and was looked on in the early 1960s as something of a model privately owned line. It is further understood that Leonard Heath Humphrys had discussions with the Derwent Valley's General Manager and potential users.

Mr Pickin then suggested that as the Beeching plan would leave a wide area without a delivery service for small traffic, the K&ESR could pick up the traffic using Tenterden as its main base. In view of the Society's aims, this seemed a reasonable proposition, with no comment on it being recorded in the minutes of the meeting. Had the original aims of the scheme been successfully pursued, it is not impossible that the K&ESR would have attempted to run such services.

Mr Penny asked what type of company it was proposed to form, although the prospectus clearly stated that it could be private or public and that Counsel's advice was awaited on this point. Furthermore, the Chairman of the meeting had, of course, already touched on the subject. It seems odd that such an astute gentleman as Mr Penny should have raised the subject. Perhaps he had been primed to highlight this area for the benefit of members. The Committee seem likely candidates for having done this, as towards the end of the meeting Mr Penny proposed the formation of such a company, the proposal being carried unanimously. The seconder of this motion was Malcolm Dunstan from among the volunteer force.

Len Heath Humphrys closed the meeting and informed everyone that refreshments were to be found at the station where, at least temporarily cured of their previous ailments, *Gervase* and *Marcia* were in steam. Reading the minutes of that afternoon, indeed recalling any of the early general meetings, one is struck by the divide between the lofty aspirations voiced in the Town Hall and the on-site reality known to the forty or so regular volunteers. *Marcia* and *Gervase* might be in steam, but bearing in mind the events described in the previous chapter, they could have been running on another railway.

A Financial Sub-Committee was set up as a result of the SGM and enough money had been subscribed or guaranteed (although still not the full amount required) for the Society to have accepted BR's offer to sell the line subject to contract. Once a sale contract had been agreed, occupation and use of the railway would be permitted pending completion.

The Society's solicitors were working on both the details of the contract as well as bringing the K&ESR Company Ltd into legal existence. Once formed, the Company, which it had been decided would be a private company, would take over negotiations. Optimism was still running high and it was expected that the line would become the property of the Company at the beginning of 1964.

In the meantime, and rather nearer to the grass roots (in both senses of the phrase), Ron Wheele, a Brighton businessman, had, together with his brother Vic, offered to buy the K&ESR a Terrier. The exact locomotive had not been decided at that stage and, in any event, its release from BR service depended on the closure of the Hayling Island branch.

By this point, a small group of Society members who lived in the Surrey area had emerged under the leadership of Roger Crombleholme, a prominent member of the Narrow Gauge and Light Railway Society. Roger had the idea of buying Terrier-sized industrial locomotives from the ironstone mines in the Midlands and fitting them with vacuum brake equipment to work passenger trains. This now seems to have been part of the natural development of the steam railway movement. At the time it was close to revolutionary.

Scouting trips to the ironstone country revealed two locomotives which would be available rather sooner than No. 3. Both were 0–6–0 saddle tanks – an advance which seemed a quantum leap after the vagaries of *Marcia* and *Gervase* – and both were in the ownership of the Park Gate Iron and Steel Company of Sproxton, Lincolnshire. The older of the two was a Hunslet named *Hastings*. Built in 1888, she had served with the contractors building the Manchester Ship Canal and later moved to another firm in the South (where she had acquired her name), before going to Sproxton. *Hastings* had been virtually out of use since 1957 and her boiler fittings had been subjected to frost damage during the extreme conditions of the previous winter.

The second locomotive was a relatively modern Manning Wardle 0 class (built 1917) which had spent its entire working life with Park Gate, firstly at Charwelton in Northamptonshire and subsequently at Sproxton. She was named *Charwelton* in honour of her first home and was in excellent condition, requiring only the fitting of vacuum brakes to make her suitable for use on passenger trains. She even had a slight Southern connection as she bore a strong family resemblance to her elder (Manning Wardle Q class) sister which had belonged to the Freshwater, Yarmouth and Newport Railway on the Isle of Wight and had subsequently been SR No. W1. The price for *Charwelton* was £280 and £250 was wanted for *Hastings*.

In 1963 the total sum was a twenty-year-old's salary and probably represented the annual income earned by the average volunteer. Urgent steps needed to be taken if *Hastings* and *Charwelton* were to be secured.

This was the point at which the Kent and East Sussex Locomotive Trust actually came into existence. This new body was formally constituted at a meeting in Maidstone on 7 November, its first task being to make sure the two 0–6–0s were obtained for the K&ESR. The *Rother Valley Railway* for August–December 1963 described the Trust in some detail:

> . . . [it] is completely independent of the Society, and at present consists of some five individual members together with the Industrial Locomotive Society and the Narrow Gauge and Light Railway Society, both bodies having sent representatives to the meeting. It is intended that all corporate and individual members of the Trust shall subscribe towards the purchase of the engines such sums as they can afford, and the engines will become the sole property of the subscribers. They will be loaned or rented to the Railway Company for use on the line. At present the existing members of the Trust have subscribed some £300 – sufficient to purchase one engine and spares, but in order to secure the second engine at least as much again is needed. The Trust therefore invites any interested members to join in helping to purchase these engines, anyone so joining becoming part owner of them.
>
> It is also intended, subject to the agreement of the Company, Society, and any other interested bodies, that the Trust shall own all the other historic rolling stock which may be used on the line, thus ensuring that if, at any future date, any unforseen difficulties should necessitate the sale of the railway, the rolling stock, not being the property of the Company, could not be disposed of . . .

The address given at the end of this item was Tony Hocking's house, which, for those who knew this to be the case, gave a feeling of the Trust being part of the 'family'. Trusts were nothing new in railway preservation and this one certainly seemed a good idea on both financial and practical grounds. The inclusion of third-party organizations in its structure comes, even now, as a surprise. For the sake of consistency, the Society passed the ownership of *Dom, Gervase* and *Marcia* to the Locomotive Trust.

On the lighter side of motive power matters, the Rother Valley Railway's correspondent, who we met in connection with the tramcar, had once more rushed for his Basildon Bond. This time he asked if anyone who saw *Marcia* could believe that it belonged to a railway which was intended to a practical means of conveying people and merchandise in the latter half of the twentieth century. He added that, if what appeared to be a trend towards eccentricity continued, he would feel obliged to withdraw and seek for a sensible private enterprise project to support.

One wonders what the gentleman who wrote this letter would have made of Tenterden Town station on 21 December when the volunteers marked the festive season with a Christmas party. This was the first of these uproarious occasions and among the clutter of the party was an LP sleeve with notes which read, 'Rugby songs are sung at Rugby clubs and many other places as well . . .' It appeared that railway preservation schemes had joined them.

V

The year of 1964 was a time which popular culture came to regard as the 'swinging sixties'. It has become widely accepted that changes which began after Suez had acquired considerable momentum by that time, as was evident in a wide range of social and political activity. It can be convincingly argued that the growth of the railway preservation movement owed much to these developments and in particular a willingness to challenge authority, as well as the end of conscription which left a generation of fit and restless young men with time on their hands. These were young men who, as boys, had stood by the lineside with Ian Allan's spotters' books, and had come to feel they were about to be cheated of the railway scene known to generations of their predecessors. In short, preservation was railway enthusiasm's contribution to the 'youth rebellion' of the 1960s. The times they were a-changing and the rebels had found a cause. But be it understood, none of this should necessarily be seen as incipient Thatcherism or a desire for widespread privatization. Tories there were, but the commercial aspect of the movement was a means to an end. A reasonable number of those involved regarded themselves as socialists and, if they bothered to think about it at all, justified their presence on grounds of maintaining the rail network and workers' control.

The eventful nature of the times was mirrored on the K&ESR, a brisk pace being evident soon after New Year. Some of my diary notes for 1964 have survived and those for 2 January begin with the following:

> . . . in Lee High Road [Lewisham] saw *Hastings* on [her] way to Tenterden. When I got home I rang the railway and spoke to Robin. He was surprised to hear it was *Hastings* I had seen as *Charwelton* was supposed to arrive first. He thanked me for ringing and asked me to ring again if I saw any more . . .

The Locomotive Trust (the 'Surrey' group plus several other K&ESRPS members) had not wasted any time in making initial payment for these

0–6–0STs or in arranging their transport to Tenterden. It was a very strange sight, that Thursday morning, to see an elderly Hunslet, on a low-loader, and making its way through a congested part of south-east London en route for the A20 and the open spaces of the Weald. The diary continued for Saturday 4 January:

> . . . to Tenterden today, discovered . . . both engines had arrived. *Charwelton* first . . . the transporter carrying *Hastings* having broken down . . . worked for the locomotive department as they were in need of help. . . . Helped clean *Charwelton* up a bit. . . . After dinner chopped some wood then sieved some coal and helped coal up *Charwelton* . . .

In order of their arrival, *Charwelton* had become K&ESR No. 14 and *Hastings* No. 15 (No. 13 being conveniently allocated to the Morris Railcar). Both were in Park Gate's dull brick-red livery, which was a change from the weathered green nearly every other industrial locomotive seemed to carry. This red-brown shade was, not surprisingly, also rather the worse for wear, although *Charwelton*'s paintwork was serviceable and could, with some effort, be brought up to middling BR standards. *Charwelton* was soon put to work, as again shown by the diary, this time for Sunday 12 January:

> . . . rang up and spoke to Derek [Dunlavey] who said it wasn't snowing at Tenterden and to see if the train was running. Had dinner early and left for Tenterden – snow all the way down. When we arrived the first train was coming back. Spoke to Derek who said as he stopped speaking [to me] it started snowing . . . went from level crossing to level crossing [by car] as far as Northiam.

The next diary entry was for Saturday 25 January, but before considering this the reader is asked to remember, the somewhat fraught use of the station building as volunteers' mess accommodation. Some Committee members were muttering about conditions in the booking office, describing them as 'intolerable', and the sight of the Secretary attempting to type letters amid piles of food and blankets was becoming a standing joke. Words like 'squalor' were heard and on Saturday nights half a dozen bodies snored on the floor while the air always seemed to be filled with the aroma of baked beans and stale socks.

Dennis Pope had even been known to ensconce himself for the night in a platelayer's hut between Rolvenden and Wittersham Road, which, with all respect due to someone who is no longer with us, came as a relief to some people – Dennis had a pile-driving snore! The platelayer's hut has in a curious way become his memorial, for a younger generation now know the area around it as Pope's Cottage.

The alarming habit had developed of cooking food in unpunctured tins. (Health and Safety at Work?) A future director of the Tenterden Railway Company, whom we shall not name, applied this treatment four times to one tin of baked beans and sausages which were never actually eaten once they were cooked. On the fifth occasion the long-suffering tin gave way and exploded, demolishing the gas stove and splattering red-hot beans all over the booking office ceiling.

The answer to these problems was found at Ashford Works by Dave

Sinclair, a Society member who worked there in the Carriage and Wagon Department. For some years a grounded coach body, which dated from SE&CR days, had been in use as a store and lecture room. When this was finally pensioned off it was acquired for the princely sum of 10s (50p) and taken to Tenterden for the use of the volunteers. A mound at the end of the platform was levelled off and a base of old sleepers prepared. To do this it was necessary to remove a large and elderly tree. This was removed, although it left a substantial root still in place. Much labour was expended in digging out the root but it finally had to be removed with the assistance of *Charwelton*. At Ashford, Dave Sinclair sawed the coach into two halves and transport was arranged by Mike Farley, another member, and school friend of Derek Dunlavey, who made available lorries belonging to his family's haulage business.

The coach was duly delivered on Saturday 25 January, the diary indicating that the first half arrived about 11.00 a.m. By the end of the day it had been re-assembled, was ready for use and was indeed slept in that night. The join in the middle leaked somewhat but the coach did have a stove and was tolerably comfortable. The stove eventually developed various faults and was replaced about eighteen months later, a suitable substitute having been 'found' at Horsmonden station on the abandoned Hawkhurst branch and brought to Tenterden in the boot of my car.

Some people still complained about squalor, but at least it was at the end of the platform, together with its familiar odour – a blend of grease, stale sweat and cold tea – as well as a clutter of sleeping bags, blankets and unwashed dishes. Order now returned to the booking office, except that volunteers at first needed to continue to use the gas stove. Kevin Blakiston laid on electricity soon afterwards and some time later running water arrived as well. This was at least an improvement on trying to wash under the single tap by the station building.

Around the time the coach arrived the Dave Clark Five were winging their way up the charts with a number called *Glad All Over*, which in an age of unforgettable music was memorable only for its thumping rhythm. Every time this song was played by whichever pirate station the coach radio was tuned to, a loud thumping of volunteer feet would begin and the aged structure would creak and shake. Fortunately for the continued survival of the coach, and after a sequel appropriately titled *Bits and Pieces*, the Dave Clark Five sunk out of sight.

The partition in the coach was quickly moved back to provide further sleeping accommodation and the remainder left as storage for the Permanent Way Department, though the department was pushed out altogether as the number of volunteers increased. The partition was eventually demolished, its last use being in a much mutilated condition several years later when it served as the entrance to something called the 'Rother Valley Buffet', which was where the food and drink was kept. In the end this went as well, and even more sleeping accommodation was crammed in by the railway's bunk builder, Terry Heaslip, who in his working life was another BR employee. The bunks made use of old carriage cushions and were quite comfortable either to sleep or sit on, although their design appeared to owe something to one of the volunteers' favourite films – *The Great Escape*. A source of tinned food at trade prices was found, orders were picked up each Saturday and the goods purchased during the week. The Webb brothers sold the resulting groceries to the volunteers, the profits going into Society funds.

With companions around, the coach could be quite cosy, if a little basic in its amenities. Spending the night in it alone could be an eerie experience as Dick Beckett once found out when he awoke to hear a great crashing around at the far end. No movement was visible in the gloom and Dick made a great rush for the light switch, only to discover that the cause of the disturbance was not the ghost of a discontented passenger but a moth in a paper bag.

Much track work was in progress during the early part of the year. The Northiam loop was being relaid and the oddly variable platform height was receiving attention. At Bodiam the bulging platform face was demolished in preparation for rebuilding and blocked drains were cleared at various locations. Keying-up was completed along most of the line (loose and missing keys had been a contributory factor to the uneven track near 1029) and an officer from the Longmoor Military Railway had examined the four bridges on the line most likely to cause trouble. The Society was, of course, hoping for free attention to these structures. Large amounts of signalling and point-operating equipment, including the six-lever frame from Churn Lane siding on the Hawkhurst branch, were obtained from the contractor demolishing that line and efforts were being made to get three-quarters of a mile of concrete sleepers and a quantity of telegraph poles from the same source.

During early April a redundant set of points was dismantled at Tenterden and moved down the bank to Rolvenden. This was the beginning of the revival in the fortunes of that historic site which, happily, has continued down to the present. The points were intended to serve the second road of the proposed engine shed which, even then and on the recommendation of Mr W.H. Austen, it was intended to build on the station yard side of the line. (Tenterden had been considered in 1962, but rejected on the grounds of too little space and the problems the high water table would cause with pits.) The site of the original works and shed were by that time occupied by a Mr Terry who built garden sheds, but the position of the turnout that had once served these was still available for purchase. It was at that spot Charlie Kentsley set up home on the K&ESR in an example of that classic of improvisation, a prefab bungalow. During the mid-1960s many prefabs were coming onto the second-hand market in kit form as their local authority owners over-eagerly replaced them with tower blocks. The prefabs had been designed to have a short life but they were immensely sturdy and proved ideal for Elsie and Charlie Kentsley. Their cosy home was often open to the volunteers who found it a welcome contrast to their own quaint but rudimentary accommodation. Charlie also brought with him his live steam miniature railway, which he assembled alongside the line, and a workshop which housed his lathe and other power tools. These were soon in use for the more precise jobs being undertaken by the Loco Department.

Meanwhile, the Wheele brothers' offer to buy the railway a Terrier had firmed up into not just any Terrier but No. 3 itself. The purchase of the

Volunteer group enjoying the Kentsleys' hospitality outside the Haven at Rolvenden in 1964.
On the left are Elsie Kentsley, Charlie (standing) and Ron Cann (sitting in front) (Chris Lowry)

locomotive was preceded by an official inspection while she was in steam at Eastleigh. Ron Wheele, Charlie Kentsley, Robin Doust and Derek Dunlavey travelled to Hampshire in Ron Wheele's VW Beetle. No. 3 was driven up and down for her new owner to see and Robin Doust filmed the occasion on 9.5 mm cine film. This footage turned up many years later in the loft at Tenterden Town and was subsequently transferred to video. The purchase price for the locomotive was £750, including delivery to Robertsbridge. It had been pointed out to BR that it was asking more than twice the price paid to the Park Gate Company for *Charwelton*, broadly speaking a comparable locomotive. Although this did not result in a reduction in price, BR did agree to deliver No. 3 free of charge and also supply a full bunker of coal into the bargain. Mr Wheele and the Society were given about one week's notice of the Terrier's arrival, the journey from Eastleigh beginning on Friday 10 April. No. 3 travelled via Havant and was stabled overnight at Brighton. The following day she continued her journey to Robertsbridge, at a maximum speed of 25 mph, via Polegate, Hastings and Crowhurst, her journey summed up by the headboard she carried for the occasion – 'Returning Home to the K&ESR'. No. 3 arrived at 1.30 p.m. to be greeted by a large crowd, the emotional and symbolic nature of this event hardly needing to be spelled out. She could not work up the line at that stage and had to remain in Robertsbridge yard. She was, however, not idle for long, as *Pride of Sussex* was due for repair and for a short while No. 3 shunted the line to the Mill with her BR decals obliterated and all numbers painted out except for the '3'.

No. 3 she might have been once again, but as *Bodiam* she was incomplete without her nameplates. These had fortunately survived their removal in 1937 and one now came from Mr Lawson Finch and the other from no less an institution than the Museum of British Transport at Clapham. They were subsequently replaced by replica nameplates when one of the originals was returned to its owner.

The efforts of the first three years suddenly seemed to be paying off and the arrival of No. 3, although deeply symbolic, was not the only cause for apparent optimism.

There was also another circular to members on the reverse of the note informing them of the arrival of No. 3. It began: 'Since the Special General Meeting in September last year, an offer of financial support has been received which your Committee feels to be sufficient of an improvement on the proposal considered in September to offer every prospect of success.' What it did not say was that Mr Davis had withdrawn from negotiations by this stage and that the new offer came from George Pickin, who many people had seen for the first time at the previous AGM.

As the Wealden spring began to blossom into summer, an editorial in the *Rother Valley Railway* told the membership that 'the day [is] rapidly approaching when trains will once again be running on the Kent and East Sussex'. A second Terrier was in the offing (more about this later) and another Manning Wardle 0–6–0ST, *Sir Berkeley* which was built in 1891. The latter locomotive was the property of the Narrow Gauge and Light Railway Society, which had, of course, members in common with the Surrey Group and was also a corporate member of the Locomotive Trust.

The rolling stock side of the K&ESR was nowhere near so advanced but was beginning to show signs of activity. The purchase of a GWR railcar was again being pursued, two Pullman cars once used on the Hastings line were being seriously considered, and an SE&CR bogie corridor coach was expected to arrive before too long. (This belonged to a member of the failing Westerham Valley Railway Association, about which more later; the coach went to the Keighley and Worth Valley Railway.)

The two Pullman cars had been spotted by Alan Dixon in a siding at Walton-on-Thames carrying the dreaded 'condemned' mark. They were the last of the wooden-bodied type built to restriction '0' dimensions. They had taken part in various special trains over the K&ESR and had seen their final service with BR on the 'Ocean Liner' expresses to Southampton. Unfortunately they had already been sold to a Welsh scrap merchant, but Len Heath Humphrys quickly contacted the firm and persuaded them to resell the coaches to the Society for £265 each. When the Southern Region was asked to deliver the coaches to Robertsbridge, it replied that as they had been sold for scrap at a price including delivery to Wales, then to Wales they must go! The cars actually went into the scrapman's yard, only to be reticketed and sent all the way back to Robertsbridge. The £110 this cost was met by the K&ESRPS.

The Pullman cars subsequently arrived at Tonbridge, where Robin Doust spotted them one night on his way home to Tenterden. He promptly left the train and walked over to the yard for a closer look. Unable to resist the temptation, he made his way between wagons standing in the yard until he could gain access to the Pullmans and promptly climbed inside. Although by that time repainted green and numbered in the standard coach sequence, it soon became apparent from a brass plate on the vestibule door that the original Pullman number had been 185. (The car had been named *Theodora*, the other vehicle having been No. 184, *Barbara*.) Robin soon realized that No. 185 was an old friend in which he had breakfasted while travelling from Tunbridge Wells to London in steam days.

While he was inspecting both vehicles, Robin was horrified to hear someone else on board, and, conscious of his position as a trespasser promptly took refuge in one of the kitchens. Hearing scratching noises, he peeped out and was shocked to see a BR shunter prising the mirror from the vestibule door frame. Forgetting his own status, Robin marched up to the thief, demanded to know what he was doing and threatened him with dire consequences in his capacity as a representative of the owner. The poor man was horrified at being caught red-handed and never thought to query Robin's presence. Pleading for mercy, the shunter promised never to touch a withdrawn coach again and was duly seen off the premises before Robin sneaked away himself to resume his interrupted journey to Headcorn and Tenterden.

But it was not from BR but the extensive, and then closing, railway system at Woolwich Arsenal that the very first items of rolling stock came. The pride of this purchase was an LNWR (North London Line) four-wheeler of 1911, an absolute gem which cost the Locomotive Trust £50. Delivery of the 'Woolwich coach' was delayed, but not so the six three-plank open trucks of various origins which cost £15 each. The money was raised by Locomotive Trust members.

Armed with several working locomotives and a small but useful amount of rolling stock, the opportunity was taken to run a works train. This was to be the most ambitious movement over the line since closure and the train was to be made up of *Charwelton*, the six wagons and, once again, *Dom* in the role of brake van, but with some of her upper panels removed to allow extra visibility. The chosen date was Whit Sunday 16 May and the plan was to run to Northiam with rails for the new station loop, load up with rubble and proceed to Salehurst, where the rubble would be used as a first step in the replacement of the halt platform. My diary shows that activity connected with the train had started by Saturday 2 May and that wagons were being loaded up at Tenterden on that date.

Unusually for a bank holiday, Whitsun 1964 provided three days of golden sunshine. Maidstone and District's express service E3 from London delivered me to Tenterden at around 11.00 a.m. where, after the short walk to the station, I found the loading up of the train was still in progress. This continued as the day grew very warm indeed and lengths of rail were, with the aid of *Charwelton*, hauled aboard the wagons, some of which had their ends temporarily removed to allow this. *Charwelton* was in steam, marshalling the train with its load of track components, and when at the end of the afternoon this was complete, her fire was dropped and she was stabled on the siding behind the mess coach.

The volunteers then had the remainder of the evening to themselves. And what a glorious English evening it was, mellow and with the heat absorbed during the day reflecting from walls and pavements. From the coach came the smell of cooking and the sound of young people laughing or simply talking to one another too loudly. Expectancy was in the air and there was an atmosphere which almost amounted to celebration. Vaughan Williams' *Folk Song Suite* would have formed an appropriate background, but it is not this but a quite different type of music which recalls that evening. Dave Webber had asked a few of us round to his house so that we could listen to a then recently released LP by a startling rhythm and blues-based group, the Rolling Stones. For so many of us who knew the K&ESR in the 1960s, the music of the time, its fads and its fashions do not have London as a setting but the Rother Valley, Tenterden and the surrounding countryside.

Although food could be obtained at the station, this was usually regarded as little more than a snack and Tenterden High Street, never short of licensed premises, offered attractive alternatives. At that time the volunteers' favourite pub was the Eight Bells, a hostelry which served excellent food over the bar and had as a landlord an ex-RAF sergeant, known throughout the town as 'Happy'. This gentleman and his wife, Kay, were firm friends of the railway and more than a little tolerant of the lads from the station. Having heard all that the Stones had on offer, Dave Webber and his friends joined the others for a few jars. The evening no doubt included, as usual, a visit to the fish and chip van, run by a character named Horace, in the High Street. Then it was back to the station, with a deep, rich quiet hanging over the town.

The coach was very crowded that night and (despite a Committee ban) several people went back to sleeping in the booking office. An early start was made the next morning, and the first man awake was Kevin Blakiston, who began lighting up *Charwelton* as the sun rose over the town. Everyone was issued with a circular explaining what was intended during the course of the day, the words 'This is not an excursion train' underlining the serious intent.

The train eventually set off mid-morning, *Charwelton* running bunker-first and making easy progress down the bank to Rolvenden. For many of the volunteers this was, except for very short journeys, their first trip over the K&ESR. Being Whit Sunday, there were many cars on the roads and, although there had been no advance publicity, word had somehow got around and there were numerous railway enthusiasts at every station. At Rolvenden advantage was taken of the water crane before the train ventured out across the marshy Rother Levels where the trees lashed the side of the train and intruded into *Dom's* cab. The train slowly crossed 1029 and steamed along, cutting its way through the undergrowth, the condition of the line keeping the speed down to 10 or 15 mph. It was a strange sensation to travel over the line in a train. The railway, particularly at the Tenterden end, was familiar enough, but it was ground-level familiarity, the familiarity of the grass and the weeds and the track, of the fishplates and sleepers. But this was to view the line from coach height and see the overgrowth and dereliction not as part of the railway, but as something which could be overcome.

The Rother Bridge was crossed and Northiam came into sight. It was midday, the sun blazed out of a clear blue sky and the volunteers were

Whit Sunday 1964. Charwelton *enters Northiam with a permanent way special. The photograph was taken from the 'brake van' (i.e.* Dom*) (Photographer not known, Malcolm Dunstan collection)*

beginning to suffer from sunburn and thirst. A crate of soft drinks had been brought down from Tenterden and Ricky Lawrie did a brisk trade before three wagons with the components for the loop were detached and the rubble for Salehurst loaded up. Then it was on to Bodiam where more rubble was available. With the hop fields passing on either side, this was the first train to reach that part of the line for three years. But at Junction Road things started to go wrong. It had been realized that not enough volunteers had stayed at Northiam and Dave Sinclair was waiting with his van to take a party back to that station. No sooner had this problem been overcome than the footplate crew realized *Charwelton* was going to run short of water before too long. There was a rapid retreat back to Rolvenden, the train and crew heading for the water crane as fast as they dared! When the locomotive returned another problem had arisen – a shortage of coal. It was decided to abandon the whole operation and haul just one wagon back to Tenterden, three wagons plus *Dom* being left in the siding at Junction Road.

To make up for the lack of coal, wood from tree-cutting which had been loaded aboard the wagons was used as fuel in a repeat of the previous year's problems with *Gervase*. This was something for which *Charwelton* had most definitely not been designed. To ride up Tenterden Bank in an unfitted wagon, with no brake van and dodging showers of red-hot wood ash was an experience not to be easily forgotten!

After this further debacle there was a certain amount of muttering in the ranks about 'organization' but it said much for the corporate spirit which had already built up that nobody appeared to clear off to some other scheme – with one exception. Proposals for army co-operation had got as far as a Territorial Army unit appearing on the line, for some ill-defined purpose, while the Whit Sunday train was running. They were never seen again. Following the events of Whit Sunday, most people were fairly exhausted and the following day (a bank holiday) was used for 'rest and recuperation' in the form of a trip to the Elham Traction Engine Rally. This was quite appropriate as a Garrett engine present was owned by a well-known member of the Society, Mr Ronald Cann of Folkestone.

Movement of the works train resumed two weeks later and this time the rubble actually got to Salehurst. Unlike the first attempt, this train was run on a day of incessant drizzle which resulted in a tarpaulin being erected as a tent on one of the wagons. Memories remain among those present of logs being chopped up within this shelter against the possibility of another fuel shortage.

VI

In the first half of 1964 events had taken an unexpected turn and in relating this part of the story it is necessary to refer back to the period preceding the April circular letter informing members of the offer made to the Society by George Pickin.

Following a sudden and inexplicable demand from the Southern Region for confirmation that the Society would be in a position to complete the purchase of the railway, it became necessary to form a '£100' Private Company very quickly. Six directors were appointed from the Society's Committee in order to get the Company functioning. These were Messrs Cook, Doust, Humphrys, Kentsley, Penny and Watkins.

Mr Pickin states that, in February 1964 and while he was in South Africa on business, he wrote to the Society simultaneously making two offers. The first of these was a straightforward takeover bid for the Company for £27,720. The second and alternative offer was for a lease-back arrangement, also involving £27,720 for 3 per cent over Bank Rate. This was intended to out-manoeuvre Mr Davis (who, unknown to Mr Pickin, had withdrawn from negotiations) and, as mentioned in the previous chapter, appeared rather better than Mr Davis' offer, not least because a lease of only five years did not form part of the package. (Mr Pickin has pointed out that any lease he granted would not have been renewable for ever. He was not, however, prepared to put himself in a position where he would never see his money again while the value of the rent vanished with inflation.)

In March Mr Pickin received a letter telling him he could rely on his offer to 'pay BR £27,720' being accepted and giving him the date and the time the K&ESR Board would be meeting. Although he had not been told which of his alternative offers this referred to, simply that the sum he offered appeared to be enough, Mr Pickin flew to Britain. He arrived in Tenterden to find the

K&ESR Company Board about to begin their discussions. Both the K&ESRPS Report of the Committee for 1963–4 and Mr Pickin agree that by the end of the meeting the Board had agreed to the takeover proposal. There were two abstentions to the otherwise unanimous vote.

The Report for 1963–4 told members the Committee had subsequently discovered Mr Pickin's 'unorthodox intentions'. These intentions were stated at a later date to be twofold. For one thing, he proposed very few paid staff, although the Society thought more would be required. Mr Pickin has added, in information given to me, that he was unwilling to pay for copper telephone wire and ex-London Underground signalling equipment which the Society wished to install. (Both of these items are referred to in later contexts.) Secondly, Mr Pickin proposed to run a regular service of nine trains each way daily using a steam railcar. He believed a sufficiently intensive service would attract passengers. The Society believed four or five trains daily to have been the viable maximum, although this aspect does not seem to have been raised until the AGM in July. These were, as events turned out, not to be the only contentious issues in Mr Pickin's dealings with the Preservation Society.

The Board held a further meeting one week later and it was agreed that the lease-back offer be accepted instead of the takeover. On being told this Mr Pickin insisted on being given control of the Company. The Board met again a few days later and 'it was decided that Mr Pickin be asked to give an undertaking that he would not proceed with his more peculiar proposals'. When this was not forthcoming in the terms wanted, the Company Secretary then telephoned all the directors.

To quote again the Report for 1963–4:

> . . . three agreed to Mr Pickin being given control and three did not. Those in agreement included the Chairman of the Board, and they forthwith signed a resolution agreeing to Mr Pickin being given control. The Company Secretary (soon after) issued 76 £1 shares in the Company to Mr Pickin. At a Board meeting held three days later, further discussion resulted in the three directors who had signed the original resolution refusing to ratify it, but it was subsequently found that the issue of the share certificate by the Secretary under the authorization of the three directors who had signed it was valid, and that Mr Pickin had gained complete control of the Company, and through this the right to negotiate with BR for the purchase of the railway. Following this event, all six directors, together with the Company Secretary, Solicitor and Accountants all resigned simultaneously.

In conclusion, members were told that in the face of Mr Pickin's proven ability to produce £40,000 when required, and his own statement that his personal fortune amounted to an adequate sum, there appeared no alternative but to allow him to proceed with the purchase of the line.

To the reader unfamiliar with these events it may seem incredible that such a chapter of hasty decisions, equally hastily reversed, should have taken place. But take place they did and the matter has remained a sensitive subject for over a quarter of a century. It should, nevertheless, be remembered that Mr Pickin's was only the second firm offer received and that it seemed to have advantages over Mr Davis' lease-back proposal. As explained earlier, some of the Society's aims (although not ultimately realized) were, in their day, innovative and radical. The project had been in existence for three years and although supporters were many, there was no shortage of sceptics. BR was pressing to bring matters to a conclusion and, on the financial front if not among the work parties, a sense of desperation was beginning to set in.

Another remarkable feature of these events was the relative lack of recrimination against the Committee as the managers of the project – particularly on the part of the volunteers. But it was, of course, inevitable that those who were most frequently at the railway should be aware of these developments and there was no small concern that control of the Company had been lost by those who had set it up.

The response of the volunteers was to form the Rother Valley Workers' Association. This body, which had many similarities to a trade union, was inaugurated at a meeting in the mess coach on 3 May. A straightforward constitution was drawn up, although its clauses also included these:

> 3. Membership of the Association shall be open to all workers on the K&ESR, ex-workers on the K&ESR and any person elected by a straight majority at an Association meeting.
>
> 8. The purpose of the Association shall be as follows:
> a) To discuss the working of the railway, and to provide an opportunity to discuss any improvements to the working which may occur to the member.
> b) To give the opportunity for the management of the railway to inform the members of any progress made by the railway company.
> c) To present a united front in cases of: (1) Mismanagement by the railway company; (2) Victimization of members of the Association.
>   If any member of the Association is given an order which he thinks is contrary to the preceding paragraph, he should at once seek the advice of a Committee member.
>
> 9. In case of incidents which a meeting of the Association decides falls into the category of 8(c), the Association shall take any action which they consider appropriate, including, if it should be necessary, strike action.
>
> 10. Should the K&ESR Preservation Society be at any time wound up, or if the Association decides that the Society's aims no longer agree with those laid down in the Society's Constitution, as existing in May 1964, the Association shall take over the aims and activities of the Society, including that of buying, and running the railway should it be necessary or advisable.

The officers of the Association were Derek Dunlavey, Dave Sinclair, Micky Sargeant, Charlie Kentsley and, the only nonrailwayman, Ron Cann.

In my opinion this departure marked the rise of the volunteer group as a power in its own right and was an expression of group loyalty. I would also consider it to have been a reaction to the volunteers' dislike both of Mr Pickin and his proposals (a situation not changed when they later knew his proposals in greater detail). Mr Pickin for his part considers it to have been an expression of personal loyalty to the Chairman and Secretary and formed to 'smash' his operation by such means as strikes.

The situation on the K&ESR was by that time complicated by a proliferation of overlapping and interlinked groups. To recap, there was, by June 1964, the Limited Company and the Locomotive Trust as well as the Preservation Society and the RVRWA. The first mentioned did not enjoy the confidence of either the Committee or, the most active part of the membership, while the volunteers' organization had been brought into existence by force of circumstances. The Locomotive Trust was off on another tangent altogether. It was not without links into the Committee and ordinary membership (Robin Doust was an early member) but its independent status and third-party involvement made it seem just beyond the orbit of everyday K&ESR activities. By nature, the Trust tended to be made up of more affluent individuals (the minimum donation was £10, a largish sum at the time) and one has a lingering impression – albeit as a result of much hindsight – of young men in collars, ties and expensive suits, whose occasional presence sat oddly among the collection of apprentices, BR staff and sixth-formers who characterized the volunteers.

In the early part of June edition No. 6 of the *Rother Valley Railway* was issued. With it came a series of circular letters, all dated 10 June 1964, and which, if taken together, seem to signify rising panic. The first began with a very optimistic statement:

> . . . it is at least possible to say with a degree of certainty that the railway will re-open. At the time of writing, it is understood that a draft contract of sale for the line is before the BR' Board, and this will be forwarded to the K&ESR Company almost immediately. . . . The hope is that a limited service will be in operation before the end of the year . . .

The next enclosure gave Society members notice of the Annual General Meeting on 11 July and announced that Pullman cars Nos 184 and 185 had been purchased and were about to be delivered to Robertsbridge, If, however, the member was also a volunteer he would have found, on the reverse, the following:

> This letter is being sent to all regular volunteers (i.e. members of the Rother Valley Railway Workers Association), all Preservation Society Committee members and the officers of the Locomotive Trust.
>
> I regret to inform you that the various possible avenues of approach which it is hoped would enable the purchase of the line to be financed without using Mr Pickin's capital have failed to bear fruit. Accordingly, a meeting of those to whom this letter is sent is proposed for Sunday next, 14 June, to be held at the above address (i.e. Tenterden Town station) from 4.00 p.m. onwards.
>
> Mr G. Pickin has been invited to attend this meeting at 4.30 p.m. for the purpose of explaining his plans and of answering any questions which those present wish to pose.
>
> This situation has been precipitated by a direct question from BR on Monday of this week as to whether it is in order for them to proceed with the sale of the line to Mr Pickin. An immediate answer being required, and there being no other immediate hope of raising the necessary capital from other sources, BR have been told to proceed with the sale to the K&ESR Company, controlled by Mr Pickin.

The final circular letter was addressed to all members:

> Since the enclosed magazine went to press, there have been a number of changes in the substance of the offer of finance [by Mr Pickin]. Full details of these changes will be circulated during the next few days, and in any event prior to the Annual General Meeting of 11 July. However, the basic effect of the changes will be that the entire control of the railway will rest in the hands of the individual involved in putting up the capital involved.
>
> The individual in question is known to have a number of plans for running the railway, some of which are unconventional in the extreme. If the purchase of the railway is carried through by this person, it is likely that although the railway will run again, the original plans of the Society to run it as a commercial public service will never be realized.

When this fact became apparent, your Committee made an all out effort to raise the capital necessary to purchase the line by alternative means. The proposal made is that members will be invited to make guarantees, preferably of £1000 or more, as security against a bank loan, and that for such a guarantee, collateral security in the form of a Debenture for the appropriate sum secured on the value of the assets purchased would be offered. To date just under £12,000 has been raised in this way and this circular is a last attempt to save the railway in the form in which most members would like to see it. A form is attached, which members able to assist in the way mentioned above are asked to complete, and return . . .

The meeting of 14 June took place in the mess coach and Mr Pickin explained his ideas to the group of regular volunteers who attended. These met with little enthusiasm on the part of the workforce.

Between the 14 June meeting and the AGM two further documents were circulated to all members: a further letter, signed by Robin Doust as Secretary, which amounted to a position statement; and a document headed 'G. Pickin's Proposals'. The contents of both documents have, in part, been described earlier in the narrative. To include full details here might be tedious, and instead their contents are reproduced in Appendix 1. Comment needs, however, to be made on one of Mr Pickin's proposals which he called by the unfortunate name of 'railway apartheid'. This (to quote Mr Pickin's own words), '[would] permit other societies to have full rights in their own areas and run their trains over the whole line, without having any rights in the railway as a whole, but Tenterden and Rolvenden will be reserved for the Company'. In 1964, and within the context of then current ideas about railway preservation, the whole notion seemed frought with difficulty. The argument that 'there can only be one boss' was sometimes heard. While this book was being prepared, Mr Pickin suggested to me that a comparison could be made with the still extant joint operation between Amersham and Harrow on the Metropolitan line. Under this analogy, his Company would, presumably, have been in the position of the Metropolitan Railway (now LUL) and other groups in that of the Great Central Railway (Network South-east). In the 1990s the various sectors of BR are sharing the same tracks and many steam railways have another group operating on their property. One wonders if Mr Pickin was ahead of his time! Mr Pickin's description of his scheme as 'railway apartheid' did not, however, take account of the pejorative usage of the second word in everyday English. On the one hand it conjured up all the wrong images for the politically aware, while on the other it could produce mystification among those who did not share such interests.

On 11 July the Loco Department lit up their charges ready for the display of rolling stock which was fast becoming a regular part of the Annual General Meeting. A number of the other volunteers were not to get an easy day though, for during the morning a 20 ton weighbridge (obtained in connection with the proposed goods service) turned up on a lorry and had to be unloaded. This delayed the start of the meeting until 3.00 p.m.

Eventually Len Heath Humphrys, who was again acting as Chairman, brought the gathering in the Town Hall to order. The formalities of the previous AGM and the September SGM were read and approved. The report for 1963–4, which of course included the account of how Mr Pickin took the

Company over, was then read and, rather surprisingly in the circumstances, approved by the meeting. A vote of thanks to the volunteers was passed unanimously and after that the 'fun' started.

Len Humphrys continued the meeting by reporting that extensive discussions had been conducted with Mr Pickin at a number of meetings. Despite these there still remained three serious areas of disagreement. The first of these was Mr Pickin's intention, already made known to the membership, of running an intensive service, but the remaining two were even more controversial. These were that no further Light Railway Order should (or needed to) be obtained and that, despite all the attendant risks, no third-party insurance should be taken out. It was also stated that there were numerous minor points of difference and that, on every one, Mr Pickin refused to compromise. It was stated from the chair, however, that it was hoped some sort of compromise could still be reached.

In a letter to me, Mr Pickin has stated that, rather than seek a Light Railway Order, he had originally wanted the line transferred to the Company under Section 18 of the Railways Act 1921. This provision stated: 'Where an agreement has been or may hereafter be entered into for the purchase, lease, or working by one railway company of any part of the system of another railway company, the Minister may, by order, confirm the agreement, and where any such agreement has been confirmed it shall be lawful for the companies to carry the agreement into effect.'

The possibility of using such a procedure stemmed from the fact that the Robertsbridge–Rolvenden section of the Rother Valley Railway had been authorized under a private Act of Parliament in 1896. The Company had switched to the Light Railway Act when that alternative had become available later the same year and when construction had reached formation level. The original Act had never been repealed. It was Mr Pickin's contention that nowhere in the Light Railway Acts was there a provision which enabled those statutes to be used to transfer a line from A to B and that only modifications to the manner in which a line was worked could be authorized in this way. Mr Pickin was of the opinion that in this way the need for inspections or inquiries could be avoided.

Section 18 had, however, been repealed by the Transport Act 1962, and a further possibility considered by Mr Pickin was that the operating powers be transferred by means of a provision in the private Act which BR put through Parliament annually to obtain legal authority for anything from new line construction to the modification of regulations. It is beyond the scope of this volume to consider the legal arguments involved in these ideas. I shall instead only confine myself to the observation that, during the preservation era, powers have always been transferred from BR using the Light Railway Acts, this having been the course preferred by the Department of Transport and its predecessors.

With regard to insurance, Mr Pickin considered premiums for a volunteer-worked railway would be very high and

> . . . simply not worth it. In the event of a claim it would have been very difficult to sell the line up because of the statutory powers . . . Colonel Stephens was for long receiver of the

Weston, Cleveland and Portishead when the land ownership had gone because the Company had vanished about 1909, causing its lands to escheat [revert by default] to the feudal lords. But even if it was sold up it could have been bought back cheaply on a forced sale. [Letter from Mr Pickin to me.]

The Preservation Society Committee minutes indicate that Mr Pickin later agreed to insurance cover for the volunteers.

Mr Pickin had earlier had an item put on the agenda asking the meeting to consider the amalgamation of the Preservation Society with his Company. There was so little support for this idea that, at first, no seconder was forthcoming and the meeting stalled. Eventually a Mr Beacon seconded the motion and, after Mr Pickin had spoken and there had been some other discussion, the vote was taken. The proposal was defeated by seventy-seven votes to two.

The meeting then proceeded through an unspectacular consideration of the accounts. Following this a Mr Dowling raised a query concerning the issue of shares, and the Chairman explained that all money paid in following the appeal to members towards the purchase of the railway would be held until final arrangements for the purchase of the line had been made. At that time all subscribers would be asked for their permission for their money to be used. In return for this, shares in the Company (i.e. a second company, distinct from that owned by Mr Pickin) would be offered.

At this point, and after the Chairman had finished answering the question, the minutes of the meeting indicate an angry exchange between Mr Pickin and committee members on the platform. A brief pause followed, after which Len Heath Humphrys asked Mr Pickin to address the meeting but requested him to confine his remarks to matters relevant to the purchase of the railway. To quote the minutes (as approved by members at the AGM the following year – see chapter IX):

> Mr Pickin then accused the Society of trying to wreck his Company, and of plotting to buy the Company out after having done so. He went on to say that if such a thing happened, he (Mr Pickin) would take care to see that the railway was sold to the scrap merchants rather than let the Society take control of it. He accused members of the Society volunteer labour force of threatening to strike if he took over, and said that he thought the Society's continued efforts to raise capital were simply in order to enable it to buy the line from his Company after it had been wrecked.

The first person to respond was Robin Doust, who said that there was no question of the Society trying to wreck Mr Pickin's Company. The position simply was that the Committee considered that if he bought the railway he would speedily either go bankrupt or be closed down by the Ministry of Transport and that, in order to be prepared for this eventuality, the Society was continuing in its efforts to raise capital.

It was Malcolm Dunstan who spoke for the volunteers. A tall, slightly greying figure, his words came across in a clear, standard English accent underlined with a note of determination. He began by stating that he spent £70 a year travelling to the railway (the present-day equivalent is probably ten times that amount), that he worked on the line and that he did not spend good money and time working on the K&ESR simply to indulge in strikes and wrecking operations. He concluded that he felt sure he spoke for other members of the volunteer force in saying this. There was indeed a mood of approval among the volunteers which confirmed what had just been said.

There are differing opinions[4] as to what happened next. The minutes indicate (as again agreed at the following AGM) that, 'Mr Morgan then suggested that further discussions be held between Mr Pickin and the Society with a view to arriving at some compromise solution to the apparent deadlock.'

The election of the Committee followed, this proving to be a further cause of controversy. According to the minutes it was suggested that, to save time, the existing Committee be re-elected *en bloc* as there were no additional nominations. Mr Pickin strenuously objected to this procedure, as he had done the previous year, particularly in relation to Len Heath Humphrys and Robin Doust. Eventually both left the hall while their re-election was considered separately. Mr Harman temporarily took the chair and the remainder of the Committee were elected *en bloc*. There was some discussion and Len and Robin were re-elected sixty-eight votes to two, 'subject to the condition that they could be asked to resign their positions at any time by the rest of the Committee if circumstances warranted this'.

After further, and more quietly undertaken, business the meeting ended and the membership were invited to the station, where, as planned, *Gervase, Marcia* and *Charwelton* were in steam. The locomotives were under the helpful eye of Inspector Busswood, who brought with him the branch-line staff. For his services the Society paid the Southern Region £12. Returning to the station, scene of a volunteer's ordinary weekends, at the end of that

Gervase, Dom *and* Charwelton *in the loop at Tenterden Town on AGM day 1964. Note that* Charwelton *is in her industrial owners' livery, similar to the colour scheme in which she is well known thirty years later (Chris Lowry)*

afternoon had something of the quality of waking from an uncomfortable dream. The contrast between the 'politics' of the railway and the volunteer way of life, although in time to become equally intense, was never exceeded.

Two further personal memories remain from that weekend. After the visiting members had gone home and the 'regulars' were clearing up, Dave Webber let me drive *Gervase* along the platform road at Tenterden. This I accomplished without skinning my knuckles on the boiler immediately behind the notorious Sentinel regulator, but was not so fortunate when, the following day and while on a working party at Northiam, I dropped a sleeper on my left big toe! The injury was, thankfully, trivial, but ached for many years afterwards at the approach of wet weather. It seems apt that this should have happened just at the time metaphorical storm clouds were gathering over the railway.

VII

At the risk of labouring the point, life in the volunteer force continued with some purpose despite the turbulent events which were unfolding. The problem of weeds was growing more acute with each succeeding spring and summer, and during 1964 weedkiller was applied to the track along the entire length

The legendary Morris railcar at Northiam on 9 August 1964 (Chris Lowry)

from Tenterden to Bodiam. This had been achieved using a single-cylinder ex-fire brigade motor pump and a 400 gallon galvanized tank mounted on one of the wagons. The pump was of some antiquity and had been made to work by Ron Cann. An 11 ft wide spray bar with about eight nozzles was mounted on the wagon's rear buffers and used to deliver the Glamoxin weedkiller. The wagon thus equipped was hauled by *Charwelton*. *Dom*'s tank was also used to supply water and was mounted on a second wagon. The crew consisted of Ron Cann, Dave Sinclair, Dick Beckett, Alan Crotty and Charlie Kentsley. Unfortunately, there was again a danger of running out of water at Junction Road on the return journey. Guinness Hop Farms came to the rescue, however, with a tractor-driven pump which filled *Charwelton*'s saddle tank from the river but there then followed another coal shortage with, once again, the need to resort to wood and old telegraph poles!

If the weather was dry enough, controlled burning could produce at least temporary results. If this method was used, account had to be taken of lineside crops, and adequate water and volunteers had to be made available to control the fire. Within a matter of weeks the weeds would, however, grow back again. The smoke from these fires could be seen for miles and on one occasion a Fire Officer appeared at Cranbrook Road to enquire if professional assistance was required. Blackberry bushes grew in profusion in this area and one warm and mellow afternoon in early autumn, as the smoke of the control burning swirled around, Tony Adams (one of the regular volunteers) could be seen moving from bush to bush collecting the fruit before the enveloping flames reached it. The result, a couple of weeks later, was some pots of delicious jam which when sold to the volunteers added a small, but much needed, sum to the Society funds.

Resleepering and packing was carried out at various locations but the major job was the relaying of the 600 ft loop at Northiam with 95 lb rail which, together with the necessary sleepers, had been brought down on the Whit Sunday train, and the diary records work still being under way in late July. This work was very successfully completed, to the surprise of a Southern Region surveyor who had expressed his doubts about the ability of the volunteers to undertake the job. In the event they proved themselves quite capable of drilling two hundred sleepers to take the chair screws, correctly placing the sleepers, laying the rails, sawing them to length where necessary, and drilling the cut rails to take fishbolts. Much of this material for the Northiam loop had been recovered from the short remaining section of the Headcorn extension, used as a headshunt immediately north of Tenterden Town station. The original reason for lifting this track was to have the resulting material available for disposal at scrap prices. The resulting income would have gone towards the purchase of the railway (without recourse to Mr Pickin's capital), as it was worth several thousand pounds. These activities stayed just on the side of legality as, under the original plan, the scrap metal would have been sold somewhere around the time the purchase was completed. When used for the Northiam loop, the track, of course, remained on BR property. At Tenterden, the individual rails had been tipped out of their chairs, these latter components being much hidden among the weeds of the

Loading chairs onto one of the ex-Woolwich Arsenal wagons on 2 August 1964 (Chris Lowry)

overgrown trackbed. The rails were then loaded onto a permanent way trolley and taken back to the yard. There they were stored along the siding at the rear of the platform together with other rails which had been lifted from the back of the coal yard. This procedure was hard work but generally safe. One 'accident' did, nonetheless, occur, the following being Robin Doust's eyewitness account:

> An energetic group of volunteers [on the platelayers' trolley] came trundling back towards Headcorn at a considerable lick, completely forgetting that during their absence unloading the previous rail, one of the pair in the next section towards Tenterden had been tipped out of the chairs by the rest of the gang. The frantic waves of warning from those on the ground observing the unchecked return of the trolley were returned by equally happy waves from the cheerful trolley crew, whose forgetfulness was forceably brought home when the trolley ran off the end of the track at high speed. The immediately following events appeared to those on the ground to occur in slow motion, as the violently derailed vehicle distributed a shower of human bodies in graceful trajectories in all directions down the embankment, which was quite high at that point. We waited with baited breath and then hurried to count the injuries. Incredibly, everyone survived intact, with the exception of Alan Castle who had cut his tongue on his teeth and thus presented a rather gory sight which fortunately turned out to be a lot less serious than it looked.

The trackbed of the Headcorn extension finished abruptly at a large excavation made some time during the 1950s. The volunteers had become used to the occasional older enthusiast or local who generally introduced the words 'I remember when this line used to . . .' (add your own ending) somewhere into their recollections. One evening, some while after the recovery of much of the extension track had been completed, the conversation in the coach turned to the changes which had occurred on the line since the Preservation Society arrived. With a completely straight face, and aided by his rural Surrey accent, Tony Adams came out with the immortal line, 'Ar, now oi remember when this railway used to run all the way from Robertsbridge, right past 'ere – and all the way up to that big hole in the ground . . .'

Tree-cutting was another activity which featured prominently. Branches had traditionally brushed the sides of trains on the K&ESR and the lengthy period following closure had done nothing to improve matters. Some trees could be dealt with simply by lopping branches but others had to be completely felled. If the trees were not large wood-cutting could proceed very quickly with one half of the gang bringing a tree down every few minutes. The remaining members would then cut the timber into more manageable lengths for burning or removal. There were some larger trees as well and one provided a silent movie-like sequence when a volunteer succeeded in cutting off the branch on which he was sitting, fortunately without injury to himself! When work was in hand on Tenterden Bank, the practice developed of running a wagon down by gravity and using *Dom* as a brake power. Once the wagon was full of tree branches, or whatever else was being collected, both vehicles would then be returned to the station using any motive power that could be called upon.

In mid-August arrangements were made for the Woolwich coach to be delivered by road to Rolvenden, the first time any stock had been received at that site. The arrival of the coach was scheduled for 15 August, but as with previous arrivals there was a delay and there was still no sign of it twenty-four hours later. A phone call to Woolwich Arsenal elicited that the coach was just leaving; when it did arrive it became K&ESR No. 31 and the first passenger vehicle of the preservation era. As received, the Woolwich coach was complete except for its vacuum brake gear, original seating and partitioning. These last two items had been replaced by slatted seating running round the interior and, of all things, a table. The interior proved ideal, if slightly uncomfortable, for Committee meetings, although things were improved by the addition of carriage cushions to the seats. When in use the coach proved to have an exceptionally smooth ride, perhaps because of its wooden-centred wheels. It was, incidentally, not unknown for the Woolwich coach axle boxes to be lubricated with butter! The rancid variety was often available if a partly used packet was left in the mess coach during the week and it occurred to Tony Adams that it could be put to good use.

On the coach front, an ex-GWR railcar, W20, had been secured from the Western Region. The sale of rolling stock had by that date been centralized at Eversholt House near Euston and the BR department concerned (not exactly popular with the preservation movement) had taken the unusual step, for them, of offering the remaining railcars for tender rather than at a fixed price. A K&ESR party had inspected these at Swindon and at Worcester, where W20 was selected. Funds were made available, via the Appeal Trust, by a Mr

Brockman and £415 was offered. Much to everyone's surprise, this was accepted – particularly when this included delivery of the restriction 4 vehicle through the narrow Hastings line tunnels to Robertsbridge. Thereby hangs a tale . . .

The latter half of September 1964 was the beginning of the period when, to say the least, the railway's fortunes were mixed. A second Terrier, No. 32650, arrived at Robertsbridge on 19 September. She had been bought by the Borough of Sutton, the origins of this purchase not being without interest. Local government around London was at that time working towards the creation of the thirty-two boroughs on 1 April 1965. This was a chaotic period and all sorts of local emotions and traditions were to the fore. For the year prior to the amalgamations the London boroughs had a shadowy, impotent half-existence intended to smooth the transition, and it so happened that the Chief Planning Officer-designate of the new Council was a member of the K&ESRPS. A new civic centre was planned for Sutton and the local politicians cast around for a suitable centrepiece. It is not hard to guess what one of their Chief Officers suggested. His reasoning was that Sutton, like many London suburbs, had grown because of its railway. The Council would really have liked No. 32661, which had been named *Sutton* on the London, Brighton and South Coast Railway, but as that wasn't available it settled for the former *Whitechapel*. As the proposed civic centre was dimly foreseen some time in a rosy future (which the London boroughs were still trying to find twenty-five years later), storage accommodation had to be found and the K&ESRPS was only too happy to oblige.

No. 32650 duly arrived, to be met by the Mayor of soon-to-disappear Sutton and Cheam, the Borough Surveyor, and the Chairman of Battle Rural District Council. The locomotive was coupled to the two Pullmans in the bay platform, but someone forgot to extend the buffers at the end of the cars attached to the Terrier. (The Pullmans had buckeye couplings, and the side buffers were normally retracted when not in use.) As a result, the coupling between loco and coach was very slack, so that when the train moved off in a shunting demonstration, the Pullman started with a tremendous jerk, depositing the Mayor and a group of dignitaries in an untidy heap on the floor! Subsequently, as the Mayor was leaving the footplate of No. 32650, he slipped and fell several feet to the ground. Fortunately he was not seriously hurt, but he managed to break the mayoral chain on the way down and was probably glad to see the back of the railway by the time he left. It was first intended to restore No. 32650 to full LB&SCR Stroudley livery, and initially she was known as No. 50. She also, inevitably, acquired No. 61's name and became *Sutton*.

The day after the arrival of *Sutton*, Robin Doust had the task of sending out another and very different circular letter to members. Once again, its importance was such that it becomes necessary to quote the letter itself:

Since the last edition of the *Rother Valley Railway* appeared a number of vitally important events have taken place affecting the purchase of the railway. It is greatly regretted that discussions with Mr Pickin . . . have revealed his intentions on gaining control of the railway are not acceptable. The extraordinary scenes between Mr Pickin and members at the AGM have made it quite clear that it would be utterly impossible for the railway to operate in the way envisaged by the Society with him in control, and it has been agreed that there would be no point in continuing negotiations with him.

The Committee are conscious of the fact that the decision they have made is a grave one, and it is not without a great deal of thought having been given to the consequences. As most members are aware, the Committee has, over a considerable period, made strenuous efforts to raise capital by one means or another, and a tremendous effort on the part of Mr L.A. Heath Humphrys, the newly appointed Chairman of the Society, has resulted in the collection of some £10,000 in Bank Guarantees from members, in return for which, debentures secured on the assets being purchased will be issued. If a further £5,000 in guarantees can be obtained, a bank loan of £15,000 will almost certainly be forthcoming. In addition, negotiations are in progress with a view to raising a mortgage of £10,000 secured on the value of the land and buildings being purchased. These two sums together will give a total of £25,000, leaving a gap of £10,000 still to be closed. At the present time the Committee can see no way in which this sum can be raised unless a member or members are prepared to come forward now and make available substantial sums in the form of loans, or offer permanent finance in some form.

Much discussion has taken place as to possible courses of action in this situation, and the Committee has reluctantly come to the conclusion that it may be necessary to temporarily remove the permanent way from Northiam to Tenterden for an estimated period of 10 years. It has always been envisaged that the railway's main activities would be on the section from Robertsbridge to Northiam, and this section would produce a compact, profitable line as outlined in the prospectus. It is estimated the removal of the track will raise £13,000 after deduction of lifting costs, and it is envisaged that this action would leave the Society's Operating Company with a suitable working capital, and save over £1,000 per year in interest charges in the initial stages. It is not planned to sell any of the track site from Northiam to Tenterden, as this will obviously be required at a later date. At the end of a ten-year period, your Committee expect to have completed the repayment of the mortgage, and will be free to devote finance to the re-opening of the upper section. This depends to a certain extent on being able to produce satisfactory trading results and permanent capital to take the place of the initial bank loan, guaranteed by members.

It is appreciated that this course of action will be viewed with great distaste by members, but it is a course of action forced on us by the reluctance of sufficient members to come forward and support the venture financially. While it is realized that the ability of the railway to become a profit-making concern is something which will only be proved by experience, it should be emphasized that any money put into the scheme is fully secured, and that in the event of the subsequent failure of the project, all this capital will be repayable. A number of members have hinted over the last few months that they might be prepared to put some money into the scheme once they know exactly how it is to be run, and what security there is to offer.

The letter then continued with an announcement of a type which would become all too familiar to members:

BR have indicated that the sale contract for the line must be signed within the next 28 days, and this is an absolutely final deadline. If we are not in a position to go ahead by then, the line will immediately be put out to tender for scrap. In the past we have been given deadlines which have been circumvented for various reasons, but on this occasion there will be no possibility of further delay – we MUST know now exactly what support we are likely to have so that we can decide finally how to deal with the purchase when we are confronted with the need to sign on the dotted line.

Attached is a form which all members are asked to complete and return to Tenterden as soon as possible on which you may indicate whether you would be agreeable to the course of action outlined above if [only] insufficient capital can be raised, and also on which you may indicate any further financial assistance which you may be able to offer.

This letter is of interest on a number of counts. The section in the second paragraph about members' willingness (or unwillingness) to make finance available is fair comment, but needs to be qualified. The Society's aims were, as already pointed out, advanced for their time, although there was little in them that has not been achieved by one or other of the steam railways since. Given this background (and the course of events during 1964) it is quite possible potential backers, particularly beyond those most closely involved with the Society, remained sceptical.

Of those at the centre of the project, these individuals tended to be either nominally affluent but having their capital tied up in a business, or, like many of the volunteers, young and less well paid. Given these circumstances, it is hardly surprising that any rather more disposable income went to the Locomotive Trust.

It is also possible to perceive the dawning of a more realistic attitude that actually did point the way forward; the realization that it might be necessary to operate a shorter line and that achievement of the Society's full aims might take many years. The suggestion of concentrating on the Robertsbridge–Northiam section, with its main-line connection, the Hodson's Mill traffic and the attraction of Bodiam Castle, had much logic to it. It also had great personal appeal for Robin Doust and, while it is in no way suggested that this had any particular influence on the corporate view held by the Committee, the Northiam option was very much that favoured by the management end of the Society. It did not, however, take into account the magnetic attraction of Tenterden, a factor at least in part recognized by the acknowledgement that such a course of action would be viewed with 'great distaste' by members. The Tenterden-centred view was very much that of the volunteer force, for many of whom the town had become a second home. The 'Robertsbridge eastwards' view of the K&ESR perhaps belonged to the older enthusiasts who had known the line before passenger services ceased. 'Tenterden westwards' was, in the main, the perspective of those who came to know the line after closure. It would in time become the thrust of K&ESR history.

Both despite and because of the dire circumstances in which the project found itself, activity on the line seemed to move up a notch during the latter part of the year. With the arrival of the Woolwich coach, Rolvenden resumed its traditional role as a rolling stock stabling point, although there was a minor problem involved in this. BR had not actually been asked if the yard could be so used. The practical effects of this transgression were minor, but when somebody from the Southern Region was due to call on some matter or other it was thought prudent to move the coach up to Tenterden. This produced a second problem – none of the locos was available. The only possible motive power was, of all things, the Morris 20, and the old car did indeed perform sterling service as it hauled the coach up the bank to Tenterden Town at the end of a length of rope – surely the hardest task ever asked of it on road or rail. This 'train' – odd even by K&ESR standards – left Rolvenden between 5 and 6 p.m. on a fine Sunday evening and managed to reach the cutting below Cranbrook Road before the car could no longer cope. With Malcolm Dunstan acting as 'cheerleader', several larger persons bounced away on the rear bumper to try and improve traction while, once again, a dozen others pushed the coach – just as they had done with *Gervase* at much the same spot!

The Woolwich coach episode was almost the railcar's swansong. It had been continuing to prove its worth, even managing to haul rails to Northiam, these being slung between two flat trolleys which acted as 'bogies'. Each trolley required a crew to apply old sump oil to the plain 'U' bearings en route and prevent the axles seizing up under the load. But the Morris had definitely seen better days and for some while had featured a buffer-sized dent either side of its rear window. It had acquired these while being used to shunt some of the wagons, and it was during this operation that the towing chain had become caught in a point frog. This left the Morris firmly anchored and immobile while the wagon continued to run loose under its own momentum. Andrew Webb was driving and had the horrendous experience of seeing, via the rear-view mirror, the wagon bearing down on him. It was quite impossible to move the railcar and Andrew stayed at his post, as he considered this less hazardous than bailing out! The Morris progressively fell out of use and it was eventually retrieved by Brian Blackwell for use as spare parts.

The presence of Charlie Kentsley at Rolvenden meant that the yard was in many ways a safer storage site than Tenterden, and the decision was taken to move part of the stock down the bank. This was accomplished one weekend afternoon when *Charwelton* hauled *Gervase, Marcia, Dom* and the Woolwich coach down the one-in-fifty gradient in an impressively long line. I rode down in the guard's compartment of the coach. As far as I can remember, none of the wagons were moved, but as stock movements took place from time to time it should not be assumed that any particular item stayed permanently at any one site. An exception, however, was *Hastings*, the Loco Department having started work on her on the siding behind Tenterden station platform. The Loco Department also continued to use the mess coach at Tenterden, presumably because they preferred the relative comfort and comradeship of the coach to opening an even more spartan and lonelier establishment at Rolvenden.

Their continued presence had an amusing consequence which was repeated on a number of occasions. There were among the volunteers several Catholics which, on one level, added theology to the topics for informed debate over a pint and, on another, caused Messrs Dunlavey and Blakiston to attend early morning Mass on Sundays. Derek seemed to be quite good at getting up early but was often met with a lack of enthusiasm on the part of Kevin. Kevin had by this stage taken to sleeping in an iron-framed bed which he would assemble in the middle of the coach, blocking the gangway and making late-night trips to the loo very difficult. The bed was far more comfortable than the bunks and he was loathe to leave it. Derek's remedy was quite simply to demolish the bed round Kevin, who would come out with a string of expletives before staggering off to church, having in the meanwhile woken the assembled Protestants, doubters and atheists. St Mildred's was, of course, nearby and a few Anglicans felt constrained to attend, although the 'nationalized' (an apt description which soon caught on) never had the popularity of the Roman rite.

A further story told about both the gents and the mess coach (situated at opposite ends of the platform) features a sleeping volunteer. In addition to being a K&ESR member, this gentleman also served in the Territorial Army. One night the sleep of the railway's weary workforce was disturbed by a loud thumping which turned out to be the chap in question – who was slumbering on the floor – shouting and attempting to march while completely unconscious of his surroundings. It was somehow worked out that the part-time soldier (and railwayman) wanted to answer a call of nature. The problem of the resulting disturbance was solved by Derek Dunlavey who barked a series of military orders at the still-sleeping individual, marched him out of the coach, down the steps, along the platform, sharp left at the gents and then informed the somnambulist that he was where he wished to be. Once matters had been satisfactorily attended to, the process was reversed and peace returned to the mess coach. To this day the person concerned has no memory of what happened.

Charwelton had by then undertaken a fair mileage on the K&ESR, but had shown signs of an axle-box bearing running hot. The offending bearing had been duly removed and a replacement obtained. This needed turning up, which was in itself a time-consuming and tedious process. The necessary skills were to hand, and there remains an enduring memory of the lathe in Charlie Kentsley's workshop slowly turning while the ever-patient Derek Dunlavey sat with his feet up, rolled-up fag in hand, amid the swarf and the aroma of Old Holborn. The basic problem was that *Charwelton* had been designed for shunting but was being used for longer runs. This was not to be the last time that she was to be seen jacked up, off her wheels and awaiting a new bearing.

During the autumn, and in part as a response to the BR ultimatum, the K&ESR succeeded in getting a good deal of publicity both in the press and on television. The highlight of this was a press day held on 3 October. The public was invited as well and both Rolvenden and Tenterden were opened for the occasion. So many cars arrived at Rolvenden that vehicles were parked all the way up the hill, while at Tenterden Town a large crowd had gathered. *Charwelton, Gervase* and *Marcia* were all in steam and the only passenger vehicle available was, of course, the Woolwich coach (part repainted in grey primer, but with the brake end red), which was running with one of the three plank wagons. *Charwelton* hauled the first train out of Rolvenden and up the bank at 10.30 a.m. A noticeably purposeful atmosphere was apparent at Tenterden, something aided by such a small feature as the 'Tenterden–Rolvenden–Wittersham–Northiam' destination board. The train proceeded back down the bank, and made a further trip to Rolvenden before leaving for Northiam with TV film cameramen aboard. *Charwelton* was running well at this point and reached Northiam easily, where she was able to run round on the newly relaid loop. After a forty-minute break the first passenger train on the line since closure returned to Tenterden, having only to stop briefly to put out a fire among the inevitable weeds.

Gervase had meanwhile been trundling about, keeping the numerous visitors at Tenterden entertained. *Charwelton* returned to an enthusiastic welcome and the discovery that her right-hand leading axle box was running warm. The train was intended to make one further journey to Rolvenden, following which the coach would be returned to Tenterden. At Rolvenden *Charwelton* was taken off and Nos 10 and 12 substituted. The sight of these locomotives, hauling their first passenger train ever, was unusual to say the least (it was said at the time to be 'Emmett at its best'), and possibly one of the few recorded instances up to that time of double-heading on the K&ESR. The day concluded with a barbecue cooked on a shovel in *Charwelton*'s firebox. An item on the press day later appeared in BBC TV's then south-eastern news programme, *Town and Around*. Despite this, 3 October 1964 is possibly not as well remembered as it might be. It was one of the more successful events organized in the early days and, perhaps, showed what, given a fair wind, could have been achieved. It was the precursor of some things now associated with the 1970s and others which were not repeated until 1989.

The following Saturday, 10 October, the Society held an exhibition at the TA drill hall in Ashford. On this occasion the K&ESRPS played host to various other societies and model railway clubs and a number of regular volunteers turned up to man the event. The *Rother Valley Railway* later described it as a 'moderate success', although memory recalls it as having been rather more so. The portable layout of Wittersham Road was in the hall and this led to history repeating itself, in 4 mm scale, when the Society-owned locomotives which had been taken to Ashford stopped working and I had the embarrassing job of approaching a stand exhibiting Southern models and asking if the K&ESR could please borrow a (K's kit) Terrier!

The BR deadline was rapidly approaching and, out of the large number of replies which had been received to the questionnaire about operating a shorter length of line, all except three had reluctantly agreed to the proposal. As the weeks past, a resulting feeling of unease began to mount. It was, unexpectedly, relieved by one of the key national events of the 1960s – the election, on 15 October, of a Labour government. This pleased many railway enthusiasts as a Labour manifesto proposal was the dropping of the Beeching Plan, and *Railway Magazine* had actually suggested to its readers that they vote accordingly. If there was ever a point when railway enthusiasm stopped being the hobby of a middle-class minority and started to be regarded as a heritage-based interest for everyone, this was surely it. On the K&ESR the good news was that almost immediately the new Minister of Transport asked BR to suspend the sale of all closed lines pending the preparation of a proposed road/rail co-ordination plan. This was, in part, seen at the time as another delay in the progress of the scheme. But it postponed the possible need to lift the upper section. Not for the first time in its history the K&ESR had managed to survive, this time by the skin of its teeth.

When the Preservation Society first arrived on the line few vestiges of the signalling system (at best never more than very simple) remained beyond some disused posts. Thoughts were turning to correcting this situation and, surprisingly, it was decided to use colour-light equipment at Northiam and Tenterden (the latter despite the then doubtful future of the site) and to operate the points at both stations electrically. These signals had already been obtained from London Transport. It was hoped to get a supply of Westinghouse Mk III point motors from the same source, and former LT mechanical point rodding, pulleys and cranks had already been obtained. This development was very much associated with Geoff Percy, a regular volunteer who was employed as a signal engineer by London Transport and was very active during this and the subsequent period. The Southern origins of K&ESR tradition were already very influential in the Preservation Society, and the arrival of Geoff and several of his colleagues brought an at least tenuous link with the Metropolitan Railway, where the young Holman Stephens had received his training. A few eyebrows had, of course, been raised at the suggestion of colour-light signalling, but the reasoning that 'Col. Stephens would have used it' got another early airing!

No account of 1964 would be complete without mention of the telephone system, the maintenance of which was an activity characteristic of the early years. Mention has already been made that the line suffered the depredations of wire thieves. The first section to go was near Wittersham Road. The last was between Bodiam and Robertsbridge, as the Rhodesia independence crisis built up towards the middle of the decade and the price of copper went through the roof. The first attempt at restoration was between Tenterden and Rolvenden using copper wire salvaged from other parts of the line and ex-government field wire known as Don 8. Unfortunately, within two weeks 75 per cent of the recovered copper had disappeared, a circumstance which, for the moment, did not encourage further volunteer effort in this direction. The arrival of the mess coach at Tenterden led to the installation of a local line between mess and booking office, which was quite separate from the main system. The local line worked well and was popular, if only because it saved a walk if one wished to announce a meal was ready or that someone was wanted on the GPO telephone. The latter, incidentally, had a loud, clanging extension bell which could be heard over most of the yard.

Kevin Blakiston and one of the Webb brothers working on the phone system near Rolvenden in 1964 (Chris Lowry)

The increased activity at Rolvenden made restoration of the link a necessity and this was achieved by singling the remaining Don 8 (which reached as far as Cranbrook Road) and using this wire as a continuous conductor with earth return. The instruments all remained the simple 'omnibus' type once favoured by railway companies. The wire thieves noticed that fresh wire was in position and tried again, the line being dead the week after it was re-erected. They abandoned their activities when they realized the wire was not copper but the near valueless Don 8. During this frustrating period the telephone system had great popularity among the volunteers by providing a highly constructive activity in lieu of running trains. Prominent among those concerned with the early development of the phone system were the Webb brothers (who, of course, had useful professional skills), Kevin Blakiston (when not working on locomotives) and a destined to be very long-lasting volunteer, Chris Lowry.

While weighty matters were going on elsewhere in the Society's activities, some members were still given to writing to the magazine in what *Private Eye* might call a 'Tufton Bufton' style. The new subject for high dudgeon was the matter of locomotive liveries. For example:

> It is with some concern that I have heard rumours regarding the painting of our locomotive stock. Nos 10 and 12 are as we already know, in the old K&ESR blue, and the restoration of No. 15 has been commenced in this colour. It seems, however, that this is where any standardization may possibly end if some current thought is pursued. Rumour hath it that No. 3 is to be green, and No. 14 is to be lined out like a traction engine once again, in the mud colour in which she appears at present. If the Sutton 'Terrier' is restored to full Stroudley livery, as I suppose she must, we shall then have most of the colours of the rainbow represented in our motive power, with *Dom* still unaccounted for – perhaps she will be pink!
>
> This policy is of course foolish . . . what is wrong with old and very smart K&ESR blue livery? . . . May I suggest that a referendum be held before it is too late.'

Another correspondent was moved to write that railway liveries were like the uniforms of an army, that pride in the colours was an old and well-tried point of loyalty, and that the K&ESR was a railway and not a 'travelling circus.'

Most volunteers would probably have replied that while they had views on the livery question it had nothing to do with their loyalty to the railway. In mentioning (indeed reiterating) this aspect of life on the railway, it would be easy to go too far in the direction of 'We few, we happy few, we band of brothers'. The group dynamics of the volunteer force were, in general, very good, although not exempt from commonplace human fallibilities. In my experience, railway enthusiasts have tended to be either stabbing each other in the back or living in each other's pockets. On the K&ESR, and perhaps because of the easy-going nature of the times, communual living and tolerance were the order of the day. Not a few members were happy to socialize away from the railway and during 1964 Surrey members started to meet regularly at the White Hart in Epsom. Malcolm Dunstan was one of the central figures in this development. It was the predecessor of the later Area Groups, even if it did utilize the 'noggin and natter' formula borrowed from the conservative world of car clubs.

There were, nevertheless, personality clashes and people sometimes just got on each other's nerves.[5] The trying twelve months which had passed, perhaps

Working party on the line on 25 October 1964. The three members on the far left have not been identified. The author is second from the left, front row, with Ray Marlow (glasses) behind, Robin Doust (tie), Malcolm Dunstan (peaked cap), Andrew Webb (standing on trolley), Dave Sinclair, Mark Yonge and Malcolm Webb (Chris Lowry)

also contributed to an unfortunate incident which occurred at the volunteers' Christmas party. This had been in many ways a rerun of the previous year's event, except that Elsie Kentsley and Alan Crotty's mother had been prevailed upon to cook a superb dinner. These ladies left, after being suitably thanked and rewarded, and the party had proceeded on its way into the evening. A record player had been going full blast and one prominent volunteer had brought a large and varied selection of LPs with him. Late in the evening the party wound down and a 'leading member of the Society' was putting something away in the booking office loft. This, of course, involved opening the trap door which was reached by climbing on the counter – the same counter on which were the 'prominent volunteer's' large stack of LPs. With a horrible inevitability the trap door slipped from 'leading member's' hand and crashed into 'prominent volunteer's' records (actually without doing any harm at all, but that wasn't apparent at the time). The two members involved had been irritating each other for weeks, if not months previously, and there was a hideous silence among the few remaining people in the room as 'prominent volunteer' grabbed 'leading member' by the throat. Neither party involved was lacking in strength and I fully anticipated becoming a witness to actual bodily harm. Enter Derek Dunlavey who, in a demonstration of characteristic coolness and diplomacy, simply stepped between the two individuals and told 'prominent volunteer' he was in need of some sleep. Thus ended 1964 on the K&ESR.

VIII

At the beginning of 1965 George Pickin still held negotiating rights for the purchase of the line but the Southern Region remained prepared to talk to the Society. Five thousand pounds remained available from the original Appeal Trust and a further £12,000 was available through the Bank Guarantee scheme. Talks, based on the security of the guarantees, had been under way with two banks, but these had failed following the new government's imposition of a credit squeeze.

The Society now decided to rely on financial support available from among the membership. The Committee met on 3 January and Robin Doust outlined a proposal to raise £40,000 by issuing shares in a public company. The Committee decided to pursue this option and that, subject to advice from Peter Barrett, the Society's solicitor (he was also a member), the matter should be put to a Special General Meeting. Immediately after this, mention was made that an approach had been made to the Southern Region with a view to obtaining a credit sale agreement for the line (a similar idea to that supposedly raised by Mr Pickin at the 1963 AGM). The Keighley and Worth Valley had recently been offered such a facility but the SR turned the Society down. In the event, and although this was a minor diversion at the time, another of the seeds of eventual success had been sown.

The growing controversy about liveries was now making demands on the Committee's time, and for the moment it was decided to do nothing to the Terriers except get rid of all BR insignia. This storm in a teacup (or a paint pot) rather neatly illustrates the different perspectives from which the scheme could be seen. While the Committee laboured over fundamental, strategic issues, great heat was generated over something which could perhaps have waited.

The Committee met again three weeks later on 24 January and a number of items from the previous meeting came up once more. It was decided to hold a referendum on the subject of liveries and ballot papers would be sent to members. The solicitor had advised that a private guarantee company would be much easier to set up than a public company and had drawn up a draft deed of covenant which, although thought to be requiring alteration, provided a basis on which to work. Companies limited by guarantee were, of course, not new in the context of the K&ESR, this having been the future foreseen for the Society in the 1963 prospectus.

Discussion then turned to locomotives and Robin Doust reported that the last remaining 01 class, No. 31065, which had a long association with the K&ESR, had been purchased by a member. Arrangements were in hand for it to be stored in Ashford Works and for Charlie Kentsley to undertake work which would enable No. 31065 to be delivered to Robertsbridge under her own steam. Hopes ran high that the K&ESR would soon have a tender locomotive. Similarly, Derek Dunlavey mentioned that he understood the Eastleigh Carriage Works' diesel shunter (DS 600) would soon be available for a very low price (later stated to have been £25) and consideration was given to the possibility of bringing the locomotive to the line. This sensible suggestion later floundered when it was discovered that the shunter was in poor condition, but it remains the first recorded mention of internal-combustion locomotives appearing on the K&ESR under preservation.

By 7 February the solicitor and the officers had decided that the subscription payment scheme should run as a second Appeal Trust and the final wording of the deed of covenant was being determined. It had been decided to inaugurate the new scheme at a party due to be held in the Pullmans at Robertsbridge on 27 February, and that the Committee would meet in the Pullmans immediately beforehand to sanction officially the Rother Valley Railway Appeal Trust Fund. Depositors were to be given the opportunity to subscribe for shares in the new operating company. The Trustees were Ron Cann, Len Heath Humphrys and Arthur Penny. The RVR Appeal Trust was to have a limited life of five years.

Financial matters continued when Ron Cann, who was by then Treasurer, gave his regular review of the Society's meagre current account. He was shrewd in business matters and could be most incisive when his proper sense of accounting, and cost-effectiveness, led him to comment on the Society's activities. Ron, together with Arthur Penny (a civil servant of the old school) could put up something of a double act when occasion demanded, even if this made matters uncomfortable for other Committee members.

Ron Cann was an interesting character in other respects and, in addition to the previously mentioned Garrett traction engine, also owned a beautiful pre-war Mercedes Benz sports car (he was a very quick, precise driver). Ron was capable of a most remarkable feat of self control, being able to smoke a pipe for six months, stop smoking, appear six months later smoking small cigars, stop smoking again for a further six months, and so on. Above all, he was an energetic volunteer, although a full generation older than most of his part-time colleagues.

The meeting of 7 February included two other items with long-term implications. The first of these was a report prepared by Roger Crombleholme and one of his Locomotive Trust associates, David Wigley, the latter gentleman being allowed to attend the Committee because of this item. The minutes sum up their proposals concisely.

> The basis of the report was that the possibility of purchasing the whole line had receded almost to vanishing point, and that the Society should instead concentrate on trying to secure the short section from Robertsbridge to Bodiam, which section, it was said, would be likely to constitute the most paying portion of the line from a tourist point of view. Mr Doust then read a counterproposal urging that efforts be continued unabated to raise finance for the complete scheme, but that Mr Crombleholmes's plans for the Bodiam section be actively followed up with a view to instituting them if the necessity arose in the event of an eventual failure to buy the whole line. Mr Doust suggested as an alternative, that the longer section from Robertsbridge to Northiam would be more likely to be a useful stretch than that only to Bodiam, and that it might be better to concentrate on this longer stretch if an abbreviated length of line had to be considered at all. There followed a considerable amount of discussion, the final conclusion being that efforts be continued to secure the whole line, but that detailed plans be made for the purchase of the two shorter sections mentioned above, so that either could be instituted at short notice dependent on the amount of finance available at the time, and the degree of co-operation received from

BR. As a further step arising out of the suggestions in Messrs Crombleholme and Wigley's proposals, it was agreed that in view of the likely protracted delay before any final decision on the purchase of the line was reached, that an approach be made to the Southern Region for a short-term rental of a portion of the line, either from Robertsbridge to Bodiam, or from Rolvenden to Tenterden in order to run a limited service of some kind in order to stimulate interest in the scheme, build up membership of the Society and gain additional financial support. The Chairman undertook to make an approach along these lines.

It comes as a surprise to find that the idea of renting a section of track was being considered at this stage, when BR had so successfully discouraged the similar idea of lines being leased. The Crombleholme–Wigley plan, of course, went one stage further than the existing scheme to temporarily foreshorten the railway to raise capital. It ignored the existence of Tenterden as a strong counterattraction to Bodiam and, it has to be said, suggested concentrating on the very section which it would prove most difficult to re-open. The notion of operating some sort of service between Tenterden and Rolvenden, on the other hand, suggests a recognition of the appeal of the section which climbed onto the High Weald. The mood of these various proposals has much that suggests a growing desperation.

The K&ESR might be in trouble but elsewhere in the county the scheme to re-open the Westerham branch was close to collapse. Its well-organized workforce had previously formed itself into the Westerham Valley Railway Workers' Association (similar to the RVRWA). In the latter part of 1964, and in response to their respective difficulties, the two workers' groups had amalgamated. (The membership cards were headed 'Westerham and Rother Valley Railways Workers' Association' – something of a mouthful.) Derek Dunlavey reported that efforts were being made to keep the Westerham volunteers together, and the Committee agreed to approach this group with a view to them assisting on the K&ESR. This matter was not raised as a particularly major issue, but it was the beginning of a significant development.

The ballot papers for the livery referendum (locomotives only, choice of green, blue and a 'write-in' option) were sent out on 11 February. The same letter informed the membership about the seemingly positive developments regarding the 01 class and also mentioned that negotiations were in hand for the purchase of four Maunsell-designed corridor coaches then operating services between Tonbridge and Tunbridge Wells West. The cost was given at £215–£250 per vehicle and members interested in helping to acquire them were asked to get in touch.

The Committee met at Robertsbridge, as planned, on 27 February and gave its official approval to the new Trust Fund before the party began. Although this was the first social event to which members and their guests had been invited, the gathering in the Pullmans was counted a success, about thirty-five people paying £1 1s for the privilege. The bar was run by Derek Dunlavey, which led to jolly japes in the magazine about his having learned the art while watching the professional at work in the Eight Bells. (On that basis he was hardly the only candidate qualified for the job!) Hot snacks, tea and coffee were provided, although there was an inevitable panic when it was discovered that standard propane gas cylinders did not fit the Pullman adapter. The day was saved by the local propane stockist who rigged up a pipe straight from the cylinders to the cooker.

Culinary preparations were, again, in the able hands of Elsie Kentsley, this time assisted by the wife of regular volunteer and Committee member, Bill Westwood. Bill, who was another of the railway's older workers, was both respected and much liked. He soon acquired a role on the K&ESR much like that of a tolerant and understanding uncle.

The evening also included films and slides of the railway taken by Messrs Doust, Smallwood, Couchman and Wigley and, in a pointer to the most dimly imagined of futures, the magazine account of the Pullman party pointed out that the cars were available for hire to anyone who was organizing a function.

The Special General Meeting to launch the Rother Valley Railway Trust Fund was held on 6 March 1965 in the Town Hall at Tenterden. This was a fairly straightforward and quiet affair compared with the preceding AGMs, and the formation of another limited company to run the railway was foreseen. A motion to confirm the Committee's action in setting up the RVR Appeal Trust was proposed by Arthur Penny and seconded by Charlie Kentsley. It was passed unanimously.

Members were then given the opportunity to raise questions and one of these was inevitably about the livery question. The meeting was informed that the referendum showed a preference for blue but, and this was a new twist to the story, the owners of the various locomotives were not prepared to accept this, thus continuing the uncertainty over the matter. The subject of the ex-GWR railcar also came up as a number of rumours were circulating. The answer from the Society officers was that, although the railcar had been secured, BR had realized the previously mentioned problem of the tunnels on the Hastings line, but that the Society was insisting on holding it to the terms of the contract, particularly delivery to Robertsbridge. BR was considering what to do next and the possibility existed that a 1958-built four-wheeled alternative might be offered instead.

An account of the SGM appeared in the March 1965 magazine. Its arrival on this occasion, however, provided something of a surprise – *The Farmers' Line* had returned. The explanation at the time was that this duplicated and stapled publication could be produced more easily, and therefore be more up to date with the news, than the typeset and letterpress-printed *Rother Valley Railway*. It was intended that the *RVR* should continue and be devoted to feature articles rather than news. In the event it never re-appeared, although the *Tenterden Terrier*, in terms of size and style, would be its heir.

Preparation of *The Farmers' Line* (during both its first and later incarnations) was a regular task, which involved not only the cutting of the stencils but the duplication of thousands of pages which then had to be collated and stapled together. Any volunteer who was around was likely to get conscripted for the latter two tasks, although there was the compensation that it was a way of getting one's newsletter early. The next stage was envelope addressing and stuffing followed by a trip to Tenterden main post office, wherein resided a franking machine. The skills acquired from this activity proved to be more useful (though much less interesting) to me than the subjects I studied for A-level. When I joined the staff of a London borough (not Sutton) I found documents being prepared on exactly this basis, a practice which continued well into the computer age and after it had been abandoned by most other organizations, including the K&ESR.

Preparation of the newsletter had again fallen to Robin Doust. This was in addition to his many other duties for the railway as well as his studies to become a qualified librarian and subsequent establishment of a career. He accomplished all these things with a determination and maturity beyond his years, while his flow of clear and informative written English did much to aid the progress of the preservation scheme. Many of the direct quotes in this book are his words. Robin also maintained a high degree of physical fitness by the habitual use of his racing cycle, sometimes over very long distances. No one is superhuman, and there was a price to be paid for all this. Robin has himself recorded that he found the early years fascinating although arduous. I recall returning from the pub one evening together with Derek Dunlavey to find Robin Doust slumped asleep across his typewriter. On being gently woken he asked earnestly if we had any idea how long he had been asleep and admitted to having been working too hard for some time previously.

There was certainly much work to be done on the railway at the time and the following entry in the first edition of the revived *Farmers' Line* invited further members to join in:

> The volunteer band numbers about 20, most of whom turn up nearly every week, but there is need to keep twice this number occupied. Anyone keen to join a working party is asked to report in the first place to Tenterden station on any Saturday or Sunday, from where transport will be provided to the site of the day's work. Work normally begins about 11.00 a.m. and continues until sunset or about 8.00 p.m., whichever is the earlier, although members are quite welcome to arrive or leave earlier if they wish.

The stated number of volunteers was probably an underestimate and the 'transport' was the volunteers' cars. The time schedule may seem a little leisurely by current standards but was adequate for the stage the project had reached, while the starting time (more typical of Saturdays than Sundays) allowed for many volunteers having to travel some distance. The mess coach also allowed for a Friday evening arrival, a social evening and an early start on Saturday morning.

Among the projects for which extra labour was needed was the reconstruction of Rolvenden station platform. This was undertaken using old sleepers for the retaining wall and ash for the platform surface. The mound has already been compared to a Bronze Age barrow and, appropriately, treasure was unearthed during excavations – lead type used in the old printing hut which had stood on the platform and, best of all, a halftone printing block for a guide to the Shropshire and Montgomeryshire Railway. I was present when these items came to light and remember the eerie feeling as the past emerged from the earth and 'time closed up like a fan'. The rebuilt platform served until the retaining wall was replaced ready for the re-opening of the line.

The Farmers' Line also announced, in optimistic terms, the possibility of renting part of the line and made mention of a private venture, by a member living in Devon, to secure an ex-LSWR coach for use on the K&ESR. The few remaining examples of these vehicles were by then serving as camping coaches, and although this particular proposal came to nothing, it wasn't the last time an ex-LSWR coach would be proposed for the K&ESR.

By the Committee meeting of 11 April the earlier optimism about hiring part of the line was proving misplaced, Len Heath Humphrys reporting that he had unofficial word that there might be objections to the use of the level crossings but that he had suggested Rolvenden–Wittersham Road as an alternative. No implication appears to have been read into the possibility of 'objections', however, with regard to the longer-term aims of the project. Robin Doust thought this section's remote location would make it a liability and proposed Bodiam–Northiam, which only involved one small level crossing, instead. The Committee agreed to pursue this. Mr Pickin was still in the picture, as it was understood that the Southern Region had given him a further two weeks to complete the purchase of the railway.

Ron Cann's Treasurer's report is worth detailing on this occasion. It gave a snapshot of the Society's financial position at that point and was as follows:

> Monies in current account – £76 5s 11d
> Liabilities – £150 (Much of it accounted for by stock held ready for sale.)
> Original Appeal Trust – £1,980 3s 2d
> Value of Appeal Trust Assets – £1,103 (Including two Pullman cars, the diesel railcar and £100 earned in interest. It was agreed £50 of the interest be made over to the Society to help meet outstanding liabilities.)
> Rother Valley Railway Trust – £10 with £100 covenanted over a period of four years.
> [These small sums do not reflect the interest the Fund was later to create among the membership. They represent contributions at a very early stage.]

Less than good news came when Robin Doust stated that he thought BR would soon start to put the pressure on again and that the only solution was the already proposed lifting of the Northiam–Tenterden section. It was now also necessary to look at other ways of raising finance, and other disposable equipment as well as track was now considered for scrap. In addition planning permission was to be sought for parcels of redundant land (again following the example of the Derwent Valley Railway) which could be leased out, and a bank loan was to be sought on the basis of sums offered under the covenant scheme. This part of the meeting concluded with the Chairman mentioning that George Pickin might make a further approach to the Society for support. All agreed that in the event of this happening the only terms the Committee would be interested in would be a straightforward mortgage.

During the Committee meeting, Derek Dunlavey introduced the subject of the Brake Van Fund, another, but very useful, money-raising exercise (and an addition to the railway's list of subsidiary organizations!) The Fund was a consortium of volunteers who set about collecting the £51 10s (plus £50 transport) required to purchase a 20 ton, six-wheeled goods brake van. The van itself was of SE&CR origins but was coming from the internal railway system of the Royal Aircraft Establishment at Farnborough. Delivery was still to be arranged and the brake van would be on permanent loan to the railway. There was some concern among the younger and less well-paid volunteers that they were unable to contribute to the Locomotive Trust, particularly as they often used much of their available money to get to the railway. The Brake Van Fund, an idea of Derek Dunlavey and Dave Sinclair, was the result. Subscriptions could be anything from one penny per week upwards.

The following Committee meeting picked up on a number of the items covered by its predecessor but also touched on a number of issues of developing significance. In the first category the scrap drive was still being actively pursued and the weighbridge, less than a year previously the symbol of volunteer tenacity, was one of the first things considered for disposal. Plans for the lifting of the upper section of the line were making grim progress and demolition companies (not necessarily the railway enthusiast's best friends) were being contacted. The financial position remained poor, and as well as imposing a freeze on all but essential expenditure, the administration of the sales and refreshment account was re-organized and tightened up.

The second category included the first hint that *Dom, Gervase* and *Marcia* (Society-owned but in the care of the Locomotive Trust) be sold – although with the intention of keeping them on the K&ESR – to help the Trust with its outstanding debt to the Park Gate Iron and Steel Company. The immediate outcome of this was the Committee's agreement to the sale of *Dom* to a Society member. The Society's dealings with Mr Pickin had now taken a legal turn, Mr Pickin having issued a writ following a decision at an earlier Committee meeting to terminate his membership of the Society. Mr Pickin was calling for his re-instatement and the society's solicitor was handling the matter.

There is one final item which stands out in the minutes of the meeting of 9 May – Robin Doust's indication that he wished to resign as Hon. Secretary. Those who had been close to Robin in the preceding period had known that this was in the wind, but to quote the minutes:

> . . . he was thoroughly disgusted with the lack of support which he had received both from the Committee and the membership of the Society over a considerable period of time, and stating that since he had reached the conclusion that he and Mr Humphrys could not re-open the railway single-handed, and no one else seemed prepared to offer much help, he preferred to stop wasting his time on the project any further by resigning from his position as Hon. Secretary.

The whole of this statement requires detailed comment. As has already been said, Robin Doust had, since 1961, made remarkable efforts on behalf of the scheme. By any objective standard these earned him a distinguished place in the history of the railway, one, I would suggest, which approaches that of W.H. Austen. But this had taken its toll and as Robin made his statement the same strain showed on his face that had been visible on the occasion he had been found asleep across his desk. The minutes fail to mention that he also spoke of the contents of an old diary he had found which had made him realize just how much he had given up for the K&ESR. He was speaking from a position of strength. He and Len Heath Humphrys had carried much of the burden, and these were the words of a man exasperated at what seemed a lack of commitment by others.

But it was, of course, a subjective view. Others were putting much effort into the scheme, even if because of lack of experience or aptitude, or because of other commitments, they could not dedicate themselves in the way that Robin had. Comparisons are, as ever, invidious, but the work done by the Loco Department and the leading lights of the gang who relayed the Northiam loop show, in their different ways, no want of energy or enthusiasm. Managing the workforce on a steam railway can be a delicate matter. If some members had been pushed too far the railway would have had few volunteers. Despite this the fact remained that too great a reliance had been placed on Robin Doust's fiery drive and, to extend the metaphor, he was now in danger of burning out. When he finished speaking there was an awkward shifting with embarrassment on the uncomfortable seats of the Woolwich coach; this had the makings of a major crisis inside the Society. Various people agreed to undertake parts of the Secretary's duties and as a result Robin was, for the moment, persuaded to stay. Some of the devolved duties extended existing interests. Derek Dunlavey and Charlie Kentsley would deal with rolling stock matters for instance. Other changes involved new departures such as Bill Westwood's agreement to deal with miscellaneous correspondence. Prior knowledge of Robin's feelings must have had some bearing on the final development in this sad episode as Roger Crombleholme was able to say that Eddie Bye, also a member of the Trust and a former Committee member when he was Museum Curator, was willing to take on the role of Secretary. The Committee's reaction to this offer was to, in effect, keep Mr Bye's offer on 'hold' pending developments.

Much of the foregoing chapter has been devoted to the 'politics' and organizational side of the Society. No apology is offered, it having been possible to highlight this aspect as the necessary information for these months came readily to hand. Committee matters have also been dealt with in detail to give some idea of the management of the Preservation Society and partly because this was a particularly, though not uniquely, critical period. Committee deliberations will continue as the background to much of the story for a while yet, but the reader may, with some relief, be glad to turn to the next chapter and its continuing account of what the volunteer force was achieving in the station yards and out along the grass-grown tracks in the valley.

IX

Much has been already been said about the part No. 14, *Charwelton*, played in the railway's activities in the mid-1960s. She was, of course, the better of the two locomotives obtained from Sproxton and her long-time colleague, *Hastings*, required much attention to both valve gear and boiler. Work began not long after No. 15 arrived at Tenterden, by which time the Loco

Department was feeling very confident, having retrieved *Gervase* from near scrap-heap condition, and optimistic predictions were put about as to how long the job might take.

Hastings sat in the platform siding and loomed, like some reminder of the railway in the 1930s, above the weeds growing in the station flowerbed. Her saddle tank was removed to enable the Loco Department to get at the frost-damaged boiler fittings. Thirty boiler tubes were also removed. Month followed month, the department became involved in other work and the day when *Hastings* might steam seemed to recede into the distance. Unkind voices (the rest of the volunteers) could be heard saying *Hastings* was only fit for scrap, and following this 'wind-up' (a popular colloquialism which had not been coined at that date) a challenge was issued. A list with two columns of names appeared in the mess coach. The names of those members of the Loco Department who thought *Hastings* would be ready by a particular date

The precarious adventures of Hastings *saddle tank (Chris Lowry)*

appeared on one side while on the other was supposed to be the signatures of those who thought she would not. Whichever side lost was supposed to finance a night in the Eight Bells for the winners. Robin Doust (rather uncharacteristically but perhaps wishing to provide an incentive) put his name down on the side of the sceptics. Unfortunately he was only joined by 'Colonel Stephens' as well as 'James Bond', 'Harold Wilson' and a variety of other contemporary figures.

The boiler tubes were replaced, the safety valves reset and the valve gear stripped, cleaned, oiled and re-assembled. The regulator was also refaced, a task which involved removing the cast-iron dome. The removal of the saddle tank had been accomplished by the use of the breakdown crane from the local garage. This proved to be not such a good idea as the crane managed to drop the tank from a height of 5 ft, with the result that the injector water valve on one side was forced through the base. When the time came to re-assemble the locomotive the Loco Department decided to do the job itself and the tank appeared perched on many feet of wooden packing. But to the acute embarrassment of the Loco boys, the packing collapsed and the tank descended from a height of 10 ft with a horrendous clang which could be

The steaming of Hastings *on 11 April 1965. The siding is now the Pullman dock at Tenterden Town station. Note the weighbridge on the wagon behind the Ford Popular (Chris Lowry)*

heard over a wide area. Remarkably, there was no damage this time and the operation was repeated, the tank this time being elevated to 15 ft before being successfully slid across and remounted on the boiler.

Hastings was steamed for the first time on Easter Sunday 1965, and ran up and down the siding for two hours, after being ceremonially rechristened by Robin Doust with a bottle of brown ale. That evening *Hastings* acted as 'washing machine' for Derek Dunlavey's greasy overalls by means of a pipe running from the locomotive to a bucket. Robin was of course the only identifiable doubter on the list, but he did, as agreed, treat the Loco Department to its evening out. Unfortunately it had been decided during the hydraulic test, and other preliminary examinations preceding steaming, that owing to corrosion the boiler pressure would have to be reduced from 120 lb per sq. in. to 100. This reduced the locomotive's hauling capacity to a point where her utility became questionable. She later joined the other locomotives and stock at Rolvenden where, as various wags pointed out, the yard was again beginning to look as it had in the 1930s.

The troubles which had afflicted *Marcia* two years earlier had now been corrected. All of the work had been carried out by just two members of the Loco Department, Bill Westwood and Alan Castle, this being a locomotive overhauling partnership which was to continue until Bill's untimely death some years later. The cause of No. 12's ailments had proved to be very extensive wear in all pins, bearings and links throughout the valve gear. The entire motion was dismantled, drilled out and bushed where necessary before re-assembly. Once work was complete, the locomotive ran very smoothly and on Easter Saturday had succeeded in hauling the combined 43 ton weight of *Charwelton* and *Gervase* up and down a siding at Rolvenden.

BR, in the form of its Eversholt House staff, continued to be much exercised by the problem of getting ex-GWR railcar No. 20 from Worcester (where it had lain since withdrawal) to Robertsbridge. Realizing that it had made an awkward mistake, BR at first requested an alternative delivery point, but this was not forthcoming as road transport, from Tonbridge, for example, would have been expensive. The Society then heard through its contacts that a row had broken out between Eversholt House and the Southern Region, with the latter refusing point-blank the passage of the railcar. BR then threatened to cancel the contract, the Society threatened to sue and BR retired to consider the matter again.

During the year a K&ESR delegation was invited, in surprisingly polite terms, to visit Eversholt House. A formidable group, made up of Robin Doust, Derek Dunlavey, Ron Cann and Dave Sinclair, called at this Lubianka among railway offices and found themselves faced with an official who had previously hoisted the price of the Maunsell coaches way beyond their real value and who, on that occasion, had only been partially defeated. This time, however, conciliation was the order of the day and the Society found itself in a position to suggest a 1958-built railbus (worth £18,000 when new!) as an acceptable alternative. The discomfited BR official said he would see what could be done. This evidently alarmed all concerned at BR as the Society next heard that after consultations with AEC, who had built the railcar, it had been

K&ESR (ex-GER) coach body found near Rolvenden. Unfortunately its preservation was not to be (Dave Sinclair)

determined that the vehicle could be tilted sideways on its spring hangers sufficiently to allow it to clear the Hastings line tunnels, provided the opposite line was kept clear. Further developments were awaited.

Meanwhile, also on the rolling stock front, the body of an ex-Great Eastern Railway four-wheeled coach, which was believed to be K&ESR No. 20, was discovered in the corner of a field at the back of Rolvenden village. The coach body, which once contained two compartments and a guard's brake, had been in use as a shed together with a similar three-compartment brake/third. The latter coach had been demolished before its owner, who had recently bought the farm, realized there was a local Society who might be interested in his leftovers. The surviving coach body was inspected and it was first thought restoration was possible (although the internal partitions were gone) and an appeal was made for someone to finance the purchase of a suitable underframe and running gear. Unfortunately, this promising project almost literally fell to pieces. The Society had no money even to move the coach body to Tenterden and, it was feared, the structure was too fragile to withstand any such attempt. Some of the metalwork is thought to have been recovered but its present whereabouts is unknown.

Around this time it was announced that the railway was to have three ex-LNER Wickham trolleys which had been built in 1931 and were being sold off by the Eastern Region at York. The trolleys were to cost as little as £5 each and the money was being put up by David Wigley, Geoff Percy and Ron Cann. The new acquisitions were intended as a replacement for the Morris 20 and their transport to the K&ESR was being arranged.

The growing interest in the telephone system had been given a boost by the arrival of Frank Davis. A most likable person and acknowledged expert on telephone systems, Frank was then over retiring age and had worked for Telephone Rentals Ltd. It was he who had suggested the use of Don 8 wire and one of his initial suggestions was a ring-back system which enabled a caller to ascertain if the line was intact without having to wait for a reply from the other end. He found two ready-trained and very willing assistants in Andrew and Malcolm Webb. The Webb brothers were also beginning to take a hand in the administration side of the railway and, as part of the effort to relieve Robin Doust of some of his onerous load, jointly took on the post of Membership Secretary. Similarly, Derek Dunlavey took over postal sales in addition to his locomotive duties.

Meanwhile, Geoff Percy had completed his plans for the signalling of Northiam station and it was intended to forward copies of these to the Ministry of Transport for approval. Preliminary negotiations were also started with the Ministry preparatory to the submission of the Light Railway Transfer Order. It was necessary to involve the local authorities at this stage and negotiations were under way with the East Sussex and Kent County Surveyors' departments about the resumed use of the level crossings. In the interim it was hoped to run the proposed limited service on rented track by borrowing a BR pilotman.

The Society understood that it had to give BR a final decision shortly after 9 June 1965 about whether or not it wished to purchase the line. The Committee met on 6 June and considered the latest position. A member of the Locomotive Trust had contacted the Estates and Rating Department and arranged a meeting. Delegations representing both sides had attended, the Society ascertaining that Mr Pickin had been given until 10 June to exchange contracts. The K&ESR representatives were also able to put forward a scheme to purchase Robertsbridge–Bodiam only (i.e. the Crombleholme–Wigley plan) but were told that this could not be discussed until Mr Pickin withdrew and that, if it did proceed, the asking price would be £15,000.

The Committee then considered a meeting which had been held on 2 June 1965 between six of its number, Mr Pickin and his solicitor. The outcome was stated to be that Mr Pickin would be willing to co-operate with the Society, provided: Robin Doust and Len Heath Humphrys resigned; Mr Pickin's membership was re-instated; Mr Pickin was allowed to put a motion to the next AGM that the original Appeal Trust funds were handed over to the Society. (This may be a mistake in the minutes. It has been stated that Mr Pickin's Company was the proposed recipient and the account does in fact make sense when read with this alteration.) Mr Pickin was prepared to raise his portion to £30,000; no further track was to be lifted north of Tenterden Town station.

Len Heath Humphrys pointed out that it was not possible for the Appeal Trust money to be handed over under the terms of the scheme but Ron Cann suggested that Appeal Trust members be circulated to see if they would agree to their money being used to assist Mr Pickin's purchase of the line. The Committee agreed to this suggestion by a majority of ten to two.

Robin Doust then suggested a second line of approach, which was that the Society pay a 70 per cent deposit on the railway (he thought £9,000 of this was either available or could be readily raised) and in the six months it would take to obtain the Light Railway Order either raise the remainder of the money or lift the track between Tenterden and Bodiam – in effect an acceptance of the Crombleholme–Wigley plan. Robin then proposed that future negotiations with Mr Pickin be conducted on the Society's terms only, but this was rejected by eight votes to two.

Following this, and on a proposal from Ron Cann, George Pickin's membership of the Society was re-instated. The penultimate item of interest was the secondment of Eddie Bye to the Committee and agreement that he would become Secretary (with Arthur Penny as Chairman) if Mr Pickin signed a contract with BR to purchase the railway. As we shall see, these were eventualities which were never to occur.

The final item was, however, another step along the road to the future. Derek Dunlavey had been contacted by Mr Corbins of the Westerham Valley Railway Association who had asked that the Committees of the two organizations meet. This was agreed to.

Immediately after the Committee meeting there was the first of two further meetings which, while not part of the formal proceedings, were appended to the minutes. The first of these was a meeting in the Woolwich coach with Mr Pickin, who had been waiting outside. In addition to reploughing a number of furrows already covered, Mr Pickin was informed that his conditions had been met and he confirmed he was prepared to invest £30,000 if necessary.

An interesting side-issue raised during this meeting was Mr Pickin's intention to obtain the ex-Shropshire and Montgomeryshire Railway locomotive *Gazelle* and run it with a special coach, six seats (as prior to Col. Stephens' ownership) and a return to 2–2–2T wheel arrangement. This last change would have been aided by a replacement boiler and, if necessary, larger cylinders.

The minutes of this after-meeting also state that Mr Pickin was told that when he committed himself with BR, Messrs Heath Humphrys and Doust would resign, to be replaced by Mr Penny and Mr Bye respectively, this having been decided by the Committee the same day. Mr Pickin was not satisfied with this and would not consider the Society was behind him unless they resigned immediately.[6]

The second meeting was held during the following day's traction engine rally at Elham. The Society had a stall there, plus a miniature live-steam line run by Charlie Kentsley and, of course, Ron Cann's Garrett. A large party again drove over to represent the K&ESR, and as a number of Committee members were present the opportunity was taken to meet (in the back of Dave Sinclair's van!). The main points arising were that Len Heath Humphrys said that he was willing to circulate the subscribers to the first Appeal Trust for their views on Mr Pickin's proposals but repeated that his powers were limited. Both he and Robin Doust stated they were unwilling to resign until Mr Pickin committed himself with BR.

The last Committee meeting to be related in this sequence occurred on 4 July 1965, as usual in the Woolwich coach at Rolvenden. The Southern Region had extended Mr Pickin's deadline until 16 July and the possibility of the Society going ahead with a shorter length of line without his help was again discussed. In particular, Len Humphrys said that BR had suggested to him that a price of £10,000 be agreed for the freehold of the entire line and that the line, including track, as far as Northiam be bought at a price based on what BR received from the sale of the upper section of the line, after putting this out to tender. There was some discussion about the financial details of trying to get BR to let the Society lift the track within the period allotted to the obtaining of the Light Railway Order. Although negotiations for the purchase of the line continued to hang in this limbo, this phase was, in fact, drawing to a close and, as already hinted, developments involving the Westerham group were much more positive.

As a preservation venture the Westerham Valley Railway Association was slightly the junior of the two schemes, having been formed in October 1961, although it had been built around the branch passenger association which had come into existence some years earlier, initially being run in parallel with the preservation group before joining with it. According to all the conventional wisdom the Westerham scheme was ideal. The branch was a line of moderate length, with a main-line junction, a neat terminus at Westerham, no level crossings and a definite possibility of commuter traffic. It was also just beyond the Greater London area and there was a strong body of opinion that it was the more viable of the two schemes. During its existence the WVRA purchased an H class 0-4-4T (never delivered to the Westerham line but to Robertsbridge yard instead) and was said to have an effective administrative organization. Some mild rivalry had existed with the K&ESR, but the two groups tended to be mutually sympathetic and there was some overlap in membership. That said, most individuals had a primary loyalty to one railway or the other. Westerham, however, came to nothing when Kent County Council purchased the line from BR for road-building. Today, part of the route lies beneath the M25.

In his book, *The Westerham Valley Railway*, David Gould wrote of the line as having a 'sad little history'. This captures a mood of melancholy which seemed to hang around the branch even in its BR days and is described much less economically in my poem, 'Westerham Station':

> Autumn always reminds me of Westerham,
> Edwardian atmosphered houses
> Across the road from a station which seemed
> To be the overgrown creation of someone
> Making models of the South Eastern mood.p
> Blunt end of a withering branch, peeling
> Grubby green and light stone paintwork
> Like leaves fallen from summer heights to dirt
> Grained cement surfaces; restful melancholy,
> The withered dried up end of Victorian
> Dream time, fenced in its own soot encrusted
> Railings; a late spring grafting which
> Never took and was overdue for pruning.
> Westerham was a cold dry season before winter.
> Autumn always reminds me of Westerham,
> Edwardian atmosphered houses
> Across the road.[7]

The two schemes were also somewhat different in character. No doubt because of their locations, the K&ESR seemed 'county' and Westerham 'suburban'. Having used these two words, haste must now be made to explain that they are meant in their least pejorative senses. Something similar to the then atmosphere on the K&ESR is to be found in the less controversial aspects of H.E. Bates's *The Darling Buds of May* (the railway sequences of the television adaptation were filmed at Tenterden in recent years), with its blend of Londoners escaping the conurbation and local people following a lifestyle dating back to the 1930s. Westerham seemed to owe something to all the least backbiting and most positive aspects of the world of model railway clubs. The K&ESR was more free-wheeling but had done a great deal with its rolling stock and on its line. Westerham had, through no fault of its own, been unable to do the same but was thought to be strong on management and publicity.

It was realized that it would make a great deal of sense if the two schemes amalgamated and the Westerham members moved to the K&ESR. The Westerham Committee, accordingly, attended the K&ESR Committee meeting on 4 July and the two bodies jointly considered the possibilities open to them. The WVRA already had a commitment to Mr Pickin to present his proposals for the K&ESR to its members at a Special General Meeting on 21 July, and that it felt the need, in good faith, to keep to this. It would also be putting forward the proposal for a Northiam – Robertsbridge service without using Mr Pickin's money and said this would carry its recommendation.

Item seven of the minutes reads:

> The suggestion that an amalgamation of the two Societies be recommended to their memberships was then made, and all those present agreed that this would be in the best interests of all concerned. Accordingly, it was agreed that a meeting of a small group of members of both committees meet in Tonbridge during the following evening to discuss details of such an amalgamation. A further point made by the WVRA, concerning whether the H class loco could be used on the K&ESR was then dealt with. It was said that the engine could be used on certain sections of the line without restriction, and that future bridge reconstruction . . . would enable the engine to be used without restriction on the section of the line between Robertsbridge and Northiam.

A little later Charlie Kentsley suggested that as Mr Pickin now had a time limit he might be more willing to accept the Society's terms. The WVRA took the opportunity to discuss this in private before Mr Pickin, who was present at Rolvenden, was invited into the meeting. He was told that the Society was prepared to co-operate fully with him if he agreed to make mortgage finance available as discussed by the Committee on 11 April and afterwards communicated to him in writing. Mr Pickin declined to accept and, when informed that there seemed little point in continuing the discussion, left the meeting.

The Annual General Meeting for 1965 was held on 14 August. The Annual Report was able to state that East Sussex County Council had no objections to the re-use of the level crossings, subject to provision of various additional safeguards, and that Mr Pickin's offer to buy the line had expired. In the circumstances the Society had confirmed its willingness to carry through the purchase and an answer from BR was awaited. Leonard Heath Humphrys picked this point up during his introductory remarks at the meeting by saying that BR's proposals were expected daily. He then re-iterated the importance being placed on the RVR Trust Fund and that Northiam would probably now be the limit of operations. (The even shorter option of Bodiam under the Crombleholme–Wigley plan seems to have been abandoned by then.)

The Chairman then set targets for the restoration of services – Bodiam at Easter 1966 and Northiam at Whitsun. It cannot be too strongly emphasized that this was not as unrealistic as hindsight might suggest. Much work had been undertaken on the lower section, the weak bridge 1029 was not involved and the Society had, or would soon after receive, the rolling stock needed for a service over the shorter mileage. On a slightly lighter note it was, nevertheless, the latest manifestation of an old answer to an old question. Right from the beginning of the project anyone asking when the line would re-open was invariably told 'Next year'.

The pleasant surroundings of Tenterden Town Hall then began to echo to the usual reverberations of a K&ESR AGM. The minutes of the previous AGM were read but Mr Pickin objected to their accuracy where they referred to himself. He suggested a number of amendments but as no seconder was forthcoming the minutes were adopted as circulated. Ron Cann's Treasurer's report explained away a slight loss by using the 'one year against another' theme then popular with governments embarrassed by nationalized industries, before the meeting turned to the proposed amalgamation with the WVRA.

It had been anticipated that this would have been in the nature of welcoming retreating comrades to the next hill-top fort (albeit a beleaguered one). This was not how events developed. No sooner had Mr Ranson of the WVRA stated the case for amalgamation and there had been a burst of applause, than Arthur Penny was on his feet. Both he and Ron Cann (who also spoke, supporting him) had, subsequent to the Committee meeting on 4 July, reconsidered their personal attitudes regarding the proposal and come to the conclusion that the WVRA had little to offer the K&ESR, since the H class could not be of much use on the line and that he understood the Westerham group had little in the way of useful equipment. (The WVRA also had some coaches available to it – the previously mentioned ex-SE&CR vehicle and some Metropolitan Railway Dreadnoughts – which were the property of Association members. All this rolling stock went to the Keighley and Worth Valley Railway because of later developments and not because of opposition to the amalgamation.) Mr Penny also suggested that the disorganization resulting from a revised constitution could not be justified and that the Westerham members should simply be invited to join the K&ESRPS.

Col. Horsfield then spoke in a conciliatory manner, pointing out that the main point was to secure the support of the WVRA in the best way possible. Malcolm Dunstan represented the majority view in the K&ESR volunteer force when he said that co-operation on a proper basis seemed the best plan, rather than one organization simply swallowing another. The anti-amalgamation lobby then received further support from a Mr Woody who described the WVRA as a 'dying organization' with whom there seemed little point in amalgamating. Damage limitation was needed by this stage and was provided by Robin Doust, who repeated the advantages, and Len Heath Humphrys (from the chair), who reminded everybody that members were not being asked to take a final decision there and then. After some debate it was decided to refer the matter back to the Committee for consideration before again putting the matter to the Society.

No sooner had the amalgamation issue been safely deferred than Mr Pickin was insisting on putting forward his proposals again. He managed to speak at length, repeating all the same ideas that he had spoken on at the previous year's AGM, but it was apparent, after this had gone on for some while, that there was a certain restiveness in the hall. Eventually Mr Pickin was interrupted by Dick Beckett who said that, while he appreciated Mr Pickin's right to put forward his proposal, he should be either asked to co-operate with the Society or 'refrain from meddling in its affairs'. Mr Pickin's reply was to reiterate his plans all over again. The restiveness in the meeting was becoming marked by this stage and only ended when Col. Horsfield proposed that Mr Pickin stand down and allow the meeting to continue. The meeting agreed with that and Len Heath Humphrys ruled George Pickin out of order and requested him to sit down.

The existing Committee was then re-elected *en bloc* once again and before the meeting suddenly took another unexpected turn. Greg Goodman, one of the regular volunteers, spoke. Turning to the minutes again:

> He had gained the impression from what had been said by Mr Pickin, and from other information disclosed at the meeting, that the Society's progress had been very much retarded as a result of Mr Pickin's interference in its attempt to reach an agreement with BR over the purchase of the railway, and it seemed to him that Mr Pickin's continued association with the Society was most undesirable. He therefore proposed that Mr Pickin's membership be terminated. This proposal was seconded by Mr Morgan.

A number of questions were raised by Mr Scarlett, who was thought to be a new member and unaware of Mr Pickin's previous associations with the Society. (It is now known that he was in fact a publicity man working for Mr Pickin.) The minutes continue, 'The matter was put to the vote, it was agreed by 29 votes to 8, with 13 abstentions, that Mr Pickin's membership be withdrawn.' After all the problems caused by the Committee's withdrawal of Pickin's membership and the heart-searching about his re-instatement (which it has to be said had not been reported to the general membership), the meeting had decided to reach its own conclusions on the matter! George Pickin, not surprisingly, questioned the AGM's entitlement to take such a step and Len Humphrys, equally unsurprisingly, agreed to take advice before implementing the decision.[8]

After the meeting had finished and the visiting members had gone on their way, a group of volunteers were sitting in the mess coach going over the events of the afternoon. Remembering that local reporters had been at the meeting, Robin Doust wondered what the *Kent and Sussex Courier* would say the following week. 'Uproar at Rail Society Meeting?' suggested somebody. There was hardly a pause before someone else added, 'For third year running.'

The hopes which Len Heath Humphrys had placed on the Rother Valley Railway Trust Fund at the AGM continued to be stressed, and a calculation appeared in *The Farmers' Line* explaining that if everybody in the Society covenanted to give 10s per week the line could be paid for in four years. This was neither laughable nor fanciful. The sceptical are reminded that twenty-five years later the equivalent sum is £5 and that property prices in the south-east have accelerated far ahead of general inflation. The same edition of *The Farmers' Line* made a pointed appeal to those who had not yet contributed. Part of it read as follows:

Naturally, a good many members have considerably exceeded the basic minimum aimed at, and we have been enormously helped by the receipt of several lump sums of from £100 to £400, which has swelled the total held in the account considerably, but now that the existing members of the scheme have shown that it can be made a most useful source of income, we earnestly appeal to every member who has not yet joined the scheme to climb off the fence on which he or she has been sitting, and to support the project fully. We can succeed most effectively if support continues to grow at its present rate, but it is most essential that support is received now, as without it the full extent of services originally planned will not be possible for a good many years to come. On the other hand, if we are successful in securing your additional support, sufficient to enable the whole railway to be bought and kept intact, we shall have acheived something which will far exceed any effort yet made in the field of railway preservation, and which could well set the trend for many more successful efforts such as our own to save for the benefit of the community a public service which is otherwise doomed to extinction.

At the end of the item about the Trust was a list of those who had contributed up to that time. It was an interesting collection of names and included a number of the regular volunteers, one or two well-known railway photographers and a few individuals who would become prominent in the railway's distant future. It also included A.B. McLeod, the man who, apart from Col. Stephens and W.H. Austen had, through his pre-war management of the Isle of Wight Railways, done more than anyone else this century to popularize small, local lines.

Work was concentrating on cutting back the heavy undergrowth and the oiling of the fishplates between Bodiam and Robertsbridge. Despite the plan to operate the lower section of the line, the project was still centred on Tenterden and Rolvenden and activity was much aided by the arrival of the Wickham trolleys. They proved very successful, although all three were never in working order at the same time. They continued in use for some years, but this is a good point in the story to relate a few of the tales surrounding them.

The trolleys' JAP V twin, 1323 cc, side-valve engines had magneto ignition and bore a family resemblance to those used in pre-war three-wheeled Morgans. Transmission was via a variable disc drive (then a term associated with low technology). The silencing arrangements were minimal, while noise level within the vehicles was such as to make conversation impossible. Their ride was very rough but they seemed to have been designed to take an enormous amount of punishment. Quite often weeds blocked the rudimentary

'Have you found the magneto ring yet?': Webb brother and Wickham trolley (Chris Lowry)

air intake and overheated the engine which then seized. The driver would simply allow the engine to cool off for a while, remove the offending grass and give a few turns on the starting handle to free the piston rings. The engine would then restart without any apparent signs of damage! The rough ride could sometimes get the better of the magnetos, which would shed a small bronze ring, resulting in a loss of all electrical power. There would then follow a game of 'hunt the ring' among the grass for the preceding 200 yd. Amazingly, it was always found. One trolley was later fitted with a headlamp powered by a car battery which was charged up midweek. The light was switched on by attaching crocodile clips to the battery. It was possible, in the early evening, to climb the ladder of Rolvenden water tower and follow the trolley's progress through the encircling dusk as the lamp weaved and flickered between the lineside trees.

One particularly horrendous story is told about the Wickham trolleys which I can personally verify as being completely true. It happened one Saturday morning as a Wickham was merrily bowling along towards Northiam at a respectable speed. The first thing the crew knew that something was amiss was when, and in the vicinity of the Rother Bridge, there were two mild jolts under the trolley wheels. A quick glance to the rear showed that the trolley had run over two expensive-looking fishing rods which had been placed across the rails. Even worse, two large and angry-looking fishermen instantly materialized and proceeded to dance about while hurling expletives which were lost in the merry roar of the JAP engine. Readers will have noticed that, given a tight spot, the K&ESRPS generally tried diplomacy. Discretion was, however, the better part of valour and, rapidly summing up all the facts, the driver opened the throttle and kept going! No furious anglers appeared at the work site but there was some apprehension about the return journey which was delayed until dusk. But there was no blocked track, no ambush and neither did anyone turn up at Tenterden complaining.

There was, however, a sequel to the fishing rods' episode. Not long afterwards, a huge pile of concrete block sleepers from Northiam was loaded onto a flat trolley (a square wooden frame with four inverted-'U' bearings to hold the axles) and pushed back to Rolvenden by a Wickham. Robin Doust was seated on the front of the flat trolley as lookout, but long grass made a clear view of the track difficult. To Robin's horror, as the trolleys crossed the Rother Bridge at considerable speed, he spotted a sleeper deliberately placed across the track. Despite Robin's immediate call to stop, the trolley ran into the sleeper which fortunately slid along the top of the rails. Needless to say, the loaded trolley and the propelling Wickham stopped rather quickly, and Robin was acutely aware of the tottering pile of concrete blocks on the trolley behind him, threatening to crush him at any moment. It was never established whether the sleeper had been placed by one of the aggrieved fishermen, but it was right beside the old permanent way hut by the northern abutment of the Rother Bridge, from where the two luckless anglers had emerged with horror on their faces.

More conventional forms of rolling stock were also beginning to move towards the K&ESR. The ex-SE&CR brake van had reached Tonbridge, where the draw gear was found to be damaged at one end. (It is believed this occurred when the van was hump-shunted at Feltham.) BR had agreed to undertake repairs before delivery and as a result of the mishap the Brake Van Fund got both the vehicle and most of its money back! The Manning Wardle 0–6–0ST *Sir Berkeley* had now dropped out of sight (the loco went to the Keighley and Worth Valley Railway instead), but the Westerham Group's H class had been at Robertsbridge for nearly a year, there having been no other point at which it could have been accepted. The H had arrived on 17 November 1964 as part of a freight train and with the coupling rods slung in the bunker. Work had commenced on repainting her in SE&CR colours and members of the Loco Department gave occasional consideration as to how she could be lightened sufficiently to get her to Rolvenden. Completely emptying the tanks, boiler and bunker, as well as removing odd bits and pieces such as the coupling rods, was one possibility.

The four Maunsell coaches had been paid for as being in good condition by the early autumn and sat at Paddock Wood while delivery was arranged and some small items, such as roof-board clips, were removed to temporarily change them from restriction 1 to restriction 0, and allow delivery to Robertsbridge through the Hastings line tunnels. Woodwork and upholstery from the coaches were subject to the activities of thieves and vandals but there were other withdrawn vehicles in the sidings, all destined for scrap, and Robin Doust realized this was an opportunity to replace what the K&ESR had paid for anyway, as well as to provide spare parts. Robin was still living in Tenterden at that time and commuting to Kensington via Headcorn. For several weeks he broke his journey at Paddock Wood and made use of the long summer evenings to unscrew items from the condemned coaches and store them safely in the brake ends and compartments of the K&ESR stock. The station staff were sympathetic and there were no problems.

There then followed a meeting between BR and K&ESR representatives to agree the details of the move to Robertsbridge. Robin arrived to find a frosty atmosphere settled over the gathering. One of the BR officials then worked himself up into a fury about the 'army of men' who must have 'spent weeks stripping bare' the coaches and 'carefully hiding the parts'. There was great embarrassment all round and fervent denials on the part of the K&ESR that they knew anything about it. The furious man from BR had apparently failed to notice the missing items were openly stored in one of the brake ends but insisted 'it would all have to go back' while, just out of his view, his colleagues were winking and nodding at the Society members. In fact, when the restriction 1s were delivered to Robertsbridge on the afternoon of Sunday

The arrival of the Maunsell restriction 1s at Robertsbridge in 1965. The locomotive is, of course, a 'Slim Jim' BRCW type 3 (Later class 33/2) (Chris Lowry)

28 November, someone had added some green floral seating to the spare upholstery. Such were the bridges built in those days between BR staff and preservation enthusiasts and which have served the interests of the rail network rather well ever since.

One also wonders about the motives of the 'angry official', particularly as nothing (negative) subsequently happened. Was he going through the motions? This seems an appropriate moment to recall that many BR staff found their loyalties torn when it came to dealing with preservationists and that, as they saw it, they were 'only doing their jobs'. In the emotional atmosphere of the times it was easy for enthusiasts to assign the role of villain to anyone 'official'. Two former chairmen have stated that, during a part of the story to be related later, the metaphorical 'nod', 'wink' and 'helping hand' could often be found at a more elevated level in the railway hierarchy.

Meanwhile, the volunteers, under the leadership of Dave Sinclair and the Webb brothers, had been pressing on with the task of fishplate oiling, and by the end of October only about three-quarters of a mile of the lower section remained to be dealt with. The task involved unscrewing thousands of partly seized 1 in. diameter bolts. The more obstinate examples were often dealt with by one of the largest volunteers, Tiny Jones, so called because he wasn't. The fishplates themselves were persuaded to part from the rails by a well-aimed clout with a keying hammer, before lubricant, old sump oil from the volunteers' cars, was liberally applied. It was becoming apparent that a number of telegraph poles were rotten, if they had not actually fallen down, and it was intended to start replacing these. Dave Sinclair had waterproofed the roofs of the Pullman cars and the brake van had actually arrived and been added to the growing collection of rolling stock at Robertsbridge. The signalling department had been buying from London Transport again and a 24-lever electric-powered signal frame, with miniature levers and full interlocking equipment, had been acquired. There were still regular appeals for volunteers and one contained a lovely example of Robin Doust's subtle sense of humour, which says quite a lot about railway volunteers. 'Bring old clothes, or a boiler suit and some strong working gloves. You can change at Tenterden or Bodiam, so there is no need to appear like a tramp on your journey to the line.'

On a totally different front, it had been discovered that two trading stamp companies were willing to exchange these symbols of 1960s affluence for specialized equipment. Stamps were given with everything at that time and a scheme, run by Bill Westwood, was started. This proved very successful in obtaining various much-needed tools for the K&ESR.

A regular party from the Loco Department, under the leadership of Charlie Kentsley, was making regular trips to Ashford running shed, where repairs to the O1 class were progressing. Grey primer had been applied and the valve gear and motion replaced with assistance from the works staff. Among the locomotives resident at Rolvenden, the Locomotive Trust had sold No. 12, *Marcia,* to Dick Beckett, although this was entirely a money-raising exercise, as he had no intention of removing her from the railway.

The 'Surrey' group of the Locomotive Trust had meanwhile expressed an interest in 'diversifying', which, it was understood, meant lending locomotives to other societies. It had shown an interest in the Meon Valley line at Droxford, Hampshire, where the Sadler railcar was being developed, and there was some idea of the line being re-opened. The 'Surrey' group went as far as forming a company, the Southern Locomotive Preservation Company Ltd, to own its share of the Loco Trust assets, this being allowed under the provision which allowed corporate membership. An appreciable proportion of the other money held by the Trust had, however, come from other, individual K&ESR members.

Four of the three-plank wagons (paid for by SLP members) were actually moved to Droxford. The SLP company then attempted, at a K&ESRLT AGM, to amalgamate with the Trust. This was forestalled by other members, as they were worried about the possibility of the stock being removed from the railway. The SLP company then had a problem: £255 was still owed for *Hastings* and *Charwelton*, the ex-owners were pressing for payment and SLP members had much of the responsibility for meeting this outstanding debt. A solution was found by Derek Dunlavey, who suggested that the Locomotive Trust amalgamate with the Brake Van Fund, which would take over the debts. This would allow the SLP company to transfer its interests to Droxford.

A series of meetings followed, during which new Trust officers were elected and the Brake Van Fund agreed to take over the Trust. The reconstituted Locomotive Trust had Derek Dunlavey as Chairman and Dave Sinclair as Secretary. The constitution was a copy of that under which the egalitarian Brake Van Fund had operated.

By late in the year and after nearly five years of struggle, and, at times, considerable uncertainty, the foreground future began to look pleasingly bright. Following the expiry of his option to buy the line, Mr Pickin had returned to South Africa and, despite the lack of any guarantee that it would do so, the Southern Region offered the line to the Society. The Society, of course, accepted, subject to contract. The asking price for the line had also been held at £36,000 (£3,000 per mile), which came as no small relief, disused lines by then averaging £5,000 per mile. It was understood that once the contract was signed, a 10 per cent deposit would have to be paid and that the Society would have six months to obtain the Light Railway Order. Knowing this, Len Heath Humphrys and Ron Cann pressed on with the, at times, seemingly hopeless task of finding the necessary finance, but succeeded in agreeing with a bank that £15,000 would be made available over ten years at a very reasonable rate, the loan being, most generously, on the security of the property owned by a member of the Association. However, £18,000 would have to be raised by lifting the Northiam–Tenterden section. The Society had £6,000 in hand or promised through the Trust, and a major effort was to start in order to raise the remaining £5,000 towards the working capital it was anticipated would be required to get the line operational.

A Special General Meeting was called on 18 December following the receipt of the contract earlier in the month. There were two principal items requiring the approval of the membership and this was given in both cases. The first endorsed the proposals for the purchase of the railway and gave authority for the Committee to proceed with the signing of the contract. The second agreed to an amalgamation with the WVRA. At midnight on 31 December 1965, and with seemingly every prospect of success before it, the K&ESR PS, the shortest-lived of the railway's several managements, slipped quietly into history.

Notes

1. *The Kent and East Sussex Railway,* by S.R. Garrett, published by Oakwood Press, and *The Rother Valley Railway, Later the Kent and East Sussex Railway,* by M. Lawson Finch.
2. Mr Baker was referring to Southern Railway Sentinel-Cammell railbus No. 6, which had been officially withdrawn in 1942.
3. The origin of the term '1029' is obscure. It was not, as is sometimes thought, the Southern Region bridge register number – that was 2336. One possible explanation is that the bridge was 10 miles and 29 chains from Robertsbridge.
4. Mr Pickin disagrees with this account and in letters to me has commented:

> What happened at the 1964 AGM was that someone suggested re-electing Humphrys and Doust, but not as Chairman and Secretary, and the acting Chairman objected that only the Committee could decide on that, so a unanimous resolution was passed that they should resign as Chairman and Secretary so that the rest of the Committee could negotiate with me. This was quite unnecessary, since it sufficed that they should not attend the negotiations.
>
> Since Humphrys and Doust were being re-elected to the Committee and a member had asked whether they could be re-elected, not as Chairman and Secretary, and the acting Chairman had replied that it was solely for the Committee to decide who should occupy these posts it would have been useless and absurd for the meeting to resolve that they should ask them to resign if they chose (not even remove them). The only resolution which makes any sense is that they should resign as Chairman and Secretary so that the rest of the Committee should deal with me.
>
> That [the Committee] defied this by demanding that I should negotiate exclusively with Humphrys and Doust – they did not want to be consulted . . .
>
> In fact the Committee did meet without Humphrys and Doust, but adjourned to report to them and, on resumption, demanded I should negotiate exclusively with them as Chairman and Secretary.

Subsequent meetings did indeed take place with Mr Pickin. The minutes stand, however, to this day as the official record. The alternative version has been included at Mr Pickin's request.
5. During my time as a volunteer I was twice conscious of personal difficulties in this respect. The first instance involved difficulties in establishing a working relationship with a person I held in a certain amount of awe and the second an individual (not 'prominent volunteer') of whom I was, frankly, physically scared. Even this latter situation took some time to develop. Out of perhaps one hundred people encountered, this is not a bad batting average.
6. Once again, further comment has been added at Mr Pickin's request. He is of the opinion that his conditions for co-operating with the Society were agreed at the meeting on 2 June (particularly the resignation of Robin Doust and Len Heath Humphrys) but that 'the Committee tore up this agreement when they got into the presence of the Chairman and the Secretary without any reference to me, though I was standing outside'.
7. The 'cold dry season before winter' may be regarded as either the years just before Beeching or 1966–7 on the K&ESR.
8. Mr Pickin was expelled from membership again but took further legal action against the Society. The basis of his case was that the expulsion was against natural justice, i.e. that he was given no opportunity to hear the charges against him or to defend himself. The matter was later heard in the High Court, although the K&ESRPS could not afford Counsel and had to be represented by Robin Doust in his role as Secretary. The Society lost and Mr Pickin was reinstated. He remains a member of the Tenterden Railway Company.

PART TWO
The Association

X

Like most railway amalgamations, the creation of the K&ESR Association on 1 January 1966 brought changes which were, in the first instance, less than obvious. The arrival of ex-Westerham volunteers was muted by the overlap in membership and the fact that some WVRA people, such as Terry Heaslip, Gordon Laming and Stan Collier, had moved over well before their former scheme officially gave up. Furthermore, and quite understandably, the presence of the H class made Robertsbridge something of a centre for former Westerham members. It has to be said, nevertheless, that the most revealing comment appeared in the newsletter some months later. In a leading article can be found the following quote: 'We were also pleased to note that many WVRA members were able to attend and travel on the train, and we very much hope that if you were one of these, that you, too will have been sufficiently inspired . . . to take a more active part both in working parties and in the financial side of the railway . . . please let your interest extend to really practical help.' (To keep things in balance, it should be remembered that former K&ESRPS members could play the annoying dilettante as well.)

On the administrative side, the existing stationery stocks from both predecessor organizations were used up before the appearance of K&ESRPS-style membership cards and letterheads reading 'Association' instead of 'Preservation Society'. March brought the first newsletter published by the new Association, this being a largely unchanged *Farmers' Line* numbered Volume 4, Number 3 in the existing series. The leading article welcomed members, from wherever they might have come, while several pages later there was an article entitled 'How the Association is Organised'. This outline covered the Association itself, the RVR Trust Fund and the Rother Valley Railway Company Ltd which, as planned, had recently been formed to replace the lost Kent and East Sussex Light Railway Company. Four of the directors of the Rother Valley Railway were also Association Committee members. The place of the Locomotive Trust was also explained, as was the situation regarding the K&ESR Trust Fund. To quote from the article:

Originally quite a lot of money was held by the Trustees of this Fund, but on the instructions of those originally responsible for making the money available, much of it has been repaid to the original owners, who have, in many cases immediately paid the money to the permanent Rother Valley Railway Trust Fund. A number of others have preferred to make the amounts previously held in the Trust over to the Association to help with the legal expenses, etc. currently being incurred in connection with the Sale Contract and Light Railway Order. This K&ESR Trust Fund will, therefore, be shortly wound up and play no further part in the project.

The Rother Valley Railway Workers' Association was not mentioned and seems to have disappeared from K&ESR history by this point.

Len Heath Humphrys and Ron Cann continued as Trustees of the RVR Trust, Len also being Chairman of the Railway Company, with Peter Cox (ex-Westerham) as Company Secretary. The other directors were Charlie Kentsley (Motive Power Superintendent), Col. Horsfield (who advised on negotiations with the Ministry of Transport), Ron Cann, Robin Doust and Arthur Penny. The make-up of the Association Committee was particularly interesting as it indicated which way the wind was blowing in relation to the influence of the ex-WVRA members. Arthur Penny had now taken the chair (thus letting Len Humphrys concentrate on the Company job) and Robin continued as Secretary, although he now held this jointly with Dick Ranson. Ron Cann remained as Treasurer, with Charlie Kentsley and Len Humphrys being the other Committee members who had come from the K&ESRPS. Ex-Westerham Committee men were Len Hibbert, Peter Cox and, most prominently, Dave Kitton, who as Publicity Officer held the only other specific post among the Association's elected leadership.

The long job of fishplate-oiling had been completed on the lower section and, in view of the then doubtful future of the Northiam–Tenterden part of the line was not proceeding further. Rekeying was being carried out instead but, as the K&ESR was partly laid with 91$\frac{1}{4}$ lb per yd track, that produced a problem – the easily obtainable keys used on 95 lb per yd track would not fit. This problem was only solved when permission was obtained from the contractor demolishing the Hawkhurst branch to recover the smaller-sized keys from the track at Horsmonden. The Webb brothers were now leading the permanent way gang in an attack on the extensive tree growth between Northiam and Robertsbridge, ready for the replacement of the telephone wires on that section. The filthy job of clearing blocked drains and culverts was undertaken near Junction Road. This was a most necessary task as the not infrequent flooding in the Rother Valley had covered the track with silt at several points.

Work had begun on repainting the brake van, while at Rolvenden the interior fittings salvaged from a Maunsell restriction 4 had transformed the interior of the Woolwich coach. It was hoped that the 01 class No. 31065, which was still under repair, would soon arrive from Ashford, while the C class Preservation Society, whose 0–6–0 was still in service at the works and which had originally been intended for the Westerham Valley Railway, was intending to bring this locomotive to the K&ESR. The Association was in fact in a position to state that it would soon have enough rolling stock available to operate services. More would, of course, still be required and thoughts turned to the Isle of Wight where electrification was due to take place in the summer. Examples of the island's rolling stock and the ex-LSWR 02 class were considered for the K&ESR but, although some of the coaches were offered at £80 each, transport to the mainland proved impossible. The Wight Locomotive Society (later the Isle of Wight Steam Railway) of course succeeded where the K&ESR failed and it is not impossible that *Calbourne* may one day visit and be seen storming up Tenterden Bank.

The contract had not been signed as *The Farmers' Line* went to press in late February, as BR wanted to insert specific clauses regarding the exchange of freight traffic. The Rother Valley Railway Trust Fund was appealing for further contributions, as £15,000 was still needed towards the agreed purchase price, and the possibility of lifting the Northiam–Tenterden section still loomed large.

On a much brighter note, the March *Farmers' Line* included an article entitled 'Our First Trains', which, in view of the contents of foregoing chapters, was being a little economical with the truth, although it was explained this meant the Association's rather than the Preservation Society's first trains. The Southern Region had agreed to movements over the line, but a pilotman would have to be carried. The chosen dates were Easter Monday 11 April and Saturday 23 April.

During the last week of March the final version of the sale contract for the line, which now gave the Company nine months to obtain the Light Railway Order, was received by the Association's solicitors. To mark the signing a ceremony was organized on 30 March in the Mayor's parlour at Tenterden Town Hall. Apart from the Mayor, Alderman Winter, the guests included the President of the Chamber of Trade and his Vice-President, prominent local business people, the Town Clerk and representatives of the Rural District councils through whose areas the railway ran. Len Heath Humphrys spoke first, in his role as Chairman of the Rother Valley Railway Company, and welcomed those present. He was followed by Alderman Winter, who referred briefly to the part played by the Tenterden business community when the line was originally built, and the part it had played in the growth of the town. He said how much he and the other members of the council were looking forward to the line re-opening.

While the Mayor was speaking, one of the bottles of champagne intended to celebrate the event exploded, showering the wallpaper with its contents. *Après moi le deluge?* The Mayor, however, pressed on and said that he was sure that with the renewed growth of Tenterden (which was then becoming apparent) the railway would prove of value to the town. He then proposed a toast to the railway, to Tenterden and to the Rother Valley.

Much to the Association's pleasant surprise, the Southern Region allowed the special trains planned for Easter Monday and 23 April to run without supervision by a pilotman. Reports of these events appeared in subsequent editions of *The Farmers' Line*. These have an immediacy which it would be a pity to lose and the following accounts are, with the permission of their author, Robin Doust, edited, rather than paraphrased, versions of the originals.

The purpose of the Easter Monday train was to clear some of the rolling stock from Robertsbridge yard and to get it to Rolvenden, where work could be more easily carried out. Although this was officially an empty-stock working, as many members as possible were squeezed on board, and even more were recruited on the day from among those who wished to enjoy the privilege of being on the first train to traverse the Rother Valley since 1961.

Preparations for the day really got under way the previous Saturday, when No. 3 and the SE&CR brake van ran from Robertsbridge to Tenterden for the purpose of carrying out a detailed inspection of all the bridges on the line under load. This inspection was extremely satisfactory, and even those bridges which had previously been regarded as suspect were passed as safe for traffic at the speeds likely to be encountered on the line.

Early on the Monday morning, No. 3 was steamed at Rolvenden (for the first time in twelve years at that location) and left there at 9.10 a.m. hauling the brake van in which were stowed the supplies for the buffet car and all the other odds and ends needed for the day's operations. With several stops on the way to close farm crossing gates and chase sheep off the line, the train did not arrive at Robertsbridge until 10.45 a.m., with the result that there was a considerable delay while the only porter on duty dealt with the arrival of the main-line diesel trains before unlocking Robertsbridge 'A' box (the K&ESR ground frame) and clearing the points for No. 3 to enter the sidings and

Ron Cann and Kevin Blakiston watering No. 3 at Rolvenden on 11 April 1966. Note the reconstructed platform face, the re-use of the 1964 'Returning Home' headboard and the water pump used for weedkilling on the wagon behind the water crane (Dennis Ovenden)

marshall the train. This was eventually assembled in the bay platform, consisting of Pullman No. 184, 1st/2nd class composite No. 5618 and brake 2nd No. 4443. Even now there were considerable delays while the various members of the train crew and the Association's officers were pursued hither and thither by frantic journalists, ITV cameramen and BBC tape recordists. By the time all the recordings and notes had been made and the press had retired to the train in company with as many Association members as could be accommodated, the train was running just over an hour late. To the accompaniment of much enthusiastic arm waving and the clicking and whirring of innumerable cameras, the platform starter was lowered and the train pulled slowly round the sharp curve onto the branch. The first stop was at North Bridge Street crossing, where the whole operation of opening and closing the gates, and getting the train across the road, occupied less than a minute and delayed only two cars. Then it was past Hodson's Mill siding and on through Salehurst Halt, where the first reception committee of local residents assembled to wave the train through.

At Junction Road, after being flagged across the main road by the Webb brothers, the train pulled through the halt platform and stopped beside the Rother to take on water. (The K&ESR was not going to be caught out this time and a two-stroke engined pump, mounted in a tubular frame, was carried in one of the Pullman cars.) Ron Cann, acting as pump attendant, got to work and No. 3's tanks were topped up for the run on to Bodiam. Once there, the train stopped for ten minutes, and was surrounded by crowds of visitors, who seemed most enthusiastic, and were only too pleased to make quite handsome contributions to the contents of Robin Doust's capacious donations box. Then on to Northiam, where the scheduled ten-minute stop dragged on to twenty minutes, so thick were the crowds. The Sussex Police had fortunately sent a patrol car down, and several officers had their hands full controlling traffic over the level crossing, due to the many people standing about in the roads taking photographs. The train, however, finally got away, and moved out into the Rother Levels and on to the Rother Bridge, where water was again taken with the aid of the portable pump.

The next stop was at Wittersham Road. Notwithstanding the isolated position of the station site, crowds were again apparent. Many people had followed the train up the line by car, and the same faces were evident, although there were also many local people in the crowd. With the collecting box getting rather heavy, the train moved on to Rolvenden, where the biggest crowd seen up to then had assembled on the platform to watch the arrival. By the time passengers had all disembarked, to enable the train to be remarshalled before going up to Tenterden, the whole area was a solid mass of humanity, and people wandering over the track delayed shunting operations for some time. A sharp shower then drove many of those present to shelter in the Pullman car, which by then had been detached and parked in a siding. Elsie Kentsley and the catering staff proceeded to cash in on the sudden rush, while Driver Charlie Kentsley and Guard Dave Sinclair made the most of the opportunity to complete coaling up and marshalling the train in the platform again, reduced to two coaches for the ascent up the bank.

Unfortunately the prolonged wait at Rolvenden had spoilt No. 3's fire, and the gruelling climb up to Tenterden proved just a little too much for the engine, which, after some very heroic and recordable sound effects, finally came to a stand half a mile from Tenterden. A five-minute blow-up proved sufficient to recover steam and, after a little difficulty with slipping on the wet rails, No. 3 was able to pull into Tenterden after completing the climb in a most spectacular manner. Her distinctive, sharp exhaust beat must have been audible all over the town.

Once again, the scene portrayed in the *Titfield Thunderbolt*, and which has often taken place in reality, manifested itself as people rushed out of houses within sight of the line. At Tenterden the reception was quite incredible. Despite the fact that the run had hardly been publicized at all, the station was absolutely packed, and people were almost pushed off the platform edge onto the track. Cameras and tape recorders were everywhere and No. 3 had given their owners a superb chance to record an unforgettable example of steam at work as she thundered up the last stretch of line and over the level crossing into the station at a brisk 25 mph. Smiling faces were everywhere and once again the donations poured in thick and fast, until the poor collecting box (which had done sterling service with the railway since 1961) finally burst at the seams and left a trail of coins down the platform, much to Robin's consternation.

Eventually things calmed down and No. 3 was able to run round the train, and those who had travelled up boarded again for the run back to Rolvenden. The train left to the accompaniment of many shouted messages of goodwill, and arrived back at Rolvenden, where one of the two coaches was detached, and those returning to Robertsbridge crowded back into the remaining BSO, which ran back to the junction just in time to catch the 7.06 p.m. up train. After detaching the BSO, the train stewards and spare crew who had to return to Tenterden boarded the SE&CR brake van and the train finally left to return to Rolvenden after what had been a remarkably successful and enjoyable occasion, with the knowledge that a little piece of railway history had been made that day.

Another little piece of history was the arrival of the ex-GWR railcar which, after all the long delays, had been moved first to Reading and then to Tonbridge. It had stood in the west yard for a week before it was duly tilted (using numerous brake blocks which subsequently became K&ESR spares) and hauled down to Robertsbridge one Sunday afternoon by an electro-diesel (later designated class 73). This operation delayed a Hastings demu for twenty minutes, when the railcar could not be moved to a siding in time. This was the first time one of these famous railcars had been seen in south-east England and W20 became, into the bargain, the widest vehicle to travel the Hastings line before the tunnels were singled, on electrification, in the 1980s. In addition, the electro-diesel unofficially ran a little way up the K&ESR towards Hodson's Mill, the largest non-steam and (although running on its auxiliary diesel engine) the first electric locomotive seen on the railway.

The arrival of the railcar enabled it to be included in the stock movements on 23 April. The Association had thought that this open day would not be as

The second stock movement out of Robertsbridge at Rolvenden on 23 April 1966. Frank Davis is the gentleman adjacent to No. 3's bunker (Dennis Ovenden)

well attended as the first, having been too close to the Easter event and receiving less press publicity than its predecessor. In the event, and although there appeared to be fewer people around, takings by way of donations, sales and new members' subscriptions went up £200 – double the amount raised on Easter Monday.

The events of 23 April went smoothly (despite a panel falling off the railcar near Bodiam) and without even the delays caused to the Easter train by the activities of the press. The train consisted again of No. 3, followed by a 1st/2nd composite coach, the railcar and a brake/2nd open coach. These were marshalled in the bay platform in plenty of time for those wishing to travel up to have their membership cards checked and free passes issued, and for those nonmembers wishing to travel to join on the spot. The train was held for a few minutes to wait for the arrival of a service from London carrying delegates to an Association of Railway Preservation Societies conference which was to take place at Rolvenden later in the day (it was the turn of the K&ESR to host such an event) but finally departed at 11.07 a.m. Unlike previous runs, the train arrived at Rolvenden seven minutes ahead of schedule and the railcar and the open coach were detached. No. 3 took one coach up to Tenterden and the K&ESR commenced its later famous catering career by serving lunch (prepared in the Pullman and served in the Maunsell open) to the ARPS delegates and a number of visitors.

After lunch the ARPS conference was held in the railcar and there was an exchange of information and problems. Apart from everyone moaning about the latest iniquities of BR, Robin Doust revealed that he had received a letter from the commanding officer of the Longmoor Military Railway stating that the army would shortly be disposing of the various items of historic rolling stock it owned and that tenders would be invited. In the 1960s the army's attitude towards such matters had more in common with the Royal Air Force than with BR, and it was understood that it was only interested in selling to preservation groups. The possibility of a joint approach by the ARPS was considered and a sub-committee, on which the K&ESR was represented, was set up. The K&ESR later acquired various rolling stock from Longmoor, including two brake vans, its ex-SE&CR birdcage coaches and the ex-LNWR six-wheeled saloon, although not as a result of this initiative.

No. 3 and its train had made a return trip from Tenterden before again pulling into the platform at Rolvenden to take those wishing to catch the main-line service back to Robertsbridge. Once this had been successfully accomplished the last train of the day made its way up the line, No. 3 this time hauling the composite coach and the ex-SE&CR brake van up to Rolvenden. Night was falling as the Terrier and its short, mixed formation, so typical of the line's past, steamed across the Rother Levels and towards the edge of the High Weald. Someone switched the lights on, the dynamo worked and an island of light made its way through the encircling darkness.

That these trains were able to run was no small credit to all the work undertaken on the track both by way of clearing undergrowth and maintenance. Burning off grass banks, rekeying and resleepering were still taking up many volunteer hours but the track had proved quite satisfactory when the trains had been run. The BR Inspector who had examined the line before the Easter Sunday working had even gone so far as to say that the permanent way was in extremely good condition considering the limited maintenance it had received since 1961. The Association had no doubt that the line would be fit for service when the time came.

Tree-cutting had by then reached a point between Junction Road and Salehurst. The reader, perhaps aware that this section was abandoned in 1972, will wonder if this concentration of effort on the lower section was a waste of time. The answer has to be a qualified 'yes', but only from the viewpoint of many years later – the lower section appeared to have the best chance at the time. The Association (and later the Tenterden Railway Company) made some use of the resulting gains but this cannot be said of the work being carried out at Ashford on the 01 class locomotive. By April this had reached an advanced stage, including painting in green undercoat, but final application of SE&CR livery was to be delayed until the same work was carried out on the C class. It was still anticipated at that stage that it would eventually be possible to see both locomotives side by side.

While the respective owners of the C, H and 01 class locomotives might have settled on the gorgeously detailed SE&CR colour scheme, the K&ESR livery controversy would still not go away. The 1965 referendum was now overturned on the grounds that the Association had increased in size (i.e. the Westerham element had opened the subject up again) and Dave Kitton had proposed in February that freight locomotives should be blue, passenger locos Wainwright green, coaches Maunsell green, goods brakes maroon and other goods stock grey. The Pullmans would appear in Pullman livery and the railcar in the pre-war K&ESR livery which approximated to GWR chocolate and cream anyway. These colour schemes were part of an overall house style, most of which was never adopted and which caused some raised eyebrows at the time.

Furthermore, the argument had been extended to include the very title of the line and one faction wished the original title of the Rother Valley Railway to be revived. (Circumstantial evidence suggests that this was an echo of the Westerham project.) It was argued that this was more snappy for publicity purposes, but was countered by another group who said that the title K&ESR had been in use since 1904 and should be continued. Once more ballot papers were issued (printed on the back page of the April *Farmers' Line*), and this time asked three questions:

1. Which title was to be used for the re-opened railway
2. Should the locomotives be Oxford blue, apple green, or varying colours?
3. Should the carriages be brown and cream, Southern green or varying colours?

The decision, announced one month later, was to call the railway the Kent and East Sussex and, again, paint the locomotives blue and the carriages brown and cream. The decision about the locomotive livery was later overridden and apple green was adopted. BR's near-contemporary decision to change from green to blue for its own locomotives possibly influenced this, as also did the wearing qualities of that colour. In any event, apple green locomotives hauling Great Western-hued carriages re-opened the line. This lasted for some years until commercial pressures and fashions in railway preservation led to the appearance of locomotives in blue, apple green, Southern green, black, red and army green, not to mention camouflage and (in the case of *Charwelton*) the 'mud' colour of the Park Gate Iron and Steel Company. Carriages have appeared in a similarly wide range of liveries but all this has appeared to be quite popular, and the words 'travelling circus' do not seem to have been heard.

A definite sign of Westerham influence was the inclusion of a publicity item in the progress report for April. There was now a department dealing with this aspect under the direction of the energetic Dave Kitton. Apart from re-organizing and brightening up the museum (still then situated in the parcels office at Tenterden), stands had been run at a number of (presumably model railway) exhibitions. New members and extra income had been attracted by this means. The policy of regularly attending such functions represented something of a departure for the K&ESR. The Preservation Society, as related earlier, had not been unaware of the value of publicity. In addition to the activities already mentioned, the K&ESRPS had usually had wall space at the annual Model Railway Exhibition in London and I recall manning a stand, together with Eddie Bye, at the 1963 West Norwood Model Railway Exhibition. But it has to be said that the Society had seen such activities as the exception rather than the rule. The very size of the project on the ground is offered as one explanation for this slightly inward-looking (although not insular) perspective. The Westerham Valley Railway Association, by contrast, adopted an outward-looking approach, possibly as a substitute for on-site involvement. 'Outreach' (the present-day term for this public relations technique) is much used by local authorities and BR. It was little used by either in the mid-1960s and the K&ESRPS had connections with both. This was the beginning of one of the most useful contributions the ex-Westerham members were to make to the K&ESR.

Mention should be made at this point of an interesting development – the arrival of the K&ESR's first woman volunteer. Wives and mothers had, of course, been an invaluable help in traditional (i.e. catering) roles and girlfriends sometimes visited, but the arrival of Cathy Roberts was something different. Until the mid-1960s railway preservation, indeed railway enthusiasm, was very much a male pastime. It was almost inevitable that the 1960s would change that and Cathy was the first of the many women who have worked on the K&ESR on their own terms and on an equal footing with their male counterparts. Cathy's parents had moved to Tenterden several years earlier when they bought the High Street chemist's shop, which had been a pharmacy since 1790. Despite Tenterden's undoubted charms, their teenage daughter found the town a little quiet, particularly at a time when London's attraction as a centre of youth culture had never been greater. Cathy was intrigued and surprised to find that a rather more interesting group of people, many of her own age, were to be found at the station. It was not long before she could be found taking a full part in the Association's work and more than matching the efforts of the males around her.

The move of the GWR railcar (which retained its existing stock number once on the K&ESR) marked the beginning of an interest in diesel preservation which, in its own way, was pioneering. In No. 20 itself, the seating was dismantled, the panelling removed and the woodwork stripped ready for staining and revarnishing. These tasks provided volunteers with a useful lesson in both the efficacy and skin-scorching qualities of a well-known brand of paint stripper.

Although second-hand railcars were just becoming available in 1966, diesel locomotives were another matter. The K&ESR was, nevertheless, in need of such a machine, both for the projected freight service and as general reserve motive power. The Association was as a result interested to hear that two particularly historic industrial diesel-electric locomotives were about to be become available at scrap prices.

The machines in question were two 150 bhp Bo+Bo's which British Thompson Houston had built for the Ford Motor Company in 1932, and which had spent their lives, together with a sister locomotive, at Ford's Dagenham plant in Essex. They were some of the earliest examples of a locomotive style which was to become commonplace; the acquisition of one of them was exactly what the K&ESR wanted. An initial approach was made to Ford, which was favourably received, and that company said it would investigate which of its locomotives was best suited to continued use. Further early moves were made by Dr Paul Waters, who was an engineer. He went to AEI (as successors to BTH) and asked for their assistance in obtaining one of the BTH diesel-electrics. The result of this approach was that AEI purchased a locomotive for £500 and very generously presented it to the K&ESR Association.

The Association had meanwhile not been idle. Derek Dunlavey and Dick Beckett visited Dagenham and selected Ford No. 1, but asked for it to be fitted with the engine from No. 2. Ford was happy to oblige. Prior to AEI's generous help, an appeal had been made to members for money and, surprisingly for that date, considering that the object of the exercise was a diesel, £150 was raised quite quickly. This money was still needed after the locomotive had been secured as it was not possible to have 'the Ford' (as the BTH quickly, if inaccurately, became known) delivered over BR and the K&ESR had to meet the £250 cost of road transport.

Before the diesel made its appearance on K&ESR metals, another steam-orientated event took place on Whit Monday, it having been the intention to clear the remaining carriages, S4432S, S5153S and a Pullman, from Robertsbridge yard. Things had not begun well when BR had not allowed any passengers to be carried, a decision which caused considerable disappointment. The day had dawned bright and sunny and it had been planned that the train would leave Robertsbridge at 11.15 a.m. and arrive at Rolvenden at 1.05 p.m. No. 50 *Sutton* was in use and it was while she was attempting to reach S5153S, which was to have been marshalled in the train that, too fast, she approached a set of points sited on a very sharp curve and derailed.

There was no damage to either permanent way or locomotive, although Robin Doust has recalled that he momentarily feared she would topple over. The driver was also badly shaken and unable to drive again that day. When *Sutton* stopped she had only her centre pair of wheels on the track. Inevitably, a crowd gathered, thus swelling the large number of visitors who had witnessed the original incident. This was the first time anything like this had happened since the beginning of the preservation project and it could not have been much more embarrassing. Only two of the large screw jacks needed to rerail the Terrier were on hand, but local BR staff supplemented these with a $1\frac{1}{4}$ in. thick rerailing plate. The volunteers, which finally included a number of people who had only come to watch, rose to the occasion and, armed with the limited equipment available plus wooden packing, set about the task. The incident took place on a section of permanent way that the Association had not been able to work on, the track in Robertsbridge yard having been very much the responsibility of the Southern Region.

The day had turned immensely warm and while the volunteers sweated under a broiling sun it had become necessary to keep up the public's interest at Rolvenden where the train was long overdue. Fortunately *Marcia* was in steam, although Dick Beckett was only able to run her up and down a short siding. This limitation was, however, more than made up for by the tritone chime whistle which Dick had fitted and which gave his locomotive a cry out of all proportion to her size. *Marcia* was not alone in shattering the peace of the countryside that afternoon, as she was frequently answered by the GWR railcar's two-tone electric horn, to the irritation of some of those present. Not everyone objected and at least the wait enabled the Pullman car to do some business. It was 7.00 p.m. before the train eventually left Robertsbridge and even then the coach which had caused the trouble had to be left behind. After that another good run up the line was achieved and advantage was taken of the light evening to continue shunting operations until it was almost dark.

The 'Ford' BTH diesel reached the K&ESR on Friday 8 July 1966, where it became No. 16 in the stock list. She had last been used by Ford on the Wednesday of that week, was loaded the following day and travelled south through the Dartford Tunnel, which had to be briefly closed at 3.00 a.m. to allow her passage. Three low-loaders were required: one for the main bodywork and two for the bogies and spare parts. The job was undertaken by Hallet Silbermann Ltd of Watford. This was the largest convoy which the railway had brought to Tenterden and, having negotiated the High Street, the three huge vehicles were then faced with a much more difficult challenge – Station Road, at that stage still its original width. After a display of the considerable skill typical of his profession, one of the drivers succeeded in manoeuvring his transporter into the narrow road. Unfortunately, in doing this he flattened the kerb at the corner of the road beside the Vine Inn. He was promptly booked by the Kent Police. The K&ESR proved to be more forgiving when it became necessary to remove one of the station's gateposts to allow access.

No. 16 (as she may now properly be called, although she was later renumbered 40 in the K&ESR diesel locomotive series) was unloaded onto the much-used platform siding, immediately behind No. 15 *Hastings*. The method employed (which would definitely not be permitted today!) was to mount the 38 ton body on four jacks – the photographs alone look frightening – and run the bogies underneath. By the Saturday everything had been reconnected and it was possible to stage a demonstration run up the headshunt and back. As delivered the locomotive had the word 'Ford' in that company's logo style in large stainless steel letters on either side. These were swiftly removed, an act which led one of the Ford-owning Webb brothers to comment, 'If it had said Rolls-Royce they'd have been left on!'

The K&ESR was now approaching the high-water mark of the early preservation years. With the contract signed, much work under way, the basic rolling stock acquired and continuing cautious optimism, the railway had a distinctly different personality about it when compared with the abandoned branch line of 1961. Opinions on atmosphere must, of necessity, remain subjective, but in the summer of 1966 there appeared the earliest traces of the character the railway would assume in its flourishing years.

In a wider context, 1966 marked the zenith of the decade. It was also the last full year of steam on the Southern Region. The 1960s were kept swinging for a while but modern historians have noted that this happy period (which myth would endow with the same golden glow as the Edwardian era) was starting to turn sour. Earlier in the year the Wilson government was re-elected with a larger majority and promptly lost direction. Among Harold Wilson's first acts was the appointment of Mrs Barbara Castle as Minister of Transport.

XI

There were signs that a new awareness of organization had emerged. *The Farmers' Line* was giving increasing amounts of detail about where work was under way and where volunteers were needed. In answer to complaints that members were having problems finding these things out, the July 1966 edition stated that for the following two months Saturday working parties would concentrate on rolling stock repainting at Rolvenden and that Sunday activity would be concerned with tree-cutting between Robertsbridge and Junction Road. The facilities in the mess coach were recommended and details of public transport to the line were detailed. This simple advice produced results and there was an encouraging increase in volunteer numbers. By the end of the year Sunday transport by Wickham trolley was being offered from both Robertsbridge and Tenterden.

By this stage of the project it was not unusual for volunteers to spend a week's holiday working on the line. I did just this, in the company of several other volunteers, during the first week of September. I retain an enduring memory of walking up the platform (on the way back from the pub) one warm night as a huge harvest moon rose over the backdrop of darkened trees. Grasshoppers chirped in the undergrowth and there was a distant purr of combine harvesters working into the night in nearby fields. It was all quite idyllic.

Tree-cutting was largely complete by the autumn and Chris Lowry and Kevin Blakiston had finished restoring the telephone link between Tenterden and Northiam. The phone line (an omnibus system of the type once common in railway practice) was equipped with ten instruments and a number of plug-in points, including those at Rolvenden and Wittersham Road. Diodes were also built into the circuits to prevent spurious ringing of all the bells on the system during thunderstorms. This had actually happened at one o'clock in the morning and the merry clatter had sounded in earshot of everyone between Station Road and the Rother Valley Hotel. Great had been the Association's embarrassment, but Frank Davis had soon come to the rescue with a suitable design to cure the problem. The phone system continued to be single wire with earth return – it was planned to return eventually to twin conductors – and Frank had also come up with a relay device which boosted the current passing through the six-mile-long system without recourse to additional batteries. The Kentsleys now had a railway telephone in the Haven and a further device had been included with their instrument which required the ringing keys of other phones to be held down a little longer if Charlie needed to be contacted. This enabled the remainder of the system to be used without them being constantly disturbed by ringing bells.

The Loco Department now had more work on hand than ever. Charlie Kentsley had been applying his skills to some minor but vital work on the Terriers and the department as a whole was having to turn its attentions to problems of diesel maintenance. In this they were fortunate that Dick and Derek were, through professional need, becoming well versed in this field and expert assistance was also available from Peter Goddard, a garage proprietor from Ightham, Kent (not to be confused with another gentleman of the same name who had been a member of the 'Surrey' group). Peter had a varied career, which included railway signal engineering, and was one of the larger-than-life characters railway preservation seemed to attract. 'Large' in all senses of the word, he had the appearance of an old-time railwayman, including a walrus moustache that looked as if it might have been grown to protect its owner from the rigours of the weather on an open footplate.

The railcar had, since its arrival from Robertsbridge, been primed externally and several badly corroded panels had been replaced. The mechanical aspects of the vehicle had been receiving the attentions of Messrs Beckett, Dunlavey and Goddard, and both its AEC engines successfully run. There were problems, however, with one of the fluid flywheels (which was inoperative). Problems were also later experienced with the governor and drive shaft on one side. The batteries were barely usable after four years' neglect in the open; a new set would have cost £150 and an appeal was made for assistance in finding replacements.

Around this time there appeared two locomotive preservation schemes which, in different degrees, had associations with the K&ESR. The objects of their attentions were, however, a most unlikely choice for a line which then had a 10 ton axle loading. The first of these was a proposal to save a Maunsell mogul which, although it originated among K&ESR members, had, in the first instance, nothing to do with the Association. The instigators of the project were, nonetheless, grateful to *The Farmers' Line* for giving them some publicity and to the Association for allowing their leaflets to be included with the July edition. Much the same facility was made available to the organizers of an even more unlikely scheme (at least in K&ESR terms) – the preservation of a Bulleid Light Pacific. The Bulleid group had approached the Association about the possibility of display accommodation, somewhere it was inferred they would also be restoring their locomotive. The Light Pacific idea was to grow into the Bulleid Society which, because of events, became based on the Bluebell Railway after a spell at Longmoor, but with its locomotive, No. 21C123 *Blackmore Vale*, became a leader in one of railway preservation's most successful fields. The Mogul, U class No. 1618, actually went to the K&ESR in 1973 after several years on private sidings at Aylesford, but was only able to make limited movements in the Tenterden yard and station area. No. 1618 later also moved to the Bluebell Railway where it could stretch its legs effectively.

The search for finance still dominated events, and Robin Doust had been forthright during May, when, in *The Farmers' Line* editorial, he had written, 'we are still not receiving anything like as much support from members to the Rother Valley Railway Trust Fund as we could . . . the inescapable fact [is] that 6 miles [will be] abruptly terminated by the scrap man . . .' and that many of [our members] are idly waiting for a miracle to occur . . .'

Great hopes had been pinned on the possibility that part of Tenterden Town station site could be developed as a ready-mixed concrete plant, and that the resulting income from site rentals and traffic would be enough to secure the purchase of the top portion of the line. But during the middle of the year, and despite its declared support for the railway, Tenterden Borough Council refused planning permission. Given that situation, there was no option but to plug the Trust Fund even harder. The £15,000 bank loan formed the bedrock of the available money and £7,000 had been paid into the Trust. Unfortunately, the latter sum had been contributed by only one hundred members and the threat to the upper section was emphasized to prick consciences, it being made clear that small sums were just as welcome as large ones.

During September it was also decided to set up a Technical Sub-Committee under the chairmanship of Dr Paul Waters, as he was appropriately qualified for the post. The idea of such a body had first seen the light of day at the previous February's main Committee meeting and had been suggested as an emulation of previous Westerham practice. This initiative had received further impetus from among the volunteers themselves, who felt they were not receiving adequate direction from the management of either the Association or the Company. These were the first indications of a breeze which would return as a whirlwind eighteen months later. An unofficial grouping at first, the Sub-Committee who, it was agreed, would only meet with an Association Committee member in attendance, was recognized by the Association after only two weeks. Other members of the Sub-Committee represented the Permanent Way, Loco, Carriage and Wagon, and Signal and Telegraph departments, as well as a new addition, the Buildings and Structures Department. Its brief was to carry out forward planning and deal with day-to-day problems.

The October *Farmers' Line* also carried with it the outcome of another notion first suggested earlier in the year. Included with the newsletter was a specially printed circular letter which covered a number of the then current themes regarding the need for further finance. It read:

Dear Member,

I am addressing this letter to you personally as Patron of the Association. As you will know from reading the accompanying newsletter, and from past issues, a vast amount of work has been put into the bid to re-open the K&ESR during the past five years. Already those critics who forecast the early death of the scheme have been proved wrong, and now more help arrives every week in the form of additional labour and finance. By the end of the year not only will the whole railway be in a fit state to carry traffic, but £24,000 will have been raised towards the £36,000 needed to purchase the line.

This is a tremendous achievement, but unfortunately it is still not enough to enable the whole of the Railway to be bought and re-opened. If the full length of track is to be saved, a further £12,000 must be raised in the next three months. I feel you will want to do your utmost towards achieving this, and so I do hope you will support the new scheme which is explained below.

We now have nearly 800 members, and if each one was to become a Life Member £16,000 would be available to complete the purchase of the line and meet the initial cost of establishing services on it. I am therefore asking every one of you to make a real effort to become a Life Member at a subscription of £20. In return for this you will automatically receive all benefits of the Association, including reduced rates on the railway, without any further subscription for as long as you live. You will also have the satisfaction of knowing that you will have made a very real contribution to saving part of the railway from extinction. Some of you may find it difficult to pay the whole £20 in a lump sum, so if you prefer you may pay the subscription over a period of five months at £4 per month.

A form is attached for you to complete, and I do hope you will join with me in making this final effort to save the whole of this useful and historic line if you possibly can. Remember that over the next few years you would be paying the equivalent in annual subscriptions, but if you go on paying at the rate of £1 per year, you will only see half the line re-opened. If you pay the whole £20 now, that same amount of money will enable the entire line to be saved.

The letter was a reasonable summary of the state of affairs on the K&ESR but the surprise was that it was signed by the Bishop of Kingston and that the notepaper clearly stated the fact that he was Patron of the Association, the first time that members had been made aware of the existence of such a post, even though Dick Ranson had reported to the Committee on 26 February that the bishop had agreed to becoming patron.

No one would doubt the sincerity of the gentleman involved, who had probably been conscripted to the railway's aid and who was acting in the long and honourable tradition of clerical interest in railway matters. My personal recollection of receiving the letter was that it appeared a jarring and mawkish use of the *'Titfield Thunderbolt* factor'. The best that could be said for it was that, given the critical situation of the time, and like an irritating TV commercial, it made sure the recipient got the message. One wonders how effective (or counterproductive) this initiative really was, as, later in the year, it was stated that the appeal for Life Members had been disappointing and that only about sixty people had responded.

The October *Farmers' Line* also included an item by Dave Kitton entitled 'Publicity is *Your* Responsibility'. (The third word was underlined for emphasis.) Over the previous few years, many of Robin Doust's articles had not exactly lacked assertiveness when cajoling the membership, but this particular piece contained a developing note of 'hard sell' which was new. It is also worth quoting in detail:

Our urgent needs are for MEMBERS and MONEY. Developments during the past few months have resulted in a substantial increase in both, but although we have sought to exploit recent happenings to the full, and obtained good press and BBC coverage, it is clear we have only tapped a small percentage of the total potential members. Our catchment area is vast, and includes the Greater London area and the whole of the South East, as existing membership shows, but while there must be tens of thousands of serious enthusiasts in this area to whom our scheme should appeal, only about 800 have shown active support by joining the Association.

Clearly the general publicity we put out, while giving the public an idea of our progress, cannot be sufficiently personal in its appeal to stir the majority to action. While we can make the enthusiast aware of the railway, it often needs further encouragement before he decides to join. This is where YOU come in! EVERY MEMBER must be active in advertising the line at a local and personal level, carrying on where we leave off. It is up to YOU whether your friends and neighbours become sufficiently interested to join. If the Association fails to secure the whole line through lack of support, much of the blame will rest with the individual member.

Please, therefore, co-operate with us – make the fullest use of every item of news we publish and all the publicity material we prepare, draw the attention of every potential member to our activities and 'sell' the Association, and the Rother Valley Railway at every opportunity.

Here are some of the ways you can help:

POSTERS – We now have a striking new poster, size about 8 in. x 11½ in., and hope you will be able to display one or more. They can be had on paper or card, depending on their intended position, and are available now from Tenterden station. Put one up in the local model shop, the model railway club, the public library, or wherever you feel they will be most useful. If you live on a busy road, put one on a notice board at the front gate, inviting those interested to ask at your house for further details, and have a supply of leaflets ready to distribute to enquirers.

EXHIBITIONS – Encourage your friends to attend the various exhibitions at which we are participating, for this presents an ideal opportunity to capture their interest and enrol them. Details of the exhibitions at which we are exhibiting may be had by sending a postcard to Tenterden. We are always anxious to obtain space at any exhibitions, and can always provide an interesting display wherever we go. If YOUR club or society is holding a show, and you can assist us to procure a stand or display space, please let us know.

The article then went on to talk about Christmas cards and calendars. Cards were not new, the Preservation Society had them available each Christmas, but their sale, together with the more innovative calendars, had now been taken into the main publicity effort.

Much of what Dave Kitton had to say was unarguably right – the idea that the K&ESR needed to be sold to the line's potential supporters. His estimate of the numbers involved seems optimistic and nearer to the likely customers than the possible members. But perhaps the former was what he was really aiming at and he was deliberately overselling. In fact, it is possible to interpret the new tone as early glimmerings of the proactive commercial outlook the railway would later need.

These 'outreach' activities were a valuable and effective way of taking the railway to people and therefore, hopefully, attracting money to the scheme, but one aspect of this publicity drive nonetheless remains a little difficult to explain. Why, when much of the catchment area was within a couple of hours' travel of Tenterden, were people being encouraged to go to model railway exhibitions, some of which must have taken upwards of an hour to reach? From the pre-war photographers to the members of the Preservation Society, a visit to the line had often been the K&ESR's best recruiting sergeant.

October had also seen a crisis within the Committee which, once again, revolved around Robin Doust's wish to resign from the post of Secretary. He had, the membership were informed, disagreed with his colleagues over the 'organization of the working part of the Association'. Dr Waters temporarily took over the duties in addition to his chairmanship of the Technical Sub-Committee. (The disagreement was connected with the operation of the Sub-Committee.)

Saturday 12 November brought the first Annual General Meeting of the K&ESR Association, the tradition of using Tenterden Town Hall for such occasions being maintained. The mood of the meeting was one in which to address the issues of the time, even if the alarums of earlier years were not repeated. Arthur Penny welcomed members to the meeting and began the proceedings in fine style by mentioning that the statutory notices of intention to apply for the Light Railway Transfer Order had appeared in newspapers that weekend. Making application for a Light Railway Order at that time has been compared to taking a partly restored vintage car for an MOT test – one did what appeared necessary and asked for permission to operate. This contrasts with the current situation which is more like applying for planning permission from one of the more progressive local authorities – an open exchange of views at the beginning leads to constructive advice and co-operation as the project develops.

Good news came from Ron Cann, who was able to tell the members present that the Association had made a profit, a contrast to the constant deficit which the Preservation Society had laboured under in previous years. The accounts circulated were still running to the K&ESRPS yearly cycle and were complete only up until 31 May. They nonetheless showed a balance of income over expenditure of £744 6s (later revised to £1,000 for the full year). The Treasurer then explained that this happy situation was unlikely to recur as it included the ex-Westerham funds and the £400 made during the running of the special trains earlier in the year.

Ron Cann then carried on in much more cutting style and in his role as Trustee of the Rother Valley Railway Trust Fund. He deplored that only 140 of the 780 members had so far contributed and stated that these people were 'The true friends of the railway', having raised over £8,514 in twenty months. He went on to say that many of them were also among the regular volunteers but that the remaining members of the Association had done nothing except turn up when trains were running and swarm all over the track. This was hard-hitting but it expressed how the most active part of the membership felt about waverers and those who would not involve themselves. A particularly pointed remark was in respect of one member who had openly defied 'BR's request to cease trespassing upon their property' and who had 'been partly responsible for the restriction on further passenger runs being carried out by the Association'. Ron Cann closed his report by reminding members of the serious financial situation and asking them to search their consciences (and by implication their domestic accounts).

Len Heath Humphrys then spoke about the progress being made towards the purchase of the line and also laid stress on the importance of the Trust Fund, before it was Arthur Penny's turn again, this time to introduce the election of the Committee. After various names had been proposed and seconded, the new ruling body was made up of Peter Goddard, Malcolm Dunstan, Dr Waters, Peter Davis, Len Hibbert, Peter Cox, David Kitton, Robin Doust, Ron Cann, Len Heath Humphrys and Charlie Kentsley. Following the election of the Committee, members were told, the Chairman, Secretary and Treasurer were to be selected from among their number. In the event, and as Arthur Penny was no longer a Committee member, the leadership reverted to the longstanding triumvirate of Humphrys, Cann and Doust, Robin having been persuaded to return to his old position 'in anticipation of a more dynamic internal policy'.

The penultimate agenda item was consideration of the draft constitution for the Association and a good old K&ESR disagreement promptly broke out over some of its terms. Robin Doust reminded the meeting at this point that during the Preservation Society's Special General Meeting the previous year it had been suggested that the Association be formed into a company limited by guarantee, an idea which, of course, harked back to the 1963 prospectus and which was to prove to be one of the routes into the future. The Association had been running under the old K&ESRPS constitution since January and it was agreed that this should be continued until Articles of Association could be drawn up.

The meeting concluded with a question-and-answer session (mainly about the RVR Trust Fund and publicity matters), before a vote of thanks was proposed from the floor for the volunteers. This was seconded by Arthur Penny and the meeting showed the workforce its appreciation by a round of applause. Then it was back to the station for refreshments in the Pullmans.

Two of the most interesting additions to the Committee were Malcolm Dunstan and Peter Davis. Malcolm (by this stage 'Big M' to everyone) had now taken on the crucial role of Membership Secretary from Ray Marlow, another regular volunteer who had himself taken over from the Webbs some months earlier.

The election of Peter Davis was to prove one of the more significant events in the history of the railway. Peter had been a member of the Preservation Society and a volunteer for several years, was a little under ten years older than the average volunteer, and had at one time been a regular army officer. By the mid-1960s he held a management post with the cement manufacturers APCM and was confident, calm and charismatic. He drove a pre-war Alvis and his other interests included motor sport. Overall, Peter looked the personification of the type of Englishman who used to be portrayed by Kenneth Moore. This combination of characteristics and abilities was to fit Peter for a future pivotal role in K&ESR history, for he was young enough (and young enough at heart) to earn the respect of the volunteers at the same time as having an undoubted credibility when dealing with authority. One of the first things the Technical Sub-Committee had done was to appoint him as head of the Buildings and Structures Department.

An initial task for Peter was to organize a Construction and Maintenance section, this move being part of a general re-organization of working parties. It was seen that the real estate and buildings needed to be improved before a public service could be started, and also to maintain the best possible public image. Until the line was secured it was, however, decided to proceed on a maintenance-only basis, except for the construction of a badly needed Loco Department workshop at Rolvenden. Immediate tasks were foreseen as general repairs to all stations, although it was hoped to rebuild platforms and construct a loco shed at a later stage.

In the meantime, the Construction section put out an appeal for a concrete mixer, site huts and a wide variety of building materials and equipment! With Peter Davis' business connections there was, nonetheless, a ready supply of cement at staff discount prices. The section also rapidly got itself organized, not even needing to announce its intentions in *The Farmers' Line*. Instead, potential recruits, particularly those with appropriate skills, were asked to send a 2s 6d postal order to the boss so that he could circulate details of work in hand to everyone interested. It was also hoped to use this method to organize staff transport to and from the railway using volunteers' cars. The first fruits of all this activity and forethought was the arrival of a very large quantity of concrete building blocks at Rolvenden and an actual start on the workshop. That (still extant) building was very economically constructed under the water tower in Rolvenden yard, thus making use of the pre-existing concrete framework. The framework also allowed the roof to be completed first and before the foundations were dug!

When the December edition of *The Farmers' Line* appeared, the application for the Light Railway Transfer Order had gone to the Ministry of Transport, where it was to be kept until 31 December and during which period any objections could be made. By this stage the Rother Valley Railway Company had £26,000 in hand but remained £10,000 short of the minimum requirement. At that point in time it was thought that the remaining £32,500 (the full purchase price minus the deposit) would have to be paid on 31 December and that the only way to achieve this would indeed be to lift the Northiam–Tenterden section. It was an occasion for further bluntness and the membership got it on the fourth and fifth pages of the newsletter. There was no appeal to sentimentality this time, not even ad-man's campaign selling, just two letters, the first of which was printed in red so that it could not be missed. It read:

Dear Sir,

February 1965 saw the inauguration of the Rother Valley Railway Trust. It came into being after months of fruitless efforts to obtain financial assistance in raising the £36,000 necessary to purchase the railway. All the major banking houses had been approached without result and several financiers had come forward and had retired when it became obvious that we were not going to throw the station sites into their hands for development. Then, at last, it became quite obvious that if we were going to raise the price, we would have to find it from the resources of the membership list. So the Trust was born in an atmosphere of enthusiasm and great confidence. We had at that time 440 members, and we did not doubt that at least half of these would join the Trust as soon as the details were published in *The Farmers' Line*.

I was one of the confident ones and, because I knew that we would not have four years to raise the money, I made an offer to provide collateral security on behalf of the Company for a loan of £15,000. The offer was made conditional upon my name not being disclosed in case the membership failed to support me and it became necessary to withdraw my offer. Well, Sir, look at the figures! The members, there are now 780 of them, have failed to raise even a quarter of the sum necessary. If they had raised half of the price I would still have to take an appalling risk, for the property I own stands in the West End of London and was valued at the time of the offer at £85,000. It is all I possess and to use it as the Company's security would mean that I could lose it at any time if the Company failed, or the Ministry of Transport, for any reason stopped the traffic on the railway. Furthermore, my reward for this action is precisely nothing.

My view is that what would have been a risk if half the sum was raised has now become an inevitability. Look at the purchase scheme we are forced to adopt. It involves the scrapping of the Northiam–Tenterden stretch. In my view the fact that the railway serves as large a town as Tenterden gives it prestige, and that to cut it down to a Northiam terminus demotes it to very near the status of another 'Week-ends' only railway, with which we are all familiar. Nor is it only a matter of prestige. Tenterden is expanding rapidly, and has prospects of sharing in Ashford's expansion to a town of 150,000 people, as was announced recently. The Tenterden Bank is the second-steepest standard gauge bank in the country, and the railway fans would make the journey from Robertsbridge to travel up it behind a Terrier – perhaps two Terriers. But to carry this further is to lose the point of this letter! I have a message for the members and it is this. On the present financial standing I am not prepared to assist the purchase. You have until the end of December to produce more financial support. Much more. It is no use indulging in the insanely optimistic view that someone is going to buy you a railway. If I don't help the Company the railway is gone – all of it – and it will mark the death of all private efforts to save branches in this country. British Rail have been extremely patient with us for six years and, if we fail after all, they will finish with preservationists for good.

I shall be looking at the figures again about December 28th (you have only until 31st) and I am prepared to bend over backwards to help if you play your part but not otherwise. It's up to you.

Yours faithfully,

'FELIX'

'Felix' was in fact Ron Cann. Hard-hitting, possibly offensive, though this may have been (only one letter of complaint was actually received), it was exactly what was needed. 'Felix' was backed by the writer of the second letter:

> As a member who has been associated with the K&ESR project from the start, I have been very disappointed to read in successive newsletters of the poor response which has been received from members to the various fund-raising activities which have been undertaken by the former Preservation Society and now the Association.
>
> However, I am wondering whether the reason for many members' non-participation in the financial side of the venture is the result of possible doubts as to their security, if, for any reason, the railway has to close down in the future.

The correspondent went on to suggest that members might purchase eighth, quarter or half miles of track from the operating company and lease them back, thus allowing them to sell their portion of permanent way for scrap should this become necessary. It was an interesting proposal but, as matters turned out, it did not need to be taken up. The letter was signed by 'W. Robbins'. (In fact it was Robin Doust; his motive was to propose this course of action without it appearing overdesperate or merely another money-raising ploy by the Committee.)

But, as in past crises, the week-to-week life of the volunteer force seemed to continue with purpose. This was not 'insane optimism' – too many active members were Trust Fund contributors for that. Neither was it a lack of awareness. The workforce was too tightly knit and perceptive a group to remain oblivious to what was going on around them. It was rather more an expression of a quiet determination that eventually, through persistence and the efforts of individuals, the railway would re-open.

In addition to *The Farmers' Line* carrying details of current work sites, and following a suggestion at the AGM, attention was also given to organizing volunteers' transport to the line. This took the form of people willing to give lifts to Tenterden at weekends and included the names of the stalwarts one would expect such as the Webbs, Peter Goddard, Frank Davis and Ron Cann. It also included the first mention of Colin Edwards, a Maidstone member who had been with the K&ESR for three years and who was destined to become one of the most solidly reliable and quietly influential characters on the railway.

Work, and particularly track work, was being planned on the assumption that the Robertsbridge–Bodiam section would be in use by Easter. Geoff Percy and his group had temporarily changed their attentions from signals to point work and were making their way up the line overhauling operating mechanisms. By late in the year they had reached Northiam, where they set up mess accommodation in railway bungalow No. 1. It is to this general period that one of the most hair-raising tales of the early years belongs.

In addition to their track and signalling work, Geoff and the London Transport volunteers had decided to clear a considerable area of undergrowth between the bungalows and the commercial fuel depot at the back of the station. The easiest way of doing this was to burn the vegetation off, the same method already much used elsewhere on the railway. The volunteers (all professional railwaymen) were well aware of the existence of the fuel depot but were satisfied that an adequate fire-break existed between railway and private property. What they were unaware of was that large quantities of spilt fuel oil had built up in a ditch beneath the bushes. The fire was lit but, to the horror of those who thought they had started a controlled burn, there was a sudden eruption of flame which raced towards two fully laden 5,000 gallon road tankers parked in the depot, as well as the vastly greater fixed storage tanks. Had this situation not been swiftly remedied the consequences for the people of the surrounding area could have been devastating and the implications for the K&ESR, and the preservation movement generally, severe. The work gang, however, reacted with a commendable display of courage and tackled the blaze themselves, succeeding in extinguishing the flames before any serious damage could be done. But it was a close-run thing and both road tankers (which had fortunately been parked facing the railway) had the paint burnt off their radiators. The owners of the depot initially threatened legal action, but there was a subsequent police inquiry into the incident which exonerated the K&ESR and the volunteers and found that the fuel depot was to blame, having ignored numerous safety rules about spillage. The matter was quietly dropped.

One of the most famous features of the K&ESR was its numerous ungated level crossings. It was correctly anticipated that the Company would be required to do something to protect these, and the decision had been made to investigate the possibility of installing lifting barriers. The task of designing and constructing a suitably inexpensive type, operated from a trackside switch by train crews, fell to the versatile Messrs Dunlavey and Beckett. The prototype was put together in Rolvenden yard and looked very promising. Once the switch was operated, a pair of barriers were to descend across the road, blocking the full width of the carriageway. Standard red warning lights would operate at the same time, and once the barriers had descended the train would be free to cross. Having crossed the road, the train would operate a track circuit and the barriers would rise again automatically. It was hoped that the whole operation would take under forty-five seconds. The design included an electronic device intended to stop the arm from descending below the horizontal position when the operating switch was activated.

The prototype barrier managed, however, to disgrace itself in a moment of high comedy. During one particular test the lights flashed, the barrier descended, reached the horizontal plane and kept descending. In a true illustration of Murphy's law, the stop device had chosen that moment to develop a fault, and the K&ESR engineers stood there aghast as the arm reached the ground, dug into the soil and proceeded to lever the base out of its mountings! Back to the drawing board.

Back among the more normal work of the Loco Department, Peter Goddard had been fitting a new bunker to No. 3 (Dick Beckett had welded part of this to the loco, in the platform at Tenterden, on the evening of the AGM!) and Alan Parrott had applied a coat of undercoat to the locomotive. At Ashford the 01 was nearly ready for a boiler test. Diesel traction was, with good reason, taking up much time, the railcar now carrying an undercoat version of K&ESR brown and cream livery, and the Ford diesel had been off its bogies (and on four jacks and a lot of packing!) again before being re-assembled during the weekend of 10–11 September and moved to Rolvenden under its own power a week later. The buckeye couplings, which were to American standards, had been removed, the buffers repaired and the control circuits modified to allow air pressure to be automatically built up if the locomotive was left idling.

A major publicity event was anticipated for the spring when, in what was to prove a savage twist of irony, it was hoped that AEI would be able to arrange for Mrs Barbara Castle, Minister of Transport, to present the locomotive officially to the K&ESR. This ceremony was never to be.

Meanwhile, 31 December, bringing with it the deadlines set by BR and by 'Felix', was looming ever closer.

XII

A few years ago I completed a short (unpublished) novel on the theme of steam railway preservation. This drew on various sources although, inevitably, a fair amount of the K&ESR got into the story. On showing the manuscript to a friend, a reasonably favourable series of criticisms concluded with, 'The plot's OK, but, after all the problems, the story suddenly seems to end by in effect saying, "And with one bound he [i.e. the railway] was free!".' The reader is perhaps beginning to have the same incredulous feeling about the K&ESR .

The K&ESR had already had at least one such narrow squeak after the October 1964 General Election, and even the Northiam fire could not have happened in much better circumstances, with trained railway staff on hand to deal with it. Something similar happened just before New Year 1967, and when 'Felix' (whether metaphorically or in reality) came to look at the figures again he found that the letters he and Mr Robbins' had written had worked and that the membership had responded. There was one small reservation to this welcome news; many of those who contributed the extra money were the

A 'train' of Wickham trolley on Northiam crossing in 1967 (Chris Lowry)

same people who had contributed to the Trust previously. While it was appreciated that there were some people who could not afford more than their annual subscription, the last weeks of 1966 had seen several large offers of support including one for a loan of £1,000 and another for £500. The number of contributors to the Trust continued to grow, and it seemed that the December newsletter had worked where earlier efforts had failed, as members appeared to have taken the hint about Life Membership. Overall, the railway was only £3,700 short of its objective.

Equally importantly, the Association and the Rother Valley Railway Company had been granted another breathing space following delays in the granting of the Light Railway Transfer Order. When it became apparent that the deadline for obtaining the LRO and completing the purchase would not be met, K&ESR representatives were asked to attend a meeting at Waterloo and told that the Southern Region would allow them until 1 June. It was made clear that, although the difficulties of dealing with the Ministry of Transport were understood, there would be no further extension beyond that date.

It was still anticipated that passenger trains would be running between Robertsbridge and Bodiam by Easter and permanent way work was well advanced under the impetus provided by the seemingly improved position. During the first six weeks of the year it proved possible to replace over one hundred rotten sleepers near Salehurst, and Peter Davis' gang had got to grips with Bodiam station. The roof had been bitumenized, the platform canopy repaired, the gutters replaced and (cosmetic but effective though it may have been) the hedge had been trimmed down to a reasonable height. The next task was the rebuilding of the collapsed platform face.

The BTH Ford diesel was off its wheels once more, the bogies at each end having been run out. This allowed the wheels and traction motors to be removed and cracks in the frames to be welded. The Allen diesel engine was receiving new exhaust and inlet valves, together with the associated springs and the renovation of various bearings. No. 50 *Sutton* had been the object of attention among the steam locos, her valve gear having been stripped down and the Westinghouse brake overhauled. As a preliminary to the work between her frames, the underside of this Terrier had been steam-cleaned using *Marcia* as a source of supply.

Two further locomotives arrived on the railway during the spring, the first being a Borrows 0–4–0 well tank named *King*. This locomotive had valve gear that was outside the frames but inside the wheels, a most unusual arrangement. *King* had been privately purchased from the United Glass and Bottle Company, Charlton and was only being stored at Robertsbridge, as a further 0–4–0T would have been of little use to the K&ESR. The second locomotive was of considerably more use to the railway, being another Manning Wardle 0–6–0ST, although smaller and of somewhat different appearance to *Charwelton*. *Arthur*, as this Manning was named, had been built in 1903 and had spent the latter part of its working life handling coal traffic to the APCM works at Stone, near Dartford. On retirement *Arthur* was presented to the Industrial Locomotive Preservation Society and moved to the K&ESR, where it became No. 17. Unfortunately, *Arthur* derailed while being unloaded and proceeded to sink into the mud. The K&ESR, in typical fashion, managed to change this to positive advantage, suitable publicity-attracting photos appearing in the local press. *Arthur*'s boiler was in perfect condition and the valve gear was said to require only 'slight attention' to put it into good working order. The dumb buffers would also have to be replaced by the sprung variety. Once this had been done and vacuum brake equipment added, No. 17 would be able to haul light passenger trains.

The locomotive-hauled coaching stock was also receiving attention ready for the anticipated re-opening, Robin Doust replacing split panels on the Woolwich coach, and John Smallwood painting Pullman No. 185, which was to become *Barbara* once again. This involved him using skills he had learned and utilized on a much smaller scale on the Talyllyn Railway, which was a pleasant link with the origins of the preservation movement. Such skills were, however, rare and there were serious problems regarding the other bogie coaches, which needed to be painted urgently before their condition began to deteriorate. Two were painted professionally and at no small expense, although this was minimized by someone who members were told was in the contract painting business and had arranged for his employees to do the work at cost price. The other vehicles remained untouched; an appeal was made for suitably able volunteers to come forward and two such persons actually appeared and started work on the other Pullman, No. 184 *Theodora*.

The Publicity Department's regular forays into the realms of trade stands and rivet-counting continued to produce results and this was reflected in the membership figures. A couple of ploys new to the railway but fairly unoriginal elsewhere were tried in the interests of fund-raising during these months. The first of these innovations was a dinner held at Justin's Hotel, Bodiam, organized by Peter Davis. The attractive setting, overlooking Bodiam Castle and its surrounding area, lent itself to a most pleasant evening which was enjoyed by a number of the Association's most active members and by other guests. This occasion resulted in several generous contributions to the railway, the total raised during the evening being no less that £3,000. This event seems to have been a far cry from tins of baked beans or a pickled egg and a pint in the pub – not that such things ceased – but, once again, points to the K&ESR realizing it had to live in the world of commercial necessity.

The second innovation was the introduction of a monthly Rother Valley Railway Draw. A Christmas raffle had been run each year since 1965, the draw usually being at the volunteers' party, and, at the instigation of Mr S.R. Clark of Bromley, the idea was extended to run on a monthly basis, tickets being sent out to all members with *The Farmers' Line*. Substantial cash prizes were offered and it was hoped to bring in a worthwhile income. This certainly proved to be the case in the first two months; prizes ranged from £30 to £2 10s and the Association earned £70 on each occasion. Other small-scale but useful fund-raising worthy of mention included the continued collection of trading stamps, still being handled by Bill Westwood, and by 1967 extended to include cigarette coupons and foreign coins. A jumble sale was also organized and was held in the Glebe Hall, Tenterden, on 4 March. This event was run by Doris Goddard and Elsie Kentsley and succeeded in raising £40.

Life on the K&ESR had taken on a discernible pattern during those years, and a particular feature of this was the already much mentioned practice of running works trains or empty-stock workings in the spring. The year in which it was expected that the Light Railway Transfer Order would be granted was no exception, and an Open Day and Work Weekend was organized for the Easter holiday. In a reflection of previous problems, only members actually carrying out work were to be carried on the trains.

Being Easter, the weather provided occasional showers, but the volunteers managed to carry out much work. A further 450 ft of track from the Tenterden headshunt was lifted and taken to Bodiam for re-use in the proposed passing loop. The works train was made up of two wagons and the Woolwich coach, both Terriers being in steam during the four-day period. Robin Doust had by that time completed the renovation of the coach interior, which turned the vehicle into a most comfortable form of transport. A large group of volunteers was present each day over the weekend, and at Bodiam it proved possible to remove the old siding, whose site would be needed for the loop, and level the ground for the new formation. Scrap material was returned to Rolvenden ready for sale.

Visitors had been made most welcome at Rolvenden during the weekend and been able to witness the first test run of the railcar since its mechanical overhaul had been completed, a trip which took it to Northiam and back. Shunting operations were also to be witnessed in the yard, including, at times, a train of six locomotives! The opportunity was taken to clear the running line for the operation of through trains and to get the best publicity advantage out of the placement of the rolling stock.

The Ministry of Transport was meanwhile processing the Light Railway Transfer Order and, although it been hoped to get away without a public inquiry, three objections were received and the necessary proceedings were held in Tenterden (in the Town Hall and Highbury Hall respectively) on 21 and 22 March. After all the delays, the Ministry acted with some speed in making the arrangements and, as the inquiry was held during the week, relatively few of the railway's protagonists were able to be present. The formal objections were from: The Kent River Authority, which was concerned about what might happen if the bridges collapsed into the watercourses, particularly if the Company were wound up at some future stage; The Rother Drainage Board, which voiced exactly the same concerns as the Kent River Authority; Mrs D. Lloyd of Great Dixter House, near Northiam (who was represented by her son), was concerned about the possible decay of fencing, weed growth and flooding if the railway drainage were not maintained in good condition.

In addition to the above Guinness Hop Farms made 'certain other representations' but did not formerly object. Guinness was basically sympathetic to the project but needed to safeguard its interests in respect of fences, drainage and weeds. Neither county council objected to the re-opening, provided a public need was served in so doing. The K&ESR had not been able to obtain the services of the Counsel it wished to represent it, but the view was taken that at least the railway knew where the objections were coming from. All that could be done was to wait for the Ministry to make its decision.

However disquieting the progress of the Light Railway Transfer Order might be, the financial front was now decidedly bright and the threat to the top section appeared to have finally gone away. The 'Red Letter' had continued to have an effect and yet more Trust Covenants had been received. The total capital available was as follows:

K&ESRA bank account – £2,000
Raised by RVR Trust – £14,000
Loan from Ron Cann's (still known as 'Felix') bank, secured against his property – £20,000 (this had, of course, now been increased by £5,000)
Available from other loans – £8000 .

If the money spent on rolling stock was included, the capital expended or available by mid-1967 amounted to £50,000. Not much has been said so far about the background to the story in terms of the national economy, but it should be mentioned that ever since October 1964 the government and country had endured one of the worst credit squeezes on record. It would not be appropriate to discuss the political and historical reasons for this, but it needs to be added that the regular payments by members into the Trust persuaded the bank to grant the loan in the first place despite such difficult circumstances.

Ron Cann had recently bought a delightful Georgian house near the railway, and, as this historic property required a great deal of work, he considered he would have to relinquish his position as Association Treasurer and also as administrator to the Trust Fund. He would, however, be remaining as a Trustee and a Committee member and was to be replaced as Trust Administrator by Arthur Penny. An appeal for a new Treasurer was made in *The Farmers' Line*, but, as so often in such circumstances, there were no takers and his name continued to appear in the officer list. A little later in the year Peter Cox resigned from the position of Company Secretary, although remaining on the Association's Committee, and his place was taken by Len Heath Humphrys.

By the middle of the year the blazing summer weather matched the K&ESR's mood of expectation, a mood which, at the time, many thought was better founded than any of its predecessors. In the wider world it was also the so-called 'summer of love' which, for all their common origins in the upheavals of the 1960s, seemed far removed from railway preservation in south-east England. In the Middle East the Six Day War caused a momentary alarm about oil supplies. Much less far away, on the Bournemouth main line, the remaining Bulleid Pacifics thundered towards the end of Southern steam. There was a strange, golden sadness about the period, but in the quiet rural corners and grass-grown yards of the steam railway movement there seemed every possibility of creating something which was of the present but rooted in the things that were passing.

In June *The Farmers' Line* recorded that, 'It is irritating that news of the Light Railway Order has still not been received from the Ministry, although we understand that there should not be much longer to wait before the outcome of the application is announced. All being well, we hope to get in at least a few weeks' operation this summer, and this will probably prove possible if the Order is granted by mid-July.'

Previous to this, over the Whitsun holiday weekend, diesel locomotive No. 16 had been substituted for the Terriers used at Easter. She had hauled further lengths of rail to the lower end of the line and proved the value of modern traction by being instantly available and not requiring regular stops at every river crossing. Below Bodiam, resleepering continued and Junction Road was reached by 18 June. The Construction and Maintenance section had set about replacing fencing in the area and, following Mrs Lloyd's complaints, the permanent way gang had cleared drains and culverts between Northiam and Bodiam. All this was assisted by the rugged and long-suffering Wickham trolleys. These had now been joined by another example of that company's products, which was rather unoriginally called the 'Yellow Peril' because of its overall paint job.

The railcar, once again decked out in its former chocolate and cream, had continued to make trips between Rolvenden and Northiam, and *Charwelton* had suffered another bout of overheated axle-box bearing. No. 14's ailments this time involved the removal of the springs and valve gear as well, and to complete the list she was due a boiler inspection. A number of boiler tubes were replaced as a result. The opportunity was taken to cut away and replace the badly corroded bunker and rear of the cab, as well as to begin installing a vacuum brake ejector and the associated piping.

The six-coupled locomotives and the Bo+Bo diesel were certainly going to be needed in working order much more than the four-coupled types which seemed to cluster on the line as they did at every other preservation site. The Committee had decided to call a halt after *King* had been delivered and permission had been granted for a 1909 Hawthorn Leslie named *Met* to be stored at Tenterden. The K&ESR had quite reasonably come to the conclusion that its best interests would be served by either ex-BR or large industrial locomotives.

Throughout the preservation project the locomotive side of the scheme had always tended to overshadow the coaching stock, and by mid-1967 locomotives outnumbered coaches by nearly two to one! Work nevertheless continued to restore those vehicles which had been acquired. This particularly applied to the Pullmans and it was intended to re-install two bays of seating in each of them. An appeal for genuine Pullman armchairs appeared in *The Farmers' Line* and ended with the intriguing note, 'We will pay for these if necessary.' More coaches were obviously going to be needed and, because of the limited hauling capacity of much of the motive power, it was decided to acquire a number of elderly but reasonably light vehicles. All had been stripped internally for departmental use. Events rapidly overtook this proposal and none of the coaches came to the K&ESR. For the record they are, nonetheless, listed here. They were: an ex-North Eastern Railway 25 ton clerestory bogie coach, formerly of 62-seat capacity and retaining full gaslight fittings converted to burn Calor gas; an ex-Great Central Railway 13 ton, five-compartment six-wheeler which formerly seated forty-two; a six-wheeled saloon (again with capacity for forty-two passengers) of Great Eastern origin; and a 15 ton ex-London and North Western Railway six-wheeler seating thirty-four. It was hoped to refit these coaches using seating from vehicles scrapped by BR, and various offers of finance were received. The K&ESR Locomotive Trust was interested in the GCR coach, and the GER example was the subject of discussions with the Great Eastern Group. It is a great shame these historic vehicles never found their way to the Rother Valley.

A further three wagons of uncertain origin had been found at Reed's paper mill at Aylesford and, happily, these were acquired for £10 each and put in many years' useful service on the K&ESR. In addition, a London member had offered to put up the £250 for the purchase of an ex-LSWR seven-compartment tri-composite, then situated at Kensington Olympia, as workmen's mess accommodation, but previously used as a camping coach.

Various other areas of activity seemed to be on the up and up as the weeks dragged by without word from the Ministry of Transport. The garden at Tenterden Town station (long overgrown owing to a paucity of interest) had been receiving the attention of Mrs Waters, and was subsequently being developed by a Mr Speelman. The combined efforts of the Publicity Department and Malcolm Dunstan had reached a milestone cherished by most preservation groups, when the thousandth member was recruited. This was marked by a ceremony at Rolvenden on 22 July, when the person involved was allowed to drive one of the locomotives a short distance. He was also presented with a book donated by John Smith, the well-known proprietor of Len's of Sutton, the railway photographic and book shop.

Rolvenden had by that date developed as a major focus for visitors' attentions. The rolling stock was of course the main attraction and the post of Information Officer for the site was advertised in the newsletter. Mrs Goddard was putting in a full day's work in the Pullmans each Sunday (where souvenirs as well as food and drink were sold) and she too was appealing for assistance. Such help arrived in the form of young ladies, a development which led to at least two marriages within the volunteer force. Also at Rolvenden, Dick Beckett had made great progress with the manufacture of the first four sets of lifting barrier equipment to a modified and embarrassment-proof design.

Peter Davis' gang was continuing to make a very full contribution towards the still-expected re-opening, with progress being made on the station platform at Bodiam and the new built-from-the-roof-down workshop at Rolvenden. A weedkilling train had been run with less than expected results, even though a firm with the necessary experience had been employed in an effort to produce the maximum effect. As a result, members were informed, the suppliers of the weedkiller were conducting experiments to find out why their products had been less than effective on the K&ESR!

During the summer the K&ESR came to the attention of Granada Television which approached the Association about hiring a train for filming purposes. This was a publicity opportunity not to be missed and had a three-figure fee, plus expenses for members involved in running the train. This was correctly seen at the time as the first development in an area where the K&ESR could usefully supplement its revenues, and indeed proved to be the case, for this was the first of the many productions which have used the railway for location filming. This development caused a change of priorities, as Granada wished to make use of the newly repainted coaching stock, and resleepering had to be suspended while overhanging trees between Bodiam and Tenterden were cut back. After all the expense and effort that had gone into repainting the rolling stock, nobody wanted it scratched, even in the interests of money and publicity.

The Signals and Telephone Department was credited with a particularly symbolic achievement when Kevin Blakiston and Chris Lowry completed the last link in the overhead wiring and the telephone system was restored along the entire length of the railway. Chris was at Robertsbridge when, for the first time, he made a call through to Tenterden. Malcolm Dunstan answered in the booking office and the quality of the system proved to be excellent. (It was stated at the time that this was the first call for five years. It may in fact have been the first call since June 1961, when Robin Doust called between Rolvenden and Robertsbridge signal-box, shortly after closure.)

August had arrived and the Ministry of Transport had still not completed consideration of the Light Railway Transfer Order. Sixteen thousand pounds had been contributed to the Rother Valley Railway Trust Fund, but with the tourist season drawing to a close the re-opening had been postponed to Easter 1968. Then, on 4 September, a letter was received from the Ministry of Transport informing the Rother Valley Railway Company that the Light Railway Transfer Order had been refused.

XIII

Derek Reader had been a volunteer since the earliest days of the preservation scheme and had had the distinction of having been present at the first working party in 1961. Asked many years later about the days immediately after the Ministry's decision became known he recalled that, on arriving at Rolvenden, he was greeted with the unusual sight of a group of volunteers sitting down at the trackside in sombre mood. Even at this moment Derek could not bring himself to believe that all was lost and he asked if anyone was willing to bet him that it was not the end. But there were no takers.

The reasons stated by the Ministry for the refusal of the Light Railway Transfer Order were:

> Insufficient financial reserves to cover the possible costs which might arise in the event of some unforeseen emergency, such as the collapse of a river bridge, and that lack of finance in such an event might involve adjoining landowners or the river authorities with heavy expenses due to the railway.
> The use made of the level crossings on the railway, particularly at the A21 crossing at Robertsbridge, said to carry a heavy and growing amount of traffic, and to which the re-opening of the railway would possibly constitute a hindrance.
> That in a further ten or twenty years the amount of traffic using certain of the roads might justify their conversion into dual carriageways, and that this would require the construction of road overbridges, at the taxpayer's expense.

The Granada TV train at Robertsbridge on 15 September 1967. This scene almost suggests that the K&ESR was on the point of success rather than the brink of disaster (Chris Lowry)

The conclusion of the Minister, as stated in the letter, was that despite a certain undisputed need on public service grounds for the railway, the inconvenience it would cause would outweigh its advantages, and it should therefore remain closed.

For some years following the refusal of the LRTO there was a tendency to personally blame the Minister of Transport, Barbara Castle, for the decision, and this view has sometimes been elevated to the status of received wisdom. While undertaking the research for this book, I came across hearsay evidence that Mrs Castle may have been swayed by her antipathy to private enterprise. The former Minister's published diaries are silent on the subject and at the time of writing several years remain before the relevant government documents are released to the Public Record Office. It is, however, arguable that the Rt Hon. Lady bore no personal illwill to the scheme on either political or technical grounds. The belief that she did could easily have arisen from some Association members' party allegiancies (which was fair enough) but more particularly from a misunderstanding of the Civil Service practice (more prevalent then than now) of pretending that everything is run on the intimate scale of the eighteenth century – a most convenient way of hiding behind a politician. The LRTO was, of course, refused in the Minister's name, she certainly had the final responsibility, and Mrs Castle may well have been acquainted with the facts of the case. I suggest that the Minister was asked to endorse decisions that had been made by her officials, officials who were (and still are) notoriously pro-road transport.

The Minister's letter was considered at a combined Association Committee and Company Board meeting, together with the 22-page report of the public inquiry which accompanied it. It was unanimously decided that this was not going to be the end of the matter, but there was no small anxiety about the possible effect on members' morale, and the volunteers in particular. As a result of the meeting, a letter was sent to the Ministry of Transport. The following account of its contents is based on a special bulletin (dated September) which was issued shortly afterwards.

Concerning the ability of the Company to meet unexpected emergencies, a member of the Association had indicated his willingness to stand surety against any possible financial contingency of this nature. The member's name was given to the Ministry [it was, once again, Ron Cann] together with authority for his financial standing to be investigated through his bankers so that the Ministry could be satisfied as to his ability to meet such commitments.

The records of the Tenterden Railway Company indicate that, although the Ministry of Transport took notice of this generous offer, it was not considered adequate for the long term and that an arrangement would be required which would be available 'in perpetuity'.

The letter went on to point out to the Ministry that the report of their own Inspector, who conducted the inquiry, stated in paragraph 160, the two county councils, as highway authorities, do not consider that in present conditions the amount of interference would be intolerable, or even material except in the case of the road A21'. This indicated that, in fact, only the Robertsbridge level crossing was of any real concern. The Ministry was then informed that detailed records of the amount of traffic using the level crossing had been kept by the Association over a period covering the previous months, and the figures indicated that the county council's figures were exceedingly inaccurate. The county figures were based on a survey conducted in 1964, and it had been assumed that there should have been an 8 per cent growth each year since then. The figures quoted at the inquiry were 8,100 vehicles per summer weekday and 12,200 vehicles per peak summer weekend. Allowing for the 8 per cent growth, these should have been at least 10,000 and 15,000 respectively. In fact, K&ESR records showed that barely half these amounts were actually present on the road, and even over the peak bank holiday weekends the traffic flows were way below the county estimates. It was therefore suggested that the Minister take a careful look at the figures again, and should at least seek further information before accepting the apparently doubtful county information as a basis for reaching such an important decision.

In this connection, it was further suggested that since the really busy periods on the A21 road were confined to a narrow part of the morning and evening on a limited number of summer Sundays, that the railway agree to limit the use made of the crossing during such periods so as to minimize the inconvenience caused. Such a step would almost completely remove inconvenience from the level crossing.

The final objection, that of the expensive road overbridges which might possibly be needed in twenty years' time, apart from the fact that the Rother Valley should not be deprived of its railway for many years to come on account of a possible future development, was easily dealt with. It was suggested to the Ministry that the Light Railway Order be made for an initial period of ten years, at the end of which time a further application would have to be made to extend the powers, and this application could be considered in the light of road conditions at that time.

The letter concluded by suggesting that in view of the additional information which had become available concerning the traffic flows across the A21 level crossing, and of the other points raised, the Minister should look again at the matter, with a view to varying her original decision.

Arising out of the inquiry came one other point – that there seemed to have been a serious irregularity of procedure. It was an accepted feature of the public inquiry machinery that the Minister might seek further information on various points after the conclusion of the inquiry, but it was also accepted that she must inform all the interested parties concerned of this information and give them an opportunity to make representations on it before announcing her decision. It appeared that the question of several dual carriageway bridges being required in the future was never mentioned at the inquiry, and the Company was not told of this new information at all until the announcement of the Minister's decision.

A meeting was called of all regular volunteers during the weekend of 9–10 September. Over fifty members were present and the mood of despondency, which Derek Reader had noted a little earlier, still persisted. The Committee and Board's decision to fight on was explained but some persuasive oratory was needed – Robin Doust was prominent in this – to achieve the necessary change of mood. Once the workforce had been convinced that the fight could be continued, the details of the public inquiry report were read out. The fact then emerged that the Inspector had recommended that the LRTO be granted, subject to a few safeguards!

Matters then began to proceed very quickly indeed. Some figures about traffic on the A21 (gathered by Mr Cannon-Rogers, an older but agile-minded member of the Association) were already available. Arrangements were made to enlarge on these as soon as possible. A traffic count was set up, using the same methods employed by local authorities and which involved recording five-minute totals in north and southbound directions. Enough volunteers were found to run this count, taken at the crossing by Hodson's Mill, from 6.00 a.m. to 10.00 p.m. The necessary census forms were rapidly duplicated in members' homes and by the end of the week enough data had been gathered to indicate that the Ministry's figures were inaccurate by a factor of 50 per cent.

Other more direct action was also being taken and on Friday 15 the first approach was made to a Member of Parliament, Mr William Deedes (now Lord Deedes), who had represented the Ashford constituency for many years. The Association was represented at this meeting by Robin Doust and Peter Benge-Abbott, a local resident and active member, who also went along because of his general business experience, particularly in respect of negotiations. This combination was in itself interesting, Robin representing all that had been achieved since the early days of the project and Mr Benge-Abbott the next phase of the railway's history. Mr Deedes' reaction was also recorded in the bulletin:

> He read the Ministry refusal, and our comments on it, and immediately expressed the view that we had indeed been fobbed off with excuses, and he undertook to make immediate representations to the Minister and BR that the matter should be re-opened, and that no steps be taken to scrap the railway until a more satisfactory outcome had been reached. [The Association was concerned, since BR had indicated its intention to commence lifting track almost immediately once the Minister's decision had been reached.]

The Association was not slow in approaching the media either, and a press release was prepared during the week of 11 September. It was also necessary to obtain firm evidence of the public's support for the railway. Rightly or wrongly, the preservation scheme had never 'tested the water' in this respect previously, although in relation to freight services there was the traffic to Hodson's Mill and it was known that Kent Chemical Industries was interested in facilities at Tenterden. It was now decided to prepare a petition and ask for signatures in all the major communities served by the line. Petition forms had been printed as part of the same exercise which prepared the paperwork for the traffic count and a contemporary account said that on Saturday 16 and Sunday 17 Tenterden Town station resembled an army operations room. There was no shortage of volunteers and many members arrived to help in the exercise, which was most effectively organized with the aid of electoral rolls and local maps. The area around the railway was divided into sections and groups of members called at as many houses as could be reached. There was a most welcome and enthusiastic response on the part of local people. There appeared to be a widespread opinion in Tenterden and the Rother Valley that the line should re-open and this had been greatly assisted by an editorial in the *Kent Messenger* supporting the Association, the paper also printing the press release in full. In one and a half days no fewer than 3,100 signatures were collected. It was not only local people who, because of the publicity, rallied to support the cause. More new members enrolled in the Association in a few weeks than had joined over the course of the previous few months and there were generous additions to the funds of the RVR Trust. At work, Robin Doust was quietly reminded that he had spent most of two days taking (unsolicited) calls from the press!

Despite the traumatic events which were taking place, plans went ahead for the Granada TV train. In the circumstances there was considerable doubt as to whether BR would allow these stock movements to take place and these were not finally resolved until the day before the filming was due to occur. In the event the Association was able to draw the section staff on the morning of Saturday 22 September and the train was able to leave Rolvenden for Robertsbridge. No. 3, by then re-united with her nameplates and smartly turned out, hauled the two newly repainted Maunsell coaches and, once again, there were heartening demonstrations of support by local people. Aided by the local press, as well as items on television, the Ministry's refusal of the Light Railway Transfer Order was becoming a *cause célèbre* and there were numerous shouts of encouragement and good wishes.

The Farmers' Line reported:

> On arrival at Robertsbridge No. 3 took water, and then backed her two coaches into the bay platform. There was a lengthy wait while the film crew satisfied their hunger in a nearby hostelry, and during this time a number of main-line trains stopped at the station. It was most interesting to watch the reaction of the passengers on these trains on seeing the unfamiliar livery of the K&ESR train, and one first class passenger trampled on his own copy of *The Times* in his rush to gaze out of the window at the unusual sight. Passengers at Robertsbridge awaiting the London trains were equally interested, and on hearing what was happening, they all, without exception, gladly signed the Petition.
>
> The film crew had meanwhile filmed a number of shots of passengers alighting from a main-line train and boarding the K&ESR train. Having finished this sequence, the train was then filmed leaving the station, although this shot had to be filmed twice as it was noticed after the first occasion that it had left in defiance of a branch 'home' signal very noticeably in the 'on' position. However, good time was made subsequently up the line to Bodiam, where a further lengthy refreshment stop was made (television people seem to have permanent hunger pains!). The train then moved on up the line, and was shunted up and down the section from Bodiam to Northiam for several hours while shots were taken inside the coaches for several sequences. It was most interesting to see the special floodlights and cameras designed to work off 24 volts, and which were plugged into the carriage lighting sockets in order to carry out the filming.
>
> Eventually, the scripted sequences were completed, and the film crew and actors bade us a very satisfied goodbye (after signing the Petition, of course) with hopes that this would not be the last time they would be immortalizing the railway on film. The title of the film is *Sarah*, and we understand that it is likely to be screened by Granada during December. Having satisfactorily completed the day's work, and incidentally earned a

three-figure charge into the bargain, the train was worked back to Rolvenden and a very successful day brought to a conclusion. The occasion also did much to boost the morale of our working members, and the sight of the really superbly turned out train served to renew determination that every possible way of keeping the line open should be pursued to its ultimate conclusion. We certainly hope this determination will pay off.

Viewed from many years later the Granada train somehow seems to encapsulate the will of the K&ESR to survive, both as a physical entity and a group of individuals. That such an event should have taken place at a moment of extreme crisis, and with such success, exemplifies that strange and already commented on capacity for the railway to exist almost regardless of the storm clouds which raged around it. Nor was that train the only movement over the line during the autumn months.

The Robertsbridge P class had suffered a crack in its firebox shell and the boiler had been removed for welding. This presented Hodson's Mill with a serious problem as it was, most commendably, still receiving heavy freight traffic. Mr Dadswell took the logical course and requested assistance from the Association. Hire terms were agreed and No. 50 set off for Robertsbridge, where she carried out the shunting duties for a week before being replaced by diesel No. 16. The Ford's stay at Robertsbridge was to last for several months and during this time she was regularly driven by either Ron Cann or Charlie Kentsley. No. 16 earned the Association some badly needed income by these activities and could regularly be seen hauling up to a dozen grain wagons between Robertsbridge station and the mill. The irony of this was, of course, that every time the locomotive rumbled across the A21 the Association was doing exactly what the Ministry of Transport had said it would not allow.

Meanwhile, what may be termed the parliamentary campaign was hotting up. Efforts in this direction were spurred on by the Ministry's reply (dated 15 September) to the Association's letter challenging the refusal of the LRTO. Almost predictably the K&ESRA was told that the matter was now closed and that the Ministry was not prepared to consider further approaches in the case. Following the example of Messrs Doust and Benge-Abbott, other active members of the Association had been asked to approach their own Members of Parliament, and by the time of the September bulletin it was known that twelve MPs had been asked to help. One of the first had been Mr T.E. Boston, also a Kent MP, who represented Faversham. He had been approached by Chris Golding, an Association member who lived in his constituency, at the same time Robin Doust and Peter Benge-Abbott were seeing Mr Deedes.

The next step was to ask everyone in the Association to contact their MPs as well, either in writing or at their weekly surgeries. The first problem which had to be dealt with was the possibility that an MP might refuse to touch the problem because it was outside his or her constituency. This could quite simply be disposed of by pointing out to uncooperative MPs that their constituent was affected and he or she did live in the right place (and by implication had, or would soon have, the vote). Ron Cann was to deal with queries which MPs might have.

The general strategy at this stage was that, although there was no appeal procedure against the refusal of a Light Railway Order, the Association hoped to get the Minister to reconsider her decision. Failing that, it was intended to apply for another Order. It was reasoned, therefore, that the more public and parliamentary support which could be obtained the better. Every member was supplied (via the September bulletin) with the following letter, which individuals could adapt when writing to their Member of Parliament:

> I am writing to you as a member of the K&ESR Association in the hope that you may be able to assist us in our efforts to re-open the branch railway line between Robertsbridge and Tenterden.
>
> The Association recently applied to the Ministry of Transport for permission to re-open the railway, and has now received a reply from the Ministry refusing to grant the necessary Light Railway Order which would enable the line to run. Members of the Association would accept the decision if it appeared that there were sound reasons for it, but in fact it appears that no good reason exists, and the Ministry seems to have simply seized on some plausible excuses to reject our proposals, and now refuses to even discuss them.
>
> The Association now has some 1,200 members, and we have between us raised a total of £36,000 towards the purchase of the railway – a tremendous achievement for a voluntary organization. Some £7,000 has also been spent on rolling stock to run on the line, and this will be wasted if it does not run again. In addition, dozens of our members spend weekends and holidays on constructive work to make the line operational again.
>
> The Association has always hoped, through the efforts of its members, to be able to provide a normal public transport and freight service as well as special trains for tourists in the summer, and it is intended that the subsidy provided in cash and labour by our members would enable the railway service to be provided for the benefit of local people. We have always felt our aims to be entirely in the public interest, and designed to offer a public service without any drain on public funds. Now, however, the whole scheme is threatened with failure, and we very much hope that you will be able to assist us in having the matter considered again in some way.
>
> I enclose a copy of a recent press release, which sets out the Association's position in the matter, and if you would be good enough to read this, I think you will appreciate why we feel the matter has been seriously mishandled, and that we feel that the Ministry has behaved in a very high-handed and unjust manner. Unfortunately there seems to be no more conventional way of approaching the Ministry for further consideration of the matter, and in the meantime, BR are threatening to remove the track in order to entirely prevent any further effort being made to run the railway again. We have already approached Mr W. Deedes, MP for Ashford, and Mr T.G. Boston, MP for Faversham, and they have agreed to take the matter up for us, but we would be most grateful if you would reinforce their approaches to the Minister and BR by contacting the Ministry yourself. I should add that I have some financial interest in the organization myself, and to this extent feel justified in asking for your help as one of your constituents, even though the actual railway is, of course, not in this constituency.

Public support was further reinforced by a second petition for signature by the general public outside the confines of Tenterden and the Rother Valley, and these were to be returned to the Association by 4 October. By the time the October *Farmers' Line* was typed (on the fifth of the month) no fewer than 4,000 signatures had been collected using another addition to the growing collection of special paperwork which was being circulated to Association members. In order to gain an even better response the deadline for the petition was extended to 21 October, the day set for the Annual General Meeting.

The October newsletter brought the unsurprising news that, in the circumstances, work would be concentrated on the rolling stock at Rolvenden, where *Charwelton's* overhaul and the repainting of the Pullmans was continuing. That edition of *The Farmers' Line* concluded with an ominous item entitled 'Future Policy' which, while talking brightly of problems being overcome, had to admit to the possibility of defeat. Consideration was being given to tentative plans for a line of retreat in the event of the Association having to abandon the railway. It had been suggested that an alternative line be sought, but BR was actively discouraging preservation schemes. It had already made clear to the Association (during the course of a meeting at Waterloo) that there was virtually no chance of any other line being made available. Another, minimal, possibility was the purchase of Rolvenden station and the establishment of a museum. BR would, however, not sell a reasonable length of track on which the rolling stock could operate and this solution appeared most undesirable. The only other possibility was a repeat of the amalgamation tactic used at the time of the Westerham collapse, a course of action rendered somewhat difficult by the lack of a suitable partner. As a fall-back position, arrangements had been made for temporary storage, if the need arose, on a private railway 'elsewhere in southern England'.

At 2.35 p.m. on 21 October, 150 members gathered for the first General Meeting of the Association since the refusal of the Light Railway Transfer Order and, on this occasion, Peter Davis was in the chair. For the first time the venue was other than Tenterden Town Hall, the meeting being held in the Youth Centre, Highbury Lane (also owned by the Borough of Tenterden). Once the preliminaries were out of the way Ron Cann was able to point out that the Association's financial turnover had reached nearly £5,000 for the first time, an achievement which was very much tempered by the critical situation. The existing Committee was re-elected *en bloc* without objection to the procedure. For the record, these were Len Heath Humphrys (Chairman), Ron Cann (Treasurer), Robin Doust (Secretary), Malcolm Dunstan (Membership Secretary) and Dave Kitton (Publicity Officer). Other Committee members were Peter Davis, Charlie Kentsley, Peter Goddard, Peter Cox and Ralph Brockman. The meeting then turned to consideration of the position in which the project now found itself.

This part of the meeting began with an account by Robin Doust of the moves which had been made since 4 September. Peter Davis then invited questions from the floor and the first of these requested the names of those MPs who had agreed to support the Association, and a list of twenty-six individuals was read out. Despite the statement in the October *Farmers' Line*, the possibility of moving to an alternative line came up again and, after several locations had been suggested, the Chairman undertook to investigate these.

Shortly afterwards, Mr Cannon-Rogers (who was to demonstrate an uncanny knack for apt remarks over the next few years) suggested that a court injunction be sought to prevent the demolition of the track. The idea was not entirely new, as Robin Doust was able to reply that the possibility was already under consideration, but this was among the earliest shots in a whole new series of battles. Arthur Penny asked if the deposit paid on the railway had been returned and was told that it had but that the cheque had not been cashed pending legal advice. Another suggestion which might have seemed a good idea at face value was that the land should still be purchased even if the track was lifted. This was not possible, however, as BR was bound to offer redundant land to local authorities. Even if the counties involved had bought the land on the railway's behalf, the K&ESR would still have required a Light Railway Order which, as the Ministry would not agree to this, would bring the whole matter back to square one. In answer to a further question it transpired that, although BR was reviewing the Robertsbridge mill siding for closure, it had said in writing that it intended to keep it open indefinitely. This would, of course, perpetuate the nonsense of the Rother Valley Railway Company being refused permission to cross the A21 at the same time as BR allowing K&ESR locomotives to do exactly the same thing.

After a few routine items had been dealt with, 'any other business' was reached and with it the return from South Africa of George Pickin (without whom no AGM seemed quite complete). The minutes state:

> 11. . . . Mr Pickin then made a lengthy speech . . . [he] . . . claimed that BR did not need a Light Railway Order[1] in order to transfer a section of railway from Robertsbridge to Rolvenden to the Association's Company, because it had been authorized by a private Act, not a Light Railway Order. He also pointed out that the Railway Company, not the taxpayers, would be liable for any costs involved in constructing road overbridges across the railway. He then launched into an attack on certain members of the Committee for their handling of the matter. . . . After some discussion involving Mr Pickin and several other members, it was suggested that in order to save further time, Mr Pickin should be invited to the next convenient Association Committee meeting so that the possibility of his claims and proposals being of value should be considered in more detail. This was proposed by Mr Doust and seconded by Mr Cannon-Rogers. It was carried unanimously.

> 12. Mr Pickin then attempted to embark on a lengthy description of a special type of lifting barrier which he had devised, which he claimed would only block traffic for seven seconds at a time. Several members suggested that he desist, and Mr Glass asked the Committee to ensure that the membership be consulted before Mr Pickin was given any power to act on behalf of the Association in any way. Mr Cannon-Rogers then proposed that Mr Pickin be no longer heard, and expressed his commiserations to the Committee on having to meet Mr Pickin subsequently, as previously agreed in the meeting. The proposal was seconded by Mr Dunlavey and carried unanimously.

Towards the end of the meeting Peter Davis confirmed, in reply to a question from the floor, that everything would be done to keep both the rolling stock collection and the organization together. But in an emphatic pointer to the future, he added that the fight for the K&ESR was far from over.

About this time Robin Doust read through the Light Railways Act in detail. Noticing that the Minister appeared to be subject to a statutory duty to 'encourage' light railways, and feeling that this was the last thing the K&ESR had received, he rang the parliamentary agents who had assisted with the preparation of the Light Railway Transfer Order. (Parliamentary agents are a branch of the solicitor's profession which deals with matters relating to private Acts of Parliament and other statutory provisions (LROs for example) which affect the rights and powers of individuals and organisations.)

Robin was in London at the time and was granted an immediate appointment. But when he arrived at the parliamentary agents' offices he found that it had been assumed that he wished to arrange for the winding up of the Association's affairs. Instead, the lawyer was told that the K&ESRA Secretary thought he could see grounds for suing the Minister of Transport! Twenty-four years later, Robin could still see the look of amazement on the man's face. When, however, the lawyer had recovered his composure, he checked his Halsbury's Statutes and agreed that there might, indeed, be something in the idea.

XIV

Around the time of the AGM, news was received that BR had sold the track to Thomas Ward and Company and that lifting was due to commence on 30 October. This, the circumstance anticipated by Mr Cannon-Rogers at the AGM, was about as dire as matters could possibly get, and on 25 October a consultation was held with Mr Ian Percival QC, MP about what could be done to prevent the start of demolition. (This was a quite separate legal action from the possibility mentioned previously.) After considering the matter, Mr Percival, acting on behalf of the Rother Valley Railway Company, applied for an ex parte injunction restraining BR from lifting the track. The injunction was granted by the High Court on 27 October and a further hearing was arranged for 31 October, when BR would be represented.

The second court hearing, which involved a three-hour legal battle, ended when Mr Justice Buckley continued the injunction until the full hearing of the case. This would revolve around the question of whether or not the contract signed between the Company and BR in March 1966 was at an end. The injunction remained in force when, in early November, the next, and particularly spectacular, stage of the campaign was reached.

Meanwhile, at their meeting on 21 October, the Committee had met with George Pickin as arranged at the AGM. Mr Pickin offered financial assistance but much in accordance with his previously stated ideas. The Committee did not come to an immediate decision on this renewed offer but met again on the 27th of the month. Unusually this further meeting was held at Peter Goddard's home at Ightham. Mr Pickin's proposals were again examined but, with the dissenting voice of Peter Davis, they were again rejected. Peter's reasons for taking this view were that George Pickin was the only person in sight who was prepared to contribute large sums independent of the guarantee-backed bank loan and that lines of communication with him should be kept open. There was one further meeting with Mr Pickin at which the Association was represented by Peter Davis and Dave Kitton. There was still no meeting of minds and after that the possibility of using George Pickin's money ended. On his part, Mr Pickin still considered in 1993 that the feud with him damaged the project, affected the outcome of the first Light Railway Transfer Order application and prevented the railway being re-opened as originally planned. I will not pass judgement on issues which continue to be sensitive. George Pickin had, however, made a contribution to the growing interest in pursuing the matter through the courts. It was his contention that the RVR Company should have applied for *certiorari* (the predecessor of judicial review) in respect of the Minister's decision. He argued that under Section 7 of the Railways Clauses Act 1863, railway companies were required to meet the cost of constructing roadbridges, but that the Act does not permit demands for a bridge over a proposed (rather than an existing) road. Mr Pickin has also opined that his seven-second lifting barriers would counteract possible demands for a bridge in connection with the proposed road.

In the period following the refusal of the Light Railway Transfer Order, however, and quite separately from Robin Doust's or George Pickin's ideas, it was suggested that the Ministry's decision was legally questionable on other grounds and that the Association should sue the Minister. The Committee was receptive to anything that would enable it to combat the Ministery of Transport and was beginning to take legal action seriously.

By early November the number of people who had signed the petition forms was approaching the 10,000 mark (the final number was around 11,000) and by the 7th of the month some forty MPs from all three main political parties had contacted Mr Deedes, including Edward Heath, then Leader of the Opposition. Many of these MPs had written direct to the Ministry of Transport and all had received a 'severely uncompromising' letter in reply. Bill Deedes now felt there was sufficient interest to bring the matter up in the House of Commons. His chosen course of action was to ask the Speaker for an adjournment debate. This parliamentary procedure is a technical device which allows matters of public concern to be aired on the motion that 'This House do now adjourn', followed by the raising of whatever issue has been selected on that particular occasion. Unlike confidence motions, adjournment debates are rarely, if ever, put to the vote. They take place at the end of other business, which means they are invariably held late in the evening.

The adjournment debate on the K&ESR took place in the grim week which began with the derailment in pouring rain of a Hastings demu between Grove Park and Hither Green, in south-east London, with the loss of forty-nine lives. The scale of this tragedy, including the deaths of a number of people who had lived in the vicinity of the Rother Valley, put the problems of the K&ESR in some kind of perspective. The accident, nevertheless, lent a sombre background to the evening of Tuesday 7 November, when a number of members of the Association gathered at the Palace of Westminster to hear the matter raised in Parliament.

Dr Johnson once said that the House of Commons was the best free entertainment in London. This remained true two hundred years later, and I had certainly taken occasional advantage of the fact during my later teens, when visits to the Strangers' Gallery combined rather well with my vocational studies. This interest had, however, stayed in a separate compartment from my railway activities and to find the two now juxtaposed was, to say the least, a strange experience. The adjournment debate began at 10.15 p.m., and it has to be recorded that the House was not particularly full. Mr Deedes began by briefly recounting the railway's history and the course events had taken since March 1966. Having related the reasons for the refusal of the Light Railway

Transfer Order, he continued as follows (the following extracts from the debate are taken from *Hansard*, Vol. 753, No.7; parliamentary copyright reproduced here with the permission of HMSO):

> The Minister felt the inconvenience would outweigh the advantages. At this stage, I and a great number of other Hon. Members found ourselves involved, due to the interest and enthusiasm of members of the Association. In passing, I am bound to record the reactions of leading members of the Association to this decision and the way that they swung into action persuaded me that they were surprisingly well-equipped, and I think the Parliamentary Secretary will not deny this, to meet any emergencies or contingencies which might arise on the railway.
>
> I have practically had to open a separate office to deal with the correspondence arising out of this, and I believe the Parliamentary Secretary has had to do something of the same kind. At least I am persuaded that these people mean business. There is a disposition by the Ministry, or at least a section of the Ministry, to think that this railway will serve mainly the tourist trade, and not a very serious purpose. I could contest this if I had time, but this at least might be said. Here we are exercising ourselves about recreation for people in the countryside and elsewhere, yet we are about to consider a very large Government Bill on this subject, upon which it would be out of order for me to comment upon now. What possible sense does it make to destroy an amenity like this and then pass through Parliament a Bill designed to recreate for people the sort of amenity that this railway provides?

Mr Deedes then came to the two issues which, in his words, were 'the nub of the affair'; possible road, developments in ten or twenty years and the Association's suggestion of a temporary LRTO, as well as the dispute about the then current level of road traffic. He added that the Association had timed the delays at the crossings and found they were measured in seconds rather than minutes. On finance he referred to the offer of an Association member to stand surety against contingencies and mentioned that the assets of the K&ESR were hardly negligible. He continued:

> Suffice it to say that these people have replies which carry considerable weight. They are respectable arguments. They are not the bleatings of a disappointed body of the kind with which all Hon. Members become familiar. They are a substantial reply to the Minister's objections and misgivings.
>
> I am sorry to say the Association's replies fell on deaf ears, not because they were inadequate, but because in reality the Ministry had assumed the point of no return. It had assumed that familiar posture which, when it suits them, Ministries adopt when they are judges in their own cause: 'The case is closed. No further discussion will be entertained.'

A little later Bill Deedes quoted what he termed 'a gem of Whitehall evasion'. This was:

> The idea of an Order for an experimental period of years, although at first sight attractive, is in the view of our legal advisers, doubtfully acceptable.

Pursuing this issue further, he informed the House:

> Later, the ground was shifted a little and it was said that the BR Board did not find this proposal acceptable. I must add that the part played by the Board in this buck-passing process has been something less than distinguished. I accept that the Board has other

anxieties and preoccupations. The fact remains, however, that it sold the track, or proceeded to do so, to a contractor. On this point I must say no more, because the matter is the subject of proceedings elsewhere and I must not pursue it.

Mr Deedes then proceeded to start drawing the points of his speech towards a conclusion:

I return, however, to the second and, in my view, much the most important issue which all this raises. The principal objections raised by the Minister to which I have just referred were raised after, and not at, the inquiry. On this point a group of young people who have produced a rather good report on the report have commented that 'It seems that there has been some serious irregularity in procedure on the part of the Ministry'. [The authors of this document were Normandy (Surrey) Young Conservatives. Richard Halton of the publicity team was a member.] It is accepted that Ministers can always seek information after an inquiry on which to base their decision, but if that information is of substance they should at least inform the interested parties and give them an opportunity to make representations on it before announcing the decision.

The weighty arguments, as they seemed to the Ministry at least, about dual carriageways, and bridges, and the financial liability of the company, were not matters raised at the inquiry. Nor has the Ministry been willing to discuss these matters with the company since the inquiry. The Ministry could have made an order subject to conditions. That would have been one way round. The Ministry could have persuaded BR to accept a lease, and although I am told they do not want to, we know perfectly well that if the Ministry were to tell BR they ought to they would.

Therefore it comes to this, that on the evidence offered the inspector thought that, broadly, a case had been made out; of the three main objections raised by the Ministry, subsequently advanced, in order to justify a contrary decision, two were irregular and one was not even discussed.

This really will not do . . . [the Ministry] has done what Ministries will always do unless they are checked in this place . . . and that is, to attempt on an even issue to swing the balance with bland arguments they calculate none will challenge, and by methods which, to say the least of it, are dubious, and that is where the House of Commons has suddenly to say 'Stop', because that is really what we are here to do.

Ashford's MP then anticipated the very subject, with its suspicions of official deviousness and ineptitude, which twenty-two years later would raise the spectre of civil disorder in parts of Kent and south London. (And, ironically, raise it in connection with a railway proposal.) He wondered whether the Ministry had better reasons for their decision. He wondered if, in connection with the Channel Tunnel, there was to be a transport structure (he meant a road structure) to which the K&ESR would be an embarrassment. He hoped that:

. . . the Parliamentary Secretary will be frank about this. In some ways, I think the Ministry has had bad luck. Nine times out of ten it could have got away with all this, irregularities and all, without too much fuss, but it has been surprised, as indeed I have been, by running into a set of rather determined and really rather competent people who have set about the matter and decided to raise hell and have aroused the interest of about 40 members, at least of this House, and on both sides of it; and that is really what democracy is all about.

It is because I think that this case deserves a wider hearing that I have raised this matter in this way. Whatever the Ministry has done, at least the manner in which it was done, has been exposed. The Ministry has behaved shabbily, and I hope that it will have the sense to think again.

John Wells, MP for Maidstone, spoke briefly in support of Bill Deedes before, at 10.30 p.m., John Morris, Joint Parliamentary Secretary to the Ministry of Transport rose in reply. The written record in *Hansard* does not fully reflect the attitude which appeared to lie behind that response and a number of Association members who were present, including myself, recall that it was delivered in a dismissive and sometimes patronizing tone. Mr Morris firstly spoke of some of the details of the campaign since September before stating:

> No doubt all this is wholly admirable in terms of democracy, and I congratulate the enthusiasts. As the Right Hon. Gentleman said, this is what democracy is all about. The case might usefully be studied by those who take the view that the people of this country are helpless pawns in the hands of the bureaucracy. However, in our admiration for the pluck and determination of the Right Hon. Gentleman's constituents, we must be careful not to get the basic issues out of perspective.
>
> The main objections – the road delays and the prospect of bridges – were all discussed at the inquiry. At all events, I want to try to remove some of the emotional irrelevance which has become thickly encrusted round the affair, and to set out clearly what the Minister's position is in relation to light railways, why she decided not to grant this Light Railway Order, and, finally, why, in spite of all that has been said during the last two months, she does not propose to reverse or modify her decision. [The reader is advised to view these references to Mrs Castle in the light of the earlier comments about administrative fictions.]

Mr Morris pointed out that the Minister was empowered to make a decision on the basis of facts found out 'both by local inquiry and such other means as she thinks necessary'. He then said there were three important points he wished to make before returning to the details of the case:

> I hope that I need hardly say that my Right Hon. Friend the Minister is in no way opposed to the operation of light railways as such. On the contrary, Hon. Members will know that there are several light railways operating in different parts of the country, some run by private railway associations and preservation societies, and some by industrial firms, and many of them have been given considerable technical and legal help by the Ministry. I take issue with the Right Hon. Gentleman about the strictures he made against the Railways Board, because it gave substantial help in this case.
>
> Nevertheless, running a light railway is not a basic constitutional right. The case for being allowed to do so has to be established in the light of all the circumstances.

The Joint Parliamentary Secretary then reminded the House that it was not the Minister's function to rubber-stamp recommendations of the Inspector but to weigh up all the arguments, and also that there was no specific provision in the Light Railways Acts to allow for the granting of a temporary order. He then raised issues which were, in the following two years, to have far-reaching consequences both on the course of dealings with the Ministry and the Railways Board and also on the internal 'politics' of the K&ESR:

> As early as May, 1966, the light railway company, which had approached the Ministry for preliminary guidance, was warned in writing that any proposal to re-open level crossings over these busy main roads was bound to raise grave objections . . . re-opening a line with problems like the K&ESR could only be justified if there were a clearly established public transport need, sufficient in scale to outweigh the disadvantages to road users. . . . The

company chose to ignore these warnings that the proposals to re-open these level crossings would cause difficulties. Indeed I doubt whether ordinary members of the Association . . . were told of the risk.

Mr Morris was correct on the latter point, but this raises the question of how much weight should have been attached to the letter in question. Much of the letter stated points which were already widely known or anticipated. There was, indeed, a paragraph which pointed out the possibility of 'serious objections' to the re-establishment of the level crossings. This ended with a (rather ambiguous) sentence which might, in retrospect, be considered potentially worrying. It was the suggestion that the Society (*sic*) might wish to take the Ministry's points into consideration in deciding whether or not to enter into any financial commitments in advance of the Minister's decision.

The remainder of the debate reiterated issues which had already been covered, or are mentioned elsewhere in this account, before Big Ben struck 10.45 p.m. and the Deputy Speaker adjourned the House.

Then it was out into the gloomy November night and a sense of anticlimax mingled with bitter disappointment that the Ministry of Transport showed no sign, even after the matter had been raised in the House of Commons, of softening its position. The evening's events were briefly mulled over in the St Stephen's Tavern across the road, before the conversation drifted onto a discussion of the Hither Green derailment. Across the river, Waterloo worked on bereft of the steam locomotives which had vanished a few months earlier. In August the following year British main-line steam would come to an end. Already, in the south, railway enthusiasm was entering what many would come to regard as a dreary and characterless period which would, despite the activities of *Flying Scotsman* and successes elsewhere for the railway preservation movement, last until *King George V* began the 'Return to Steam' programme in 1971. It was not an auspicious background for the course on which the K&ESR was now set.

A further bulletin was issued to members in November and this made brief mention of the events in Parliament on 7 November, as well as giving an account of a subsequent conference held with Mr Percival on the 15th of the month. The QC had been present in the Commons during the adjournment debate and had come to the conclusion that it was possible to challenge the validity of the Minister's decision in the courts. The idea of suing the Minister had, apparently, taken hold. It was, however, by no means a straightforward case and costs of at least £750 were foreseen (double if the Association lost), on top of the £500 that had already been spent to obtain the injunctions.

Strictly speaking, the Association could not, of course, deal directly with Mr Percival, a member of the Bar, as legal procedure required solicitors to act in an intermediary role. This function was again performed by the Rother Valley Railway's parliamentary agents.

The basis of the case against the Ministry centred on the English legal doctrine of ultra vires – to exceed one's powers. Statutory authority already existed to operate the line and the Rother Valley Railway Company had merely applied to have those powers transferred to itself. The Ministry (in the person of the Minister) had, in turn, powers, under the Light Railways Acts, to grant, amend, transfer or refuse Light Railway Orders. The Ministry had, however, treated the RVR's application as if it was for the construction of a new railway and most of the reasons put forward for the refusal were appropriate only in the case of a new line. It was Counsel's opinion that in considering an application for a Transfer Order, the Minister was only entitled to consider whether or not the body seeking the powers was capable of carrying them out satisfactorily. In the case of the K&ESR, it appeared, the main consideration should have been whether the Company would have been able to maintain the statutory drainage obligations, weed control, fencing repairs and, of particular importance, the general safe running of the railway. The last point had never been queried except in the terms already outlined, and this aspect will be taken up later. The parliamentary agents were also able to use the uncertainty over the legal position as a further lever to prevent the track being removed. They merely had to point out that, even if the appeal against the injunction was successful, should the RVR win its case against the Minister, BR they might face a large claim for damages.

The November bulletin included a frank question to members: did they, or did they not, wish the campaign to reverse the Minister's decision to continue? A referendum voting slip to allow members to state their views (there was, of course, a vote to carry on) made it very clear that continuance of the fight would involve their financial support. The Association's funds were about £1,000 and two members of the Trust Fund had agreed to allow a further £750 to be used for covering the cost of litigation. It was with some regret that the monies in the RVR Trust had to be used at all, and Fund members were told that they could make their monies available for use if required. The preferred course of action was for Association members to contribute to a fighting fund which was being established for the purpose. The membership responded well to this and a further £1,000 in cash was sent in during the first week.

The K&ESR had meanwhile been the subject of a leading article in the magazine *Railway World*, which led to the Association having to put the record straight. The following is a relevant extract from the piece in question (reproduced with the permission of the current editor):

> The shock announcement by the Minister of Transport rejecting the application of the K&ESR for a Light Railway Order dashed any hopes that services would be resumed between Robertsbridge and Tenterden. Indeed, such was the speed of events that hardly had the decision been made when the Southern Region completed the contract for the demolition of the line. Thus the years of hard work put in by volunteers on track maintenance, fence renewal and not least the acquisition of locomotives and rolling stock have come to nought. More disturbing, however, is the fact that the Company had the capital to complete the purchase of the line from BR – a condition of any Light Railway Order application – and had already spent money on equipment. What is the position now regarding donations contributed for the specific purpose of restoration and re-opening of this line to passenger traffic now that the Minister has rejected the scheme? In a commercial undertaking the return of capital raised against the issue of shares is a difficult procedure; money already spent cannot be returned and if K&ESR contributors demand the return of donations the Society [*sic*] has a complex problem to sort out.

The Association's reply was included among the items in the November bulletin:

> Following a leading article . . . which was based on entirely erroneous information, the Trustees of the Trust Fund feel they should make it clear that all funds subscribed . . . are held in trust, and cannot be spent unless express permission to do so has been received in writing from the subscriber. Thus all money is still in the Fund untouched. The *Railway World* article rightly draws attention to the difficulties which would arise in the event of winding up an organization in which the money subscribed had been invested in shares, and it is primarily for this reason that RVR Trust subscribers have not so far been invited to take up a shareholding in the Company. If after all our efforts, it is still impossible to re-open the railway, all the Trust Funds can quite simply be refunded to the original subscribers. In the meantime, the £17,000 at present in the Fund represents the main cash assets of the organization towards the purchase of the railway, and it is essential that support for the Trust is maintained if we are to have sufficient capital available to purchase the railway if it eventually proves possible to do so.

Unfortunately, this would not be the last time during this difficult period that the Association would find itself answering unfavourable comment in the pages of *Railway World*.

Considering all that was happening, it came as no surprise that it was decided to hold a Special General Meeting and members were informed that this was to be held on Saturday 6 January 1968. The Committee was also still giving some thought to the possibility of moving to another site, and the Polegate–Hailsham route was discussed on 18 November. There was some minority support for this idea on the Committee but, as the majority of the membership wished to continue the fight for the K&ESR, nothing was to come of it. Other possible sites mentioned during discussions were Didcot (then at a formative stage), Longmoor, Quainton Road, the Bluebell line and the North Norfolk Railway. BR was approached for an estimate for moving the stock to Longmoor and came back with an answer of £500.

Legal matters were continuing to move steadily forward, and Mr Percival had, through the parliamentary agents, written to the Ministry stating the Association's case and asking for their observations. The subsequent reply cited various Acts of Parliament as grounds for the Minister's actions. A further six-page letter was then sent in reply to this contending the Ministry's assertions. On 29 November, the parliamentary agents issued a writ against the Ministry of Transport. The following day BR's application for the lifting of the earlier injunction (which prevented demolition of the track) was heard in the High Court. The proceedings lasted all day. Mr Justice Pennycuick gave judgement on 7 December but, unfortunately, agreed to lift the injunction. All was not lost, however, as he gave leave to appeal and BR agreed not to have any track removed until the appeal was heard.

With the K&ESR now taking up the time of Parliament and the courts, that strange capacity of the line and the preservation project to exist on two almost disconnected levels appeared to have become virtually institutionalized. It seemed a very long way from sunlit afternoons on the grass-grown track or frosty mornings on the Rother Levels. It seemed even further from three sixth-formers in a Maidstone grammar school.

But practical work continued even now, although out of a sense of reality this was still to be concentrated on the rolling stock. Hunslet (as successors to Manning Wardle) had supplied another new axle-box bearing for *Charwelton*, the remaining two Maunsell coaches were receiving K&ESR livery and the door locks had been replaced on the Woolwich coach. An exception, which in the circumstances showed considerable faith in the future, was the replacement of rotten timbers on some of the river bridges. Mention was earlier made of several coaches which it had been hoped to obtain but which, as events turned out, were not to join the K&ESR's stock. At this stage it was still fully intended that the NER clerestory coach and the Manchester, Sheffield and Lincolnshire six-wheeler should be purchased and these were actually paid for in November. The bleak and symbolic fate of these vehicles will be dealt with later. At Rolvenden other coaches were providing a very positive focus for the activities of the Association. The catering service in one of the Pullmans, ably managed by Doris Goddard, was proving highly popular with both passing visitors (many of whom returned more than once) and local people. For the railway enthusiast there was also the attraction of a treasurenr trove of old magazines and books. Like the Ford diesel, which was still down at Robertsbridge, the Pullmans were earning useful income.

XV

Apart from very occasional social visits, I was absent from the railway for the whole of 1968 and 1969. Such absence does, however, enable me to view the events of that period with some degree of objectivity.

The Special General Meeting took place as planned on Saturday 6 January in the Youth Centre, Highbury Lane. The records of the event describe it as 'short and sweet' with the membership agreeing, once again, to fight on. George Pickin (who was still showing the same determination to persist as everyone else and despite the earlier end to discussions) remained willing to offer assistance and his proposals were reiterated, on his behalf, by a Mr Tozer. These, however, remained unacceptable to the meeting. A further point worth noting was that the proposal to turn the Association into a Company was raised once again, although without any immediate result.

Overall, the situation remained very precarious and many anticipated that the Association would be evicted from the railway at short notice, followed by the kind of hasty retreat elsewhere which has been suffered by other societies. Given this possibility, all work on the line was abandoned entirely and, with Tenterden still in use as HQ and for mess accommodation, the volunteer force 'dug in' at Rolvenden yard, where work on the stock continued.

This grim picture was compounded by distressing news that was considered by the Committee at their meeting on 24 February. Towards the end of 1967, the ex-NER clerestory coach had been damaged in transit, and what was worse, damaged beyond repair. It was an old story; the coach had been rough-

Improvised track clearance machine in use in Tenterden yard in 1968. Peter Goddard is beyond the trolley (Chris Lowry)

shunted, with the result that one of the bogie centre castings had been pushed through the floor. To make matters even worse, BR then wrote off the MS&L six-wheeler as well, when this vehicle was run through a wagon retarder and all the bolts were sheered off its Mansell pattern wooden-centred wheels. Despite everything else that was happening to the K&ESR, BR knew it was not going to escape from this one and offered a substitute in the form of an ex-LSWR camping coach then located at Southall, the third time that a bogie vehicle originating with that company was proposed for use on the K&ESR.

After some delay the Association's appeal against the lifting of the injunction was heard but, alarmingly, the earlier decision was reversed and BR was free to commence demolition. The strength of the campaign which had been waged since September, and the support it had attracted, now seemed to pay off. In another of those hair's breadth escapes which have characterized K&ESR history, BR again agreed to leave the track down, this time until the outcome of the court case against the Ministry of Transport was known.

It comes as something of a surprise to recall that even during these difficult months locomotives were continuing to arrive at Tenterden (from whence they might have to be hurriedly removed by road). There was the existing commitment to accommodate the Hawthorn Leslie 0–4–0T *Met* and this locomotive duly arrived. From March 1968 the sidings at Tenterden were also graced by another industrial, albeit an 0–6–0 saddle tank which, apart from her venerability, conformed rather more to views on the type of locomotive needed by the K&ESR. This acquisition was *Minnie*, an 1877 product of the long-vanished firm of Fox Walker & Company which had been presented to the Industrial Preservation Group by Skinningrove Ironworks, Yorkshire. The Industrial Preservation Group included members of the K&ESRA and they appear to have been demonstrating their faith in the future course of events.

But no one was banking on anything, and at the Committee meeting on 23 March Peter Davis suggested that the NCB railway at Tilmanston Colliery (part of the old East Kent Railway) be added to the list of possible storage sites. 'Lines of retreat' and litigation were not the only matters concerning the Committee in the early part of 1968. Throughout this account many references have been made to attempts to improve the organization and management of the project, and during the spring this once again became a very live issue.

After the Light Railway Transfer Order was refused, the suspicion lingered in people's minds that an unstated reason for that decision was a lack of credibility on the part of a scheme which proposed to do so much, but do it using an infrastructure which, up until that point, had only been used by relatively small concerns. This possibility may never be finally proven, even when the Ministry of Transport records become available. Some undertone to this effect may, however, be read into the Ministry's concern that the financial reserves would not cover some unforeseen contingency. The report of the Inspector actually included the intriguing comment that the promoters of the project were 'trying to run before they can walk' and that they were trying to go forward too fast without ensuring their (financial) supply lines kept pace with their advance. I would also point to evidence in the *Hansard* record of the adjournment debate. During the latter part of Mr Morris' reply to Bill Deedes, the Joint Parliamentary Secretary referred to Ron Cann's offer to stand surety against possible emergencies, but added:

> But this highly personal arrangement, however generous, does not offer any really satisfactory permanent answer to the doubts about the company's finances, about its estimates of revenue and costs, and about its resources of management and manpower, which were repeatedly expressed during the inquiry by the spokesmen of both county councils, by the spokesman of the Kent River Authority, by two of the important landowners, and by the inspector himself in his report.

Suffice it to say that these suspicions have not diminished with the years.

There would appear to be two possible reasons for this attitude on the part of authority. Firstly, the K&ESR was a large, ambitious scheme with radical notions. There might have been better railways (the Westerham or Hawkhurst branches, for instance) on which to attempt all of the original objectives, including a regular local service and freight traffic. Secondly, there is the much more contentious issue of the human, and particularly management, resources available to the scheme.

When examining this latter point it is worth remembering that by 1968 the average age of the K&ESR's activists was still under twenty-five. As such, the individuals involved were just at the beginning of their careers and had simply not had the time to develop some of the necessary skills. The K&ESR could, in fact, have been a pointed example of the steam railway movement's early strength having been its greatest weakness – that the youthful vitality which had created it had by definition to be lacking in experience.

There were, of course, older heads among the volunteers and the Committee but, almost without exception, they offered some particular, engineering-based, skill or other expertise more narrowly focused than the K&ESR looked likely to demand. Peter Davis was, arguably, an exception to this (although he is of the opinion that, at that stage, he still had much to learn!).

As we have seen, some of the earlier attempts to tighten matters up had not been without success, Peter's Construction and Maintenance Section being one example. In addition, many would now admit that while the Westerham amalgamation did not bring all the benefits that had been hoped of it, David Kitton's publicity activities were highly effective and – when the LRTO was refused – 'in the right place at the right time'. What was now needed was an accomplished businessman, experienced in management and with the credibility and *gravitas* to deal with the representatives of BR, the State and the Establishment. Such a person was found in Peter Benge-Abbott.

Mr Benge-Abbott (together with his father S.J.) was the proprietor of seven highly successful contract painting companies and epitomized the type of businessman who had prospered immensely in the postwar era. He was forty-two years of age in 1968 and lived with his wife and family in the village of Benenden several miles from Rolvenden.

Although Mr Benge-Abbott had a liking for railways (unusual in the entrepreneurial class at any time since Beeching), he was not an enthusiast and the scheme to re-open the K&ESR appealed to him as a challenge and an opportunity for relaxation (not that he was to get much!). He had worked as an ordinary volunteer – the family had been involved in the project since 1966 – but it was he who, the previous year, had organized members of his staff to paint the Maunsell coaches and it was, of course, his guiding hand which had helped the Association establish contact with Bill Deedes at the beginning of the parliamentary campaign. Mr Benge-Abbott attended Committee meetings as an observer and to give advice from October 1967, but in the spring, and during a volunteers' meeting, held in the open air at Rolvenden, the workforce asked him to take a leading role. As a result, he was invited to become Chairman.

The minutes of the first Committee meeting, held on 21 April, at which he was in the chair already show indications of a new hand on the tiller. The first item on the agenda was the adoption of his proposal that the minutes should in future only detail decisions reached and not preceding discussion. This practice is widely used elsewhere (by local authorities, for example) and, while making life more difficult for researchers, was introduced for no more sinister reason than a desire for clarity and convenience. Similarly, it was decided to regularize the intervals between meetings by holding them at Rolvenden (the ex-GWR railcar was being used for the purpose) on the first Sunday in each month at 4.00 p.m.

In an effort to formalize the overall responsibility for work, this task was delegated jointly to Peter Goddard and Peter Davis, the first to be responsible for the mechanical side, and the second for civil engineering, permanent way and general tidyness of the areas open to the public. The sectional and departmental heads would be responsible to these two principal officers. In this connection, both were authorized to spend up to £10 each (nearer £100 at 1990s values) on materials they thought necessary to the organization of the volunteer force, but that Ron Cann as Treasurer should have the final say as to what was reasonable.

An item which particularly pointed towards more detailed control was the decision to agree that

> . . . the following weekend's work should consist of cleaning the rolling stock at Rolvenden, weeding of the track in the yard there, addressing envelopes in preparation for the next edition of the Newsletter, and repainting of the BTH diesel at Robertsbridge. The Chairman undertook to be available on Saturday afternoon in a supervisory capacity, and Mr Goddard to be responsible on the Sunday.

Hitherto, it would have been unusual for the Committee to have concerned itself directly at this level. More typical of previous deliberations was the discussion on the arrangements for the Whitsun weekend which that year had to consist of a Robin Doust-organized film show in the railcar (the film was the 16 mm *Services Will Resume*; much of it is now available on the video *Trains to Tenterden*), miniature steam rides care of Charlie Kentsley, and the regular catering and sales facilities as well as a raffle. This event followed on from four days of similar special activities, also at Rolvenden, over the Easter weekend, which had featured a film show as well as, on that occasion, a pre-war '0' gauge model railway.

Somewhat earlier in the meeting the Committee had made what was to prove a contentious decision. It was agreed that official approaches to the Ministry, BR and the county councils should be dealt with by the Chairman; in other words by Peter Benge-Abbott in person (it could also be used as a delaying tactic, the Chairman having to return to the Committee for consultation). Read as a routine item of business this appears no more than a common-sense approach to a critical area. Not everyone was to see it that way.

Once the new Chairman was installed, and according to an account he later gave the 1968 AGM, he spent a great deal of time investigating the workings of the Association. To quote the minutes of that meeting, and in his opinion, 'He became increasingly disturbed by the poor state of organization and the woolly outlook of the Association. The spirit of the volunteers was good but they and the Committee lacked direction.' Enough has already been said about attempts to improve the efficiency of an organization which intended to eventually run over thirteen miles of railway, as well as about officialdom's view of the K&ESR. Detailed comment on Mr Benge-Abbott's views will not be attempted, apart from two observations.

To begin with, it stands very much to the Chairman's credit that he did not lay the blame on the volunteers. In an era when the generation gap yawned chasm-like from Woodstock to the streets of Paris, it was not unknown for this predominantly youthful group to be the subject of not always favourable comment by some older members of the Association. The fact that Mr Benge-Abbott (or Peter B-A as he has asked to be referred to) had been a member of the workforce, and that the volunteers wished him to become Chairman undoubtedly helped in his easier relationship with them. Secondly, it should be borne in mind that by the time he began his detailed investigations the Association was just emerging from the traumatic period which began with the refusal of the Light Railway Transfer Order. It has been put to me that, after all the efforts to keep the project in existence, the pressures were beginning to take their toll. There appeared every likelihood of a lengthy wait until the court case was heard. In the circumstances, some 'lack of direction' seems to have verged on the inevitable.

By June Peter B-A's presence was having a distinct effect on the railway (he had also become an RVR Board member by that date), although there was a downbeat note at that month's Committee meeting when it was announced that it was not proving possible to organize emergency arrangements for a move to Longmoor. The NCB had also let it be known that it could not make storage space available at Tilmanstone, although it had helpfully suggested that CEGB might have suitable sidings at Richborough power station.

On a more public level, *The Farmers' Line* was beginning to take on a new look (the possibility of this had been discussed at the March Committee meeting). For the moment the newsletter stayed its old quarto size but acquired a glossy, but still monochrome, cover. Advertising was introduced, the clients for this new facility being Cathy Robert's Dad, the Tenterden Book Shop, Len's of Sutton, the Southern Mogul Preservation Society (still closely linked with the K&ESR at that stage) and somebody offering a caravan for holidays near the Romney, Hythe and Dymchurch Railway.

The change of direction was also manifest in a further internal re-organization and also in the Benge-Abbott inspired decision (on a report prepared for him by Peter Goddard) to concentrate on the Tenterden–Rolvenden section. The Chairman's commercial acumen had discerned that this was where much interest in the line lay, and the recognition of this was the beginning of a shift in emphasis, and eventually overall policy, which was to point the way ahead. It would also prove to be a not untroubled change. In particular, Peter B-A was considering whether the proposed freight and full passenger service which had been such a distinct and separate feature of the scheme should be continued. There seemed, to him, much virtue in changing to a policy similar to that of other steam lines, such as the Bluebell Railway, and aiming to run a tourist service. Not everyone agreed and Robin Doust for one, as a founder member of the K&ESR scheme, became uneasy at these suggestions. A marked difference of opinion soon developed between Secretary and Chairman, although this was not immediately apparent on the more public face of the railway. In *The Farmers' Line* editorial for June members were told:

> As a result of the changes, Tenterden and Rolvenden stations now look tidier and more respectable than at any time since the railway was closed. In embarking on the major 'spring clean' involved in this work it is our intention to show clearly that the Association has the ability to restore, quickly and competently, a stretch of line which has been more

neglected than any other section between Robertsbridge and Tenterden. We felt that to be able to say 'this is what we can do in two months' would encourage our members and go a long way towards convincing the general public of our competence and determination. It is only by gaining the confidence of the general public that we shall succeed and deeds speak louder than words. . . . this section would not be complete without some tribute and thanks being paid to the regular volunteers . . . without whose help nothing could possibly be achieved.

A major item in the June *Farmers' Line* was an article by the Chairman entitled 'Reorganization Structure, Progress Report and Membership Drive'. It reflects the state of the project at the time and is worth quoting in detail:

In considering the fresh structure that the Association needs, it was soon discovered that the various departments at present in being were running quite successfully under their present heads as at present constituted. These departments in most cases do their jobs very well and get on with the work without a great deal of chasing. They did, however, appear to suffer badly from lack of control and direction in their efforts, with the result that very many projects were started and very few completed. In order to provide the necessary direction, it was felt [advisable] to split the Association's activities into four groups, these being: Group 1 – Mechanical Group; Group 2 – Civil Engineering and Buildings Group; Group 3 – Public Relations Group; and Group 4 – Legal and Finance Group.

Dealing first with Groups 1 and 2 . . . the Mechanical Group is formed by an association of the Locomotive Department, led by Charlie Kentsley with Dick Beckett as his second-in-command and right-hand man; the Carriage and Wagon Department led by Dave Sinclair; the Telephone Department led by Frank Davis; the Signals Department led by Geoff Percy. The Group is led by Peter Goddard, who is responsible for co-ordinating and guiding their activities in the light of week-to-week Association requirements.

The second group (the Civil Engineering and Building Group) is headed by Peter Davis. Their responsibility is for the maintenance of the track and track bed, all embankments, structures, drainage, painting of buildings and general tidiness and smart appearance of the line. This group is not split into as many departments as the Mechanical Group, and will, in due course require further strengthening. At the present moment, it consists of the Permanent Way Department, headed by the Webb brothers, and what can be termed the Forestry Department under Norton Brown. Any spare volunteers are normally engaged on painting work, and here, Dave Sinclair of the Carriage and Wagon Department, tends to keep a 'watching eye' on the way they go about their job. Both Peter Davis' and Peter Goddard's groups work closely together, transferring labour one to the other in the light of the priorities which are allocated to work in hand after discussions between Peter Davis, Peter Goddard and your Chairman. Peter Davis and Peter Goddard will report to your Committee on the activities of their groups at regular Committee meetings.

The third, and probably the most important group in the whole of the Association, is the Public Relations Group [i.e. from a 1968 point of view]. This group is currently being formed and will consist of those people who have a responsibility arising out of close contact with the public or the publicizing of the Association's activities. These contacts are considered to be of the highest importance because it is through the activities of this group that we shall get across to the general public, the Ministry of Transport and BR, a true impression of our abilities, our determination and our desire to run a railway that will be safe, efficient, and cater for the strong public demand that exists. Final composition of this group is not yet certain, but it will include Robin Doust as Editor of *The Farmers' Line*, Malcolm Dunstan as Membership Secretary and David Kitton responsible for exhibitions and matters connected with the visual presentation of the Association's image. Nick Blake [will be] responsible for all sales and so on. This group, because of its importance, will be led by your Chairman . . .

The final group to be formed will, of course, be the Finance and Legal Group, which will consist of stalwarts such as Ronald Cann, Arthur Penny, Philip Shaw and so on.

This was one of the first mentions so far traced of Philip Shaw, another figure who was to be highly significant in the developing course of events. Philip, who had been a member of the K&ESR scheme for several years, joined the Committee the following month.

The Chairman's article continued:

> Having set up the first of the two new groups, they were very quickly presented with the target of reinstating that stretch of line from Rolvenden and Tenterden by mid-July. For this purpose, both groups have united in their efforts to smarten the section up, and have worked wonders both at Tenterden and Rolvenden, particularly when one bears in mind that little work has been done on this section since 1961 and it is very doubtful if BR did much work after 1954. The work should be largely completed by mid-July, as expected and should bring the line up to a standard where passengers could be carried within a matter of days if we were fortunate enough to be given permission to do so. Those members of the Association who have not visited the line within the last few weeks are strongly recommended to do so, particularly visiting Tenterden Town station. . . . Within the next two weeks it will be decided what will be the next target upon which volunteers will be concentrated. . . .
>
> Progress in respect of our negotiations with the Ministry of Transport has been very slow, as is hardly surprising when a matter involving legal decisions is concerned. Here we must be patient and hopeful. Where British Rail is concerned, we have of course, lost our case against them, and if they so desired, they are technically at liberty to lift the track without further delay. They have, however, responded in a helpful manner to approaches, and are prepared to consider giving an undertaking that they will not lift the track until the result of our legal action against the Ministry is known, providing the Association is prepared to give the BR Board certain undertakings. These undertakings have been considered by the Association's Committee and we are quite sure that a mutually agreeable solution will be reached within the near future. . . . This move on the part of BR is felt to be generous . . . in view of the undoubted difficulties we had to impose on them towards the end of last year.
>
> From what has been said so far, you will appreciate that far from being 'dead and buried' as some people seem to think, the Association is moving from strength to strength and the future prospects are by no means gloomy. You will appreciate that the strength of any association lies in the size of its membership, and whilst our membership has remained loyal, an increase in its strength is greatly to be desired, particularly at this time. It is therefore proposed to initiate a drive for new members . . .

The theme of change continued with the August *Farmers' Line*, the editorial picking up on the Chairman's optimistic view in the June edition by stating that the atmosphere between the Association and BR was nowhere near as hostile as it had been at the beginning of the year. For this newsletter (Volume 7, Number 1) the glossy cover was retained but the transformation was completed by adopting the then newly introduced metric A5 size. This brought the Association's journal back to a format more like that of the *Rother Valley Railway* (although the internal pages were still duplicated) and was a step in the evolution which would, years later, produce the prizewinning *Tenterden Terrier*.

Great mention was again made of the transformation which had taken place in the affairs of the railway. The following passage was written by Robin Doust, this, ironically, being the last newsletter he would edit for the K&ESR:

> The new-style magazine is yet another facet of the much wider wind of change which began with the appointment of our new Chairman earlier this year, and which has now

reached almost every aspect of the Association's operations. Many visitors have expressed amazement at the improvement in the appearance of the Tenterden–Rolvenden section of track, and a similar improvement is becoming apparent in the rolling stock.

Further on in the newsletter, a viewpoint independent of the Committee echoed the same opinion. The writer was a volunteer, Gordon Maslin:

It was on a merry Sunday in June that we (my brother and I) renewed our acquaintance with the K&ESR . Easter was our last visit, and Oh! – what a change. Never before had we seen the like. Tenterden, we are sure, has never been so spotless since the line was opened.

'But how?' we asked ourselves. Polite enquiries to Big M (Malcolm Dunstan – ed.) enlightened us to the fact that it was part of the new Public Image. Public image? – the very idea! We looked around us and surveyed the scene. Bustling activity everywhere. We shuddered.

Gone was the knee-high grass and weeds. Bright paint adorned the station and point levers. The staff quarters were cleaner than they had ever been. Gone was the sleepy branch line atmosphere, to be replaced by a spotless, efficient-looking station. We shuddered again. No more hours of quiet, peaceful bliss shall we have.

To console ourselves, we wandered down to Rolvenden. Here things seemed to be normal. Everything was moving at its usual slow, easy pace – or was it? Hardly five minutes had passed when Peter Goddard press-ganged us, in a very polite way of course, into the weeding party. By the time we had recovered from the shock, weeds were flying from our hands onto the trolley.

Maunsell, *with Dick Beckett in the cab, at Marks Cross en route for Rolvenden (Chris Lowry)*

As everyone does, we retired at lunch time. By now our two heads had a bet on to see whose could spin the fastest. But two codeines from Dave soon put paid to that wager. So we plonked ourselves down in the Pullman Car, and resigned our stomachs to the very pleasant fate of Doris's home cooking. Fantastic – not quite as good as Mum's though. Is it ever?

The progress report once again had a flavour much as it had in the days before the Light Railway Transfer Order was refused. The Loco Department had nearly completed repairs to *Charwelton*'s boiler and the locomotive was being repainted in the K&ESR's blue livery. The matter of liveries had by that date moved as far as industrial and freight locos appearing in blue and former passenger engines in apple green. No. 3 had accordingly been repainted by Bill Westwood in her pre-nationalization colour, lined out in yellow, and attention was turning to *Sutton*. The Carriage and Wagon Department was also busy applying the railway's brown and ivory livery to the last unpainted coach. An eighth coach was about to be added to the fleet as well – the ex-LSWR coach offered as a replacement for the two vehicles wrecked by BR was about to be delivered to Robertsbridge.

The Civil Engineering Group had, of course, been busy meeting the target for reinstating the Tenterden–Rolvenden section. Their activities at that end of the line meant, however, that beyond Bodiam, nature was putting matters into reverse.

The August progress report also made the first mention of a locomotive purchase which was to prove one of the milestones in the progress of the preservation project – the acquisition of the two USA class 0–6–0 tanks. The history of this American-built type is well known. It should be repeated, however, that following the displacement of the class from Southampton Docks in 1962, a number were transferred to departmental stock. Nos 30065/70 were sent to Ashford Works (by then building wagons) as DS237 *Wainwright* and DS238 *Maunsell* respectively. They continued in this role (and as the last BR steam in Kent) until April 1967, when DS237 was taken out of service. DS238 followed in June of that year, shortly before the Southern Region abandoned steam altogether. Both stayed at Ashford until sold to Woodham's at Barry in March 1968 as locomotives for shunting in their yard.

The USAs had always suffered from hot boxes when required to run more than a short distance. This proved to be their salvation, for when, during June, an attempt was made to tow them to Barry, this old problem reappeared near Pluckley – after only six miles – and a halt had to be made at Paddock Wood. The USAs were later moved to Tonbridge. There were no facilities available in the South-east to repair them, the Western Region was not keen on having this slow-moving train on its territory, and road transport to Barry was uneconomic. DS237 and 238 instead sat on the site of the former locomotive shed, where they were clearly visible to passing railway enthusiasts.

Among the many who noticed them was Dick Beckett, and it was he who persuaded the other members of the Locomotive Trust (which had just finished paying off the outstanding debt on *Charwelton* and *Hastings*) that they should acquire *Wainwright* and *Maunsell* for the K&ESR. The idea of taking the USAs to Barry had now been abandoned and they were up for sale again. During August £650 was offered for one and, much to everyone's surprise, this was accepted. A few days later a bid of £500 was made for the second and this too was successful. The Locomotive Trust raised part of the total cost among itself immediately. The remainder had to be borrowed, a fact which was subsequently reflected in advertisements placed in *The Farmer's Line*.

Wainwright and *Maunsell* were moved to Rolvenden on Friday 6 and Saturday 7 September (in that order). Their journey commenced behind a 204 hp Drewry diesel but very soon transferred to a transporter hauled by one of the handsome Scammell tractors which then characterized that form of road transport. This delivery was one of the first to be thoroughly recorded from start to finish on film, and has since become well known following its inclusion on the video mentioned earlier. One of the interesting points about this footage is its inclusion of shots of a number of the early volunteers, a feature it shares with sequences shot during the making of *Sarah* in the autumn of 1967. *Trains to Tenterden* also includes a visual record of a near-disastrous incident en route from Tonbridge. This occurred when a group of nuns travelling in a Ford Corsair took fright on seeing a locomotive in a country lane and drove into the hedge. All the world can now see this record of the traffic being stopped in railway fashion with a red flag, while volunteers from the accompanying 'chase' cars, and in railway uniform, 'rerailed' the Corsair. Both locos were greeted by large gatherings of

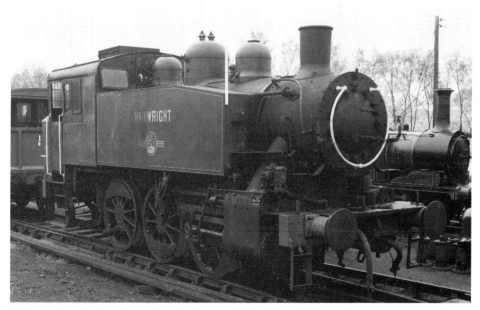

Wainwright *in Rolvenden yard on 19 October 1968. Although* Maunsell *was put into good order relatively quickly, it was to be the 1990s before* Wainwright *would be ready for steaming (Dennis Ovenden)*

volunteers, members and enthusiasts, a circumstance which, as on previous occasions, led *The Farmers' Line* to comment that it was a pity more of the latter two categories did not turn up on working parties!

The purchase of the USAs was stated at the time to be another expression of confidence in the future success of the tortuous negotiations with BR and the Ministry. But they were more than that – they marked the beginnings of a change in the railway's motive power practice. Nos 21 and 22, as *Wainwright* and *Maunsell* became, each weighed 46¹/₂ tons. As such, they exceeded the axle loading of the Robertsbridge–Rolvenden section by over 50 per cent, the same problem which attached to the H class still stuck in Robertsbridge yard. They would, however, be most useful for the fierce climb up to Tenterden Town, a section which had the more generous axle loading of 15 tons. It was also realized that something would eventually have to be done about bridge 1029 and that this was not the only structure on the line which would ultimately require rebuilding or strengthening. The future course of K&ESR locomotive policy was evolving and would free the line from its limited choice of aged ex-BR classes and equally small industrial types. This matter was considered by Peter Davis in a report to the Committee during the latter part of 1968. The full details are included in Appendix 2.

This impressive view of Hastings *on 21 September 1968 illustrates the cluttered appearance Rolvenden yard had taken on by that date (Dennis Ovenden)*

XVI

The Annual General Meeting for 1968 was held in Highbury Lane Youth Centre (which had become the regular venue for these events) on Saturday 5 October. Members had already received the accounts and the Report of the Committee. The former showed a £1,317 deficit compared with the profit made in the previous year, the main reason being the Association's decision to meet various debts incurred by the Rother Valley Railway Company. The Report was, generally speaking, a summary of previous events, but ended with this ominous note:

> . . . although differences of opinion on future policy exist even within the Committee, it is very much to be hoped that the coming year will finally see the future of the railway settled.

Reference has already been made to changes in aim and policy and that these were not achieved without controversy, although the Chairman was trying to form an organization nobody could be against. (This did not apply to the shift in motive power policy; that attracted little or no disagreement.) Some of the resulting friction belonged to the months before the 1968 AGM, but it is more conveniently related in the context of that meeting, both to prevent fragmentation of the story and because it was there that matters first came to a head.

The Chairman opened the proceedings by stating that the meeting was likely to be one of the most crucial ever. The minutes of the 1967 AGM, the accounts and the adoption of the Annual Report were all routinely disposed of before the meeting turned to the election of the Committee. The account which follows is an edited version of the minutes which appeared in *The Farmers' Line*, Volume 7, Number 2, October 1968. In order to place matters in their historical perspective I have added some commentary.

This part of the meeting commenced with a surprise, if not a shock – Peter B-A stated that he had reluctantly found it necessary to tender his resignation as Chairman. This he intended to do, with effect from the end of the AGM. Peter then referred to his personal background and pointed out that contract painting was a 'cut-throat' business. With an annual turnover of £1.5 million, it took considerable time and skill to run the companies and, with family commitments, this only left a limited time to devote to the railway. The Chairman therefore thought that the backing of a strong, realistic Committee was essential. He had made this quite clear when accepting the position of Chairman and this had been accepted by the Association.

Peter spoke of his investigations into the workings of the Association and the morale of the volunteers. He also made mention of the correspondence received from the Ministry of Transport regarding level crossings.

At a Committee meeting in August, Peter B-A had expressed his views and comments and left the Committee to think about them. He was unsure of the support which the Committee as a body would give to him as Chairman. At the following Committee meeting no points were raised about his criticisms and he felt that there had, therefore, been no apparent change of heart.[2] The Chairman felt in an intolerable position and consequently resigned both as a Director and a Committee member.

This resulted in considerable consternation on the part of most of the regular volunteers who, he said, were almost as disturbed as he was himself. As a result, Peter B-A addressed a meeting of the workforce, which expressed its support for him. Many felt that without him in the chair there was a serious risk of the Association collapsing. Peter considered that this put him in rather a 'hot seat', and there would have to be a change of attitude if he was to remain. Asked if he would accept a nomination to the Committee, he agreed, but said he would only remain as Chairman if the Committee elected at the AGM was one in which he could have confidence, and would have the respect of the volunteers.

The Chairman continued that certain names nominated for the Committee were unacceptable to him, but that there were sufficient nominations to form a Committee in which mutual confidence would exist. He then asked for questions and comments on his statement.

A member asked for examples of disagreements between the Chairman and those whom he found unacceptable. Peter said he would rather not comment on this unless pressed to do so, adding that as co-operation was essential, no purpose would be served by naming names. When asked if this was merely a clash of personalities, he replied that it was not.

The meeting then started into issues that were the nub of much of this disagreement. The next few minutes were a watershed in the history of the K&ESR and the initiation of painful changes. Arthur Penny first asked for the names of the then existing Committee to be stated, and he reminded members that the Committee elected the Chairman from among themselves. He commented that he felt that the main disagreement within the Committee revolved around the question of whether the K&ESR should be a commercial concern or a 'toy' railway. This, of course, went to the heart of what the preservation scheme had been about since its earliest days and queried whether those aims remained viable in the changed conditions of 1968. Mr Penny said he would prefer the railway to be a commercial concern and concluded by suggesting that negotiations would proceed more smoothly in the hands of a small Committee.

When Peter B-A spoke again he said that many had tried to persuade him that he was the only possible person for Chairman, but asked for other suggestions. Ralph Brockman asked what his policies would be. He replied that he had no definite policy, except to see the line re-opened in its entirety, and as a commercial proposition. This, however, could only be achieved by more 'down to earth' management, and he suggested that previous policy might have been over-dogmatic in respect of aims. The Association had to re-establish confidence in many quarters, and flexibility of policy was essential.

As has already been noted, the efforts of the workforce had been refocused on the Tenterden–Rolvenden section, 'where passengers could be carried within a matter of days if we were fortunate enough to be given permission so to do'. I must point out that no definite decision to concentrate initially on

Tenterden–Rolvenden had been taken at that stage but that thoughts were concentrating on that possibility. Robin Doust, however, remained convinced of the viability of Robertsbridge–Bodiam, with a later extension to Northiam. He was not alone in holding this view, although he was its most prominent advocate.

Mr Brockman pressed for details of how the Chairman would run the railway, for example the frequency of the services. He replied that this was a matter for the Committee. Arthur Penny then interjected that it was more important, at that stage, to get the railway than to worry about the details of operation (thus leaving the question open, at least as far as he was concerned, about what was to be run over which section). He went on to point out that the RVR Trust Fund still needed more money, and that he would like to see every member become a contributor, before the Chairman commented on the need for BR, the Ministry and other bodies to be convinced of the Association's responsibility and sound base. These things would help towards a future, more favourable decision by the Ministry of Transport. Similar railways were not having to find £36,000 outright and he suggested that this itself was probably the cause of many of the K&ESR's troubles.

Mr Cannon-Rogers then made one of the most memorable of his remarks, when he described the railway as an example of 'friendly anarchy', but went on to praise *The Farmers' Line*. With a typically succinct turn of phrase, he said that Association members should sink personal differences because Peter B–A's business experience was invaluable and that, 'Direction is essential and a smaller Committee is more efficient, although democracy demands a little more.' (Anarchy was perhaps a rather strong term to use. It was a keyword with reference to the European student activists of 1968 and possibly came more readily to mind than it might otherwise have done.)

The Chairman then changed direction slightly and mentioned the number of organizations associated with the K&ESR (i.e. the two companies, the three trusts, the change of name from Preservation Society to Association, the Brake Van Fund, etc.) and said that there were too many. He was not the first, nor indeed the last, person to comment on this and the confusion it could cause.

Peter B-A later went on to say, 'If better people arrive they should be allowed to take over.' If this statement was accurately reported, it appears a singularly unfortunate choice of words, superficially going back on his earlier, favourable view of the volunteers. It can, however, be paraphrased as, 'If more appropriately experienced and able managers arrive we should allow them to use their expertise.' This interpretation is helped by a subsequent remark from the chair that, 'The Committee still needs help from people in senior management, especially those in railway management.' I was not at the meeting but had been at least vaguely aware of the Chairman's 'better people' remark (via the published account in *The Farmers' Line*) for many years. I was sufficiently concerned about its ambiguity, however, to make a point of determining its correct meaning. The results of my investigations and the available evidence indicate that it was not meant to relate to the workforce in general and that it was not Peter's wish to exclude anyone from the railway.

The meeting then reached the point where the Committee actually had to be elected. The existing Committee members were named and indicated. The Chairman read out a list of eight individuals nominated to serve during the following year and made it clear he was only prepared to serve on a Committee made up of those persons. They were: Arthur Penny, Ron Cann, Dave Sinclair, Peter Davis, Philip Shaw, Peter Goddard, Peter Benge-Abbott and Derek Dunlavey.

He said he would prefer not to mention the other nominations unless, again, pressed to do so. To make matters clear, one of the other nominations was Robin Doust.

The proceedings thus far had taken one hour twenty minutes and, after Arthur Penny had reminded the meeting that, constitutionally, all nominations had to be put forward, a short interval was suggested and agreed to.

When the meeting re-assembled at 4.15 p.m., Dick Beckett proposed that the eight names acceptable to the Chairman should be voted *en bloc* and that everyone holding office should retain their positions. He said that he could not vote against people with whom he came into contact. He also said that if Peter B-A left he would do likewise as he felt the Chairman's presence was essential. Dick's proposal was seconded by Colin Edwards but was not voted on. The Chairman reminded everyone that certain officers had also to be Committee members and that he would not accept any other nominations than the eight which he had mentioned on a Committee of which he was the chair.

Dick Beckett then amended his proposal to exclude the Secretary (and thereby comply with the constitution), before Arthur Penny formally proposed that the remaining nominations be put forward. Once this had been duly seconded, Peter B–A stated that he did not wish to restrict the number of the Committee to eight, but wanted to leave room for more experienced people who might come on the scene later. He referred to earlier AGMs which had set the precedent for electing the Committee *en bloc*. It would save parading names in public if the eight nominations he favoured remained and the others withdrew. At this point one of the nominees withdrew. It was then suggested that the eight should be voted *en bloc*, and then a vote be taken as to whether the two remaining further nominations should be put forward. Arthur Penny suggested that all ten names be put forward one by one. Derek Dunlavey then asked if the two people involved would withdraw; they declined.

Chris Golding then proposed that the eight nominations should be voted on before any consideration be given regarding the remaining two. This was seconded, voted on and agreed with one dissenting vote. Another warning note was then sounded when Dave Sinclair made a statement similar to Dick Beckett's by saying that he too would leave the Association if anyone other than the eight named people was appointed to the Committee. Shortly afterwards the individuals involved were voted into office unanimously.

Peter B-A invited the other two nominees to speak. It must be reported here that Robin Doust stated that he was puzzled by his exclusion from those acceptable to Peter B-A and said he felt his only offence was some disagreements. When the vote was taken neither Robin Doust nor the other nominee were elected.

The following day, and after considering the matter overnight, Robin Doust resigned from the Association and withdrew his support from the Rother Valley Railway Trust Fund.

From what had been said during the AGM, these developments had obviously been building up for some time. The resulting shock was, nonetheless, apparent from the first page of the subsequent edition of *The Farmers' Line*. There was a frank admission that the newsletter had been produced during 'much rushing round and making do'. Not surprisingly, it was realized that this situation was neither 'efficient nor ideal', and an appeal was made for a new editor. The post of Secretary had, however, already been filled from within the Committee and marked a further stage in the quiet rise of Philip Shaw. The phrase 'quiet rise' is here used quite deliberately, for, like a British Prime Minister to whom it has also been applied, the new Hon. Secretary replaced an individual to whom, many would argue, much was owed and after a disagreement about future direction. This curious parallel can also be further extended as, like John Major, Philip Shaw had a financial background – he was a chartered accountant. Neither was Philip new to the steam railway movement; he had previously worked with the Welshpool and Llanfair Railway. Over the following few years his expertise was to be of great use to the K&ESR. One of his proposals, made known towards the conclusion of the AGM, was the possibility of reconstituting the Association on a charitable basis to allow advantage to be taken of the consequent tax benefits. Legal advice was being taken on this. In the meantime Peter B-A had offered to stand a £6,000 security against the loans which it was still anticipated would be taken out for the purchase of the railway.

But the crucial matter of the court case remained unresolved, and with it the issue of the relationship with BR and the Ministry of Transport. The Transport Minister had now changed to the much more pro-rail Richard Marsh (he was later Chairman of the BR Board) but, quite correctly, he had answered an enquiry from Terence Boston MP by stating that he could not agree that further discussion would be fruitful at that stage, particularly as the court case was pending.

It was still possible for *The Farmers' Line* progress report for October (written by Peter Goddard) to be presented in a reasonably buoyant manner, even if the contents were indicative of the Association being bottled up at the top end of the line around Rolvenden. A major item was the work which had been carried out on DS237 *Maunsell*, which had been jacked up to allow the removal of the axle boxes for remetalling and machining. More radically, a cure was being sought for the root cause of the problem and a mechanical lubricator (obtained either from Maunsell Moguls or Stanier 8Fs at Barry) was to be fitted in place of the primitive wick-feed device.

Beyond the level crossing at Rolvenden, Peter Davis and the Civil Engineering Group were giving attention to the small river bridge (No. 2330) at that location. The abutments had been subject to severe scouring (the Kent River Board had mentioned this during the public inquiry) and this was one of the bridges which it was known would eventually require strengthening or replacement. Ironically, it was the first bridge on the section with a 15 ton axle loading. The initial work was to take steps to prevent the scouring. Elsewhere, on Tenterden Bank a gang under the control of Norton Brown was clearing drainage ditches and cutting down trees. A 'Wants List' printed on behalf of the Civil Engineering Group provides both some light relief and further comment on one of the perpetual problems of the K&ESR:

> The Association still needs tools of all kinds. . . . Anybody who is prepared to contribute tools from the following list, please bring them down to Tenterden or Rolvenden one weekend. Peter Davis will always be grateful.
> Point and chisel pickaxes; Grubbing mattocks; Spades; Shovels; Stone Forks; Logging saws; Hand saws; Axes; Scythes; Sickles; Long-handled pruners; Bill hooks; Shears.
> It is no accident that this list sounds as if we are preparing for 'jungle warfare' – the rate vegetation grows on this line has to be seen to be believed! Come down and see for yourself.

One of the happiest developments at this point was the actual arrival (during September) of the ex-LSWR compartment coach at Robertsbridge. Being a camping coach it had been suggested that it might in the first instance provide further mess accommodation, although it is thought that it was never actually used in that role.

Less happy was the publication in the September *Railway World* of a letter from the C Class Preservation Society.

This drew attention to alleged misrepresentations (it was not stated exactly what these were) regarding the C, 01 and H class locomotives. After pointing out that No. 592 was owned by the Wainwright C Preservation Society, and that both that locomotive and the separately owned 01 were well advanced in their restoration, it was confirmed that a degree of intention had previously existed to send both these 0–6–0s to the K&ESR.

The letter then stated that this had been withdrawn and the position had, more than once, been made clear to the K&ESRA that the Wainwright C Preservation Society would consider offers recieved from preserved lines when they were actually in business.

The owner of the 01 class had asked it to be confirmed that his locomotive was not to be sent to the K&ESR. (The writer of this account understands that, in the case of the 01 class, the owner of that locomotive and the K&ESRA were, and despite the work Association members had carried out, unable to come to a satisfactory agreement).

With regard to the H class tank, it was owned and was being restored by the H class Trust and was only being stored on the K&ESR.

This statement in *Railway World* resulted in *The Farmers' Line* publishing a letter from a young student named Stephen Garrett, the future writer of the Oakwood Press volume on the K&ESR. Relevant extracts are as follows:

> The rather horrible letter in this month's *Railway World* from the C Class Preservation Society, prompted certain thoughts in my mind about the role of *The Farmers' Line* . . .
> Unfortunately, *The Farmers' Line* tends to give quite a good picture of individual trees, but not much idea of the wood around them. Moreover, when the trees get cut down, as happens with the C and 01 locomotives, one doesn't hear about it in *The Farmers' Line*. Similarly, until last year, it seemed that the section of line to be reinstated first was between Robertsbridge and Northiam, and then this year, without any prior explanation,

all the attention seems to have been focused on Tenterden to Rolvenden. [I keep] coming back to the impression that the Editors are so familiar with the line they assume that the rest of the members are equally familiar.

I hope this doesn't sound like a complaint damning the magazine completely. In fact I am fairly happy with *The Farmers' Line* . . .

The Chairman answered this in the following edition of the newsletter:

. . . it is hoped to present *The Farmers' Line* in a fashion which will be more interesting and more informative to those of our supporters who cannot get to the line as frequently as they would wish.

The change in emphasis in this magazine is part of the fundamental change in outlook which started to take effect during the first half of 1968. This change has involved a tremendous amount of 'behind the scenes' work and discussion and its other visible effects are the change in emphasis where reinstatement of the line is concerned, and reflects the outlook of the line under a new Chairman. . . . Our relationship with the C Class Preservation Society has improved to a great extent since their letter which was published in *Railway World*, and your Committee feel that a firm and friendly basis for future co-operation (if possible) has now been established.

Despite this improvement the Chairman's hopes were not to be realized – the C class went to the Bluebell Railway. The extracts from Stephen Garrett's letter and the Chairman's reply have been included here because they touched on issues which contributed towards an unfortunate confrontation which was now building up. But before turning to these events it is, instead, a pleasure to draw attention to the following which was to be found towards the back of that dispiriting October edition of the newsletter:

A WORD OF THANKS

Peter and Doris Goddard would like to thank their sincere friends amongst the volunteers who gave up a considerable amount of their spare time in order to come to Ightham and help clear up the mess left by the unexpected floods which swept through their garage and home on Sunday September 15th.[3] This spontaneous act of friendship is greatly appreciated.

These words could be left to speak for themselves, but they emphasize, once again, the bond which had grown between the K&ESR's most active supporters and was the railway's greatest strength.

XVII

Through the latter months of 1968 the Committee continued to consider the adoption of charitable status for the Association and a formal change of aims. Away from the railway, Dave Kitton and his publicity team had, during the previous few months, run stands at exhibitions at Wallingford, Reading, Crawley, Staines, Norbury, Beaconsfield, Maidstone and London. This carrying of the K&ESR banner over such a wide area had resulted in much

With her Bodiam *nameplates restored, and decked in apple green livery, No. 3 stands outside the Haven in September 1968 (Dennis Ovenden)*

valuable publicity and additional revenue. Dave was being greatly helped in this work by Richard Halton. It was Richard who had come up with a highly enterprising second-hand model railway scheme. Under this, members donated their unwanted or surplus model railway equipment to the Association; the rolling stock, or whatever, was reconditioned (by Richard) and the resulting profit, when items were sold on at the next exhibition, was added to the railway's funds.

The court case against the Ministry of Transport still remained unheard, but there was a continuing quiet optimism among Association members in general, perhaps resulting from the relative, if routine, stability which had replaced the excitement of a year earlier. This was somewhat shaken by the arrival, in mid-December, of a letter from the Southern Region informing the Association that no additional locomotives were to be delivered to Rolvenden and that only minimal maintenance was to be undertaken on the existing stock. Furthermore, it soon became apparent that work on the track was also to stop (due to insurance and safety concerns), various of the bungalows and cottages around the line – which had belonged to the old company – were to be demolished and, after all the effort that had gone into its installation, the telephone system was to be dismantled. The Chairman, in accordance with his normal practice, personally took these matters in hand.

While negotiations were under way to deal with these new problems, the

Committee had pressed on with its consideration of future policy. This was finally resolved at the Committee meeting on 5 January 1969, it being agreed at the same time not to call a meeting of members to discuss the changes but to circulate details instead.

The consequent Statement of Policy Aims should have reached members about three weeks later, together with the January edition of *The Farmers' Line*. In the event, dispatch was delayed until March due to a delay in the supply of the now separately printed magazine covers. This was hardly a good start for what was supposed to be a decisive change of attitude but it later proved to be fortuitous. Even when sent to members the Statement had to be posted separately, and expensively, from the main magazine mailing. The full text is reproduced below and the following are extracts from an accompanying note:

> The Committee are in full agreement that these aims represent a practical, realistic and attainable set of objectives, and we are convinced that the principles and ideas which are outlined are those which we can command the support of all reasonable and far-sighted people. . . . The Committee is particularly concerned that Association members should let them have their comments and suggestions, all of which will be considered, and wherever possible, included in any amendments there may be to this policy.
> . . . If we can create sufficient interest [in] and support [for] this policy, the Ministry of Transport may well feel that the preservation of the line in accordance with this fresh set of aims is very much in the public interest.

Statement of Future Policy aims from the Committee of the Kent and East Sussex Railway Association

1. The Association will change its present constitution and organization to provide a basis for the establishment of the whole enterprise as an approved charitable trust.
2. We shall aim to preserve the Robertsbridge–Tenterden line in perpetuity in order to provide permanent facilities for the people of this country and particularly those resident in London and south-east England to maintain and operate a steam-powered light railway.
3. To provide the essential source of revenue for maintenance purposes, tourist services will run over each section of the line as it is restored to a satisfactory condition. Revenue from all sources will be used exclusively for the upkeep of the line and the continued improvement of facilities.

Reasons for these Policy Decisions

(a) CHARITABLE STATUS

It is felt desirable to obtain charitable status as this will involve a degree of independent control in perpetuity (through the Charity Commissioners) and make it possible to establish an organization which may have in its governing body representatives from those authorities most immediately affected, i.e. Ministry of Transport, British Rail, county councils, etc. Individuals and organizations wishing to contribute to this enterprise will be able to do so with greater confidence if charitable status is obtained.

(b) PRESERVATION OF THE ROBERTSBRIDGE–TENTERDEN LINE

This standard gauge line is, we believe, the only original rural light railway to have survived in this country. Steam-operated railways and rolling stock have become a historical rarity, producing a tremendous volume of interest and support from both the general public and the youth of this country. The present Committee is very conscious of the tremendous effort and energy which young people are prepared to contribute, under responsible control, towards reviving and maintaining this enterprise. It is felt that the opportunity of channelling this enthusiasm into an activity which is of interest to many millions of people, should be given a chance of succeeding.

(c) REVENUE

Considerable revenue will be required in order to restore this line to a satisfactory condition, to provide adequate facilities for voluntary labour and to support the organization necessary for its control. A proven source of sufficient finance is to run a steam-hauled service which would be attractive to tourists and this would be done as each section of the line was restored to a satisfactory condition, commencing with that between Tenterden and Rolvenden. The extent of the service offered would be entirely dependent on public demand.

The list of outside organizations which might have been represented on the 'governing body' is intriguing. All these were eventually won over, but their direct participation was not to be. One wonders if in the case of the Ministry (the regulatory body) this would have been ethical.

The reference under item (b) to the part played by young people seems a further indication of the Chairman's unusually appreciative view of the often maligned virtues of the postwar generation. It is also particularly pleasing to find this attitude being taken on a corporate level by an organization concerned to seek favour with 'the powers that be' and to be seen as 'respectable'.

The Committee met once again, this time at Tenterden Town station, on 2 March and considered the Chairman's report of his negotiations with the Southern Region. He was able to tell his colleagues that:

a) The Association would not be required to dismantle the telephone system.

b) The bungalows at Northiam would not be demolished as long as they remained unoccupied.

c) A proposal by the Association to buy the Rolvenden site (i.e. as a safeguard and in advance of the rest of the railway) would first have to be referred to the Ministry of Transport.

d) Subject to satisfactory guarantees to BR with regard to insurance and safety, the Association would be permitted to resume maintenance of the track.

e) BR had been wishing to increase the rents paid by the Society. No decision had been made as to the date for the commencement of increased rents on the various station sites. The matter remained in abeyance.

The Committee agreed to mention items a), b) and d) in the form of a supplement to the magazine (as *The Farmers' Line* was now increasingly referred to). The magazine itself appeared about a week after the Statement of Aims. The supplement (actually a covering letter) apologized for the delay but added that this had resulted in the 'silver lining' of the Committee being able to announce some of the results of the Chairman's efforts. It also went on to say that the Association had been able to supply BR with satisfactory safeguards in respect of its liability should the K&ESRA be involved in any accident and that this had been backed up with details of the Association's public liability insurance policies.

A new magazine editor had been found in the person of Alan Dixon. The Progress Report was able to state that work, led by Rodney Packham, had commenced on the LSWR coach at Robertsbridge (window glass, utilizing material from ex-GWR coaches which had also been at Southall, was being renewed and the wooden bodywork thoroughly inspected) but that the weather and the short daylight hours were naturally restricting work. Clearance of the undergrowth between Tenterden and Rolvenden was, however, nearing completion.

Most interestingly, work was under way to produce a rule book for the K&ESR. One initial draft had already been discarded, but a great deal of work had been put into a second version and this looked quite promising. At the same time a series of lectures had commenced which also looked forward to the eventual operation of a passenger service. Subjects included titles such as 'How and why vacuum brakes work', 'Duties of Shunters and Guards' and 'Coupling and uncoupling of coaches and wagons by the proper and safe methods'. It was intended to expand this programme into a proper training course for operating staff, the lectures being interspersed with instructional films. Other subjects covered included safety, track maintenance, locomotive firing, the workings of injectors, buckeye couplings and the maintenance of boilers. Arrangements were also being made for the St. John's Ambulance Brigade to provide a first-aid course.

A letter in this first magazine produced by the new editor was unerringly accurate in its analysis of the rolling stock needs of the line and, indeed, of the whole steam railway movement. After outlining the motive power situation on the railway, the letter continued:

> . . . passenger accommodation of a sort can be provided by the seven and one half locomotive-hauled carriages currently on the line, but none of these vehicles is particularly suited to the task of carrying the large numbers of people likely to descend on the line during a summer season, once it is open.
>
> While one can see the need to acquire locomotives from the ever dwindling number available, surely the time has arrived when attention should be focused upon coaching stock, particularly of high seating capacity. Locomotive-hauled stock of this type must become as scarce as the steam locomotive itself in the near future, with the steadily increasing use of diesel and electric multiple units by British Rail.
>
> Should the Association not therefore concentrate its attention upon the acquisition of passenger stock now . . . I have in mind particularly the BR standard locomotive-hauled compartment coach, numbers of which have been made redundant by BR modernization in recent years . . . it seems to me that this is exactly the right high-density passenger carriage, which the line will certainly need . . .

This letter was signed, anonymously, by someone calling themselves '30931', which suggests one of the King's Wimbledon group (No. 30931 was a 'Schools' class of that name).

Alan Dixon had also been able to include an article by Peter Davis, describing that Committee member's recollections of the K&ESR in the period between nationalization and the withdrawal of passenger services in 1954. The article, 'Farmers' Line Reminiscences', still makes interesting reading today. It illustrated well Peter's deep affection for the line's past as well as his personal commitment to its future. That commitment, together with his managerial ability, had been recognized by the Chairman, who was increasingly coming to use Peter as his deputy, and volunteers from 1968–9 remember the inspections of the line, and work in progress, jointly undertaken by Messrs Benge-Abbott and Davis.

Although Robin Doust was no longer an Association member, he remained aware of events on the railway through friendships, the railway press and the enthusiasts' 'grapevine'. After the great efforts he had made during the first seven years of the preservation scheme, many were greatly saddened by the turn of events, and there was much regret, which was shared by Peter B-A, that he did not feel that he could remain involved. Robin may, himself, have regretted his action in withdrawing his support from the scheme; he certainly never lost his concern for the K&ESR. Part of this concern was his continued adherence to his belief that the railway should be opened from the Robertsbridge end.

In March 1969 Robin attempted to withdraw his resignation on the grounds that it had never been accepted. As in many voluntary bodies, it was not Association practice to acknowledge letters of this kind. It could have been argued that as *The Farmers' Line* was no longer circulated to him this constituted an implied acceptance. The Committee considered the matter but decided they could not reinstate his previous membership. In addition, and taking all the facts into account, the Committee exercised their prerogative and decided that they could not accept any application from Robin to rejoin.

During April Robin Doust circulated a letter to a hundred members whose addresses were known to him. This drew attention to the Chairman's practice of conducting negotiations alone and alleged that all maintenance on the railway had been banned, no further rolling stock deliveries were to be allowed, rents on the station sites were to be raised by 500 per cent and that some of the buildings on the railway were to be demolished. The letter went on to invite the fifty signatures necessary to call a Special General Meeting to discuss these issues. (Robin was able to take this action as the Constitution did not state that an SGM had to be called by a member, only requested by fifty people who were fully paid up.) The members circulated included me, and I recall feeling distinctly nonplussed. The contents seemed, on the one hand, consistent with a negative interpretation which could be read into some of the material in *The Farmers' Line* (up to the January edition), and, on the other, was at odds with a rather brighter view of the same facts aided by the opinions of a volunteer I was still meeting on a fairly regular basis. For someone who was not a member of the workforce at the time, neutrality seemed the best position.

While the Committee were still absorbing this, the April edition of *The Farmers' Line* was published. The timing of letter and magazine make it unlikely that the latter was in any way influenced by the former, but with the new editor firmly in the saddle, this is a good moment for a detailed look at the contents. Like all house magazines, one purpose of *The Farmers' Line* was to 'talk up' the organization and Alan Dixon was achieving this very well indeed. The magazine was obviously the work of a different hand, but he had accomplished the change without too much of a jolt. Further feature articles (not always on K&ESR subjects) were now appearing and a photographic competition was also announced.

The Public Relations Group continued to go from strength to strength, Richard Halton's Guildford exhibition having proved a great success, and another member of the group, Frank Goodwin, was intending to run a stand at several traction engine rallies, a type of event which the K&ESR would attend for some years. It was also hoped to have an Association stand at a Clapham Transport Museum Sunday opening in September.

With regard to overall strategy, two linked items in the April edition are worthy of being related in detail. The first was Alan Dixon's editorial:

> It is almost eight years since a preservation scheme was first mooted, in June [*sic*] 1961.
>
> Eight years on, it is interesting therefore, to review the situation in the light of what has gone before, as well as casting an eye to the future.
>
> In eight years, what exactly has been achieved, you may ask, for we still do not own the railway. This is indeed the case, but the fact that the railway is still there at all, is a tribute to the perseverance, enthusiasm and loyalty of all K&ESR Association members, past and present. As a result of their tireless and unceasing effort during this time, a great deal has been achieved that is more positive.
>
> Maintenance and repair work has been carried out along the entire length of the line which has served not only to prevent the railway from returning to nature and becoming a permanent eyesore, but has also made a little easier the task of preparing the line eventually to take a regular train service once more.
>
> More tangible evidence of eight years' loving care and hard labour is to be found grouped together in Rolvenden yard. Here, locomotives of many shapes and sizes have come to be assembled, starting in 1962 with the two humble Sentinels from Merstham, and culminating recently with the arrival of the more glamorous tank engines from America.
>
> The nucleus of the fleet of passenger carriages is also in evidence, already sporting the beginnings of Colonel Stephens' original chocolate and cream livery for the line, and sundry items of rolling stock have also been collected. In addition, a vast quantity of material and equipment so necessary for a project of this scope has been acquired.
>
> What of the future? Later in this issue of *The Farmers' Line* our Chairman reviews the situation in very frank terms, which we feel sure will be welcomed by all our readers, as a positive situation report.
>
> The future is still uncertain, but while there is life there is hope. Determination is probably the facet of the Association's corporate character which has helped to carry the project this far, and to this we must now add the quality of patience, for with the inevitably slow progress we will make during the coming months, patience will be of primary importance.
>
> Patience must eventually be rewarded with success, however, and it will be even more interesting eight years hence, to review eight years of more positive progress, including the re-opening under the Association's auspices of the first sections of the K&ESR , this last of Colonel Stephens' light railways, to a public service once again.

Peter B-A's article, 'Taking Stock', included the following:

I must start with a word of thanks to all those members who have written commenting on our statement of policy aims. Your suggestions will all be carefully considered and used as a guide to future action.

Most members appear to be in full agreement with these aims, feeling that they represent a realistic approach to the problems we face in preserving thirteen miles of line, with several level crossings, in an age dominated by the motorcar.

What are our chances of success? This is a question everybody wants to ask, and alas, it is the most difficult to answer. It may help members if I restate the present position.

Our original contract with British Rail is now dead and buried. The only thing that saves the line from being sold for scrap is an undertaking given to us by British Rail that they will not dispose of the track and land until our action against the Ministry of Transport is dealt with.

This action is not likely to be heard before September and because of the very heavy backlog in the courts may be much later. We feel we shall win and, of course, MoT feel that they will. The Ministry are particularly interested in this action as it involves the interpretations placed on their powers under various Acts of Parliament. These interpretations have not been challenged in the courts before.

It is obvious that the battle could be a long one and is also one we cannot give up lightly since we are fighting for our very existence.

The Ministry turned us down because our interference with road traffic would 'not be in the public interest' and was 'greater than any compensating benefit our service would provide'. Our new aims would, however, produce an enterprise which would be very much in the public interest to support, this being a self-financing and self-supporting Youth Adventure Project. Such a project appeals enormously to the young people of this country. . . . Such a project has to be a continual challenge and here the length of the line, which so many people point to as a grave disadvantage, will in fact be of great benefit. . . . Progress. . . . will be slow and unspectacular . . . our members will have to rely on their convictions to keep morale up but as long as we do not lose heart we shall win.

A section of *The Farmers' Line* which continued much as previously was the Progress Report, and with this should be associated a letter (dated 18 January 1969 and published in the April edition) which the Chairman had received from the H Class Trust. This announced that it was pulling out of Robertsbridge and was moving to Ashford Shed, where the Steam Centre was then in its embryonic stage. It stated it might come back to the K&ESR if the line re-opened. It never did, of course, and when the Ashford Steam Centre closed the H Class went to the Bluebell Railway.

The Progress Report itself gave news of work continuing, or having recommenced, on many of the projects mentioned in earlier editions, and the Manning Wardle *Arthur* was receiving a general overhaul. There were, however, indications of the restrictions which BR had been trying to impose. Movement of stock had, for instance, been totally forbidden, the Southern Region having gone to the extraordinary length of chaining a sleeper across the Robertsbridge end of Rolvenden yard. It was equally impossible to get out the other way either, as the SR had requested a halt to work on bridge 2330 which had reached the stage where the span had been removed. Weedkilling was hampered by the prohibition on movement, and although the telephone system was not to be dismantled, neither was it being expanded at that point in time. Overall, and despite the continuing clearance work up Tenterden Bank, Rolvenden yard took on something of a besieged feeling.

These restrictions bring us back to the points made by Robin Doust in his circular letter to the hundred selected members. It might, of course, have happened that his efforts were stillborn. But they were not, and on 5 May the requisite fifty signatures were sent to Philip Shaw in his role as Secretary. Robin later stated he had further signatures in reserve. To have achieved this kind of response would seem to indicate that his targeting was fairly good and that he had identified a significant if, as it later proved, minority viewpoint. Individual motives for supporting the request for an SGM appear to have ranged from misapprehension of the situation to genuinely, if privately, held misgivings about Association policy. Motives are also known to have included personal loyalty, something which had always been one of the strengths of the scheme. Sadly, this situation contained many of the elements of true tragedy.

Almost simultaneously, on 7 May, Ron Cann resigned from both the Committee and the post of Treasurer, his resignation to be effective from 31 May. The consternation resulting from these things was felt not only in the Committee but in the volunteer force as well. To make matters worse, the names of a group of regular volunteers appeared among the fifty on the SGM petition. This incensed a further group of volunteers who then set about issuing a reply to the fifty signatories, the following being taken from the resulting letter:

> We are writing to you as regular volunteer members of the K&ESR Association, who are disturbed to find your name on a list of members calling for a Special General Meeting in response to a circular letter from Mr Doust to discuss current developments concerning the railway. Some of us also received copies of his letter and were able to discount most of the points which Mr Doust raised and to clear up any other points with the Committee. As we have been unable to ascertain whether you are aware of the current situation we would like to take this opportunity of letting you know our views on his letter.
>
> Taking up the points in Mr Doust's letter, we understand:
>
> (1) Regarding all maintenance on the track having been stopped, we would refer you to *The Times* dated 5 May 1969, which clearly shows work proceeding apace, which you can confirm by paying a visit to the railway. However, work ceased for a short period while the Association satisfied British Rail that it had adequate insurance cover.
> (2) Regarding the reference to station rents, we would remind you that owing to the recent Transport Act, British Rail are now obliged to show a profit, and we ourselves have not seen any figures relating to rent increases, as we understand negotiations are still in hand.
> (3) Regarding the ban on delivery of further rolling stock, we were requested not to take delivery of further stock for the moment, and currently the line is short of safe storage spaces.
> (4) Regarding the demolition of buildings on the railway, these are in fact a pair of derelict cottages at Robertsbridge which are, in any case, an eyesore.

After pointing out that Robin Doust was no longer a member and that the Chairman had been in touch with BR officials on numerous occasions, the letter concluded:

> As regards the allegation in Mr Doust's letter of a 'serious deterioration' of the Association's position, we do not, quite frankly, consider this to have been warranted by the facts.
>
> We, as regular volunteers, have complete confidence in our current management, and would be pleased to meet you any weekend to discuss any points you may have.

The signatories of the letter did not include any Committee members.

As has been said, the fifty members calling for the SGM did include some regular volunteers who must have been aware of at least some of the details in the reply. Weighing up the evidence, one can only come to the conclusion that they continued to harbour unresolved doubts. It is, nonetheless, depressing to find individuals who had been close friends and colleagues on either side of this argument. But the K&ESR was a democracy and a plurality of views was neither subversive nor dishonourable. Thus far the matter had been conducted constitutionally, but there was some concern that it should continue in that manner. Following the volunteers' letter to the 'Fifty', Robin Doust had found it necessary to write to the Committee informing them that if any pressure was put on the signatories, at least three of them were prepared to take legal action to ensure the meeting took place. Recourse to this action did not prove to be necessary.

There was also an exchange of letters between Robin Doust and the Secretary which indicated that both parties realized the destructive potential of what they were doing, and acknowledged the all-too-real likelihood of bad publicity. Behind all this lurked the issue of Robertsbridge–Bodiam versus Tenterden–Rolvenden (unstated in either Robin Doust's or the volunteers' letters). The Committee came to the conclusion that they had to hold the SGM and resolve the issues of confidence in the management and future policy once and for all.

The Committee meeting of 1 June provided a dress rehearsal for some of the issues to be raised at the SGM, which was arranged for the 28th of that month. A major item on the agenda was the consideration of Ron Cann's resignation. Mr Cann was asked to address the Committee and the following points emerged:

a) As a director of the Company and a Trustee of the RVR Trust, he was not in agreement with the way negotiations were being conducted and could not support the Chairman and the Committee in the furtherance of the then policy.
b) He did not consider that the Chairman should negotiate with BR without being accompanied by another member of the Committee or a representative of the Company.
c) When questioned about the major point of disagreement with regard to policy, Mr Cann stated that he was in broad agreement with the published policy document except that he considered that the line should be opened in stages from the Robertsbridge end, rather than commencing with the Tenterden–Rolvenden section.

After Mr Cann had withdrawn from the meeting, it was agreed to accept his resignation. The resulting vacancy was filled by moving Philip Shaw from the post of Secretary to that of Treasurer. At the same meeting it was agreed to elect S.J. Benge-Abbott to the Committee, together with Roger Crawford. The last-named gentleman subsequently became Secretary. Roger was an Edinburgh University graduate in forestry and had been a Forestry Commission Officer based at the Kielder Forest. After marrying Penny, a native of Tenterden, he later moved to the town and opened a shop in the High Street. He was a forceful character, possessed of enormous energy and enthusiasm. He was a champion of the volunteers. He believed in working and playing hard and sometimes organized entertainment after working weekends. Above all, he got things done.

The Special General Meeting was duly held, the Committee having made the sensible decision to invite Capt. Manisty of the Association of Railway Preservation Societies to chair the meeting. Members agreed to this once the proceedings commenced and also that Robin Doust be allowed to remain present and be heard.

Capt. Manisty suggested that P. B–A should speak first, followed by a representative of the 'Fifty' and that there should be a period of summing up. This was an unusual inversion of accepted procedure, and one would have expected Robin Doust's party to be allowed to speak initially. Arthur Penny raised this point but it was not accepted by Capt. Manisty. This procedural decision was otherwise never publicly challenged (a member's letter questioning it remains on file) and, in view of the entrenched positions which had been adopted, it must be doubtful whether it made any difference to the outcome.

Peter B-A first mentioned that the 'Fifty' had not forwarded any resolutions with their request for a meeting, before going on to say that the Committee was not prepared to carry on 'while subject to threats of legal action if it does not carry out the wishes of a minority group of members'. He then went on to reiterate the course of events since before the AGM and up to the volunteers' letter and Ron Cann's resignation. He pointed out that the increase in rents (agreed to at the Committee meeting on 1 June) was in accordance with a general rise then being imposed by BR and that Committee members had full details of his dealings with BR.

The K&ESRA Chairman then told the meeting that the Committee had been informed that the money in the RVR Trust Fund 'would not be forthcoming unless the purchase of the railway was proceeded with in a certain way in accordance with the wishes of the Rother Valley Company'. The Committee was unhappy about the situation where the Association had no control over either body. He felt that 'the Company's Board did not represent the views of the Association as a whole as set out in the Policy Statement'. Adhering to this statement was the only slim chance of success.

When Robin Doust spoke on behalf of the 'Fifty', he made it clear that the increase in rents was 600 per cent (£61 to £390) per annum. He further considered that, as the agreement excluded the public from Rolvenden, this deprived the Association of a valuable source of income and that a 'week's notice on either side' clause provided no security. The Association had been formed to restore the full range of services to the line and, while it had always been seen that tourist services would produce the most income, much of the support for the project had been attracted by the proposal for such a full range. The Policy Statement said nothing about regular services.

Mr Doust disliked the decision to concentrate on opening Tenterden–Rolvenden first. This would be a truncated railway giving only a tourist service and would require replacing 1029 and the worst track before any further extension. Re-opening Robertsbridge–Bodiam would maintain the main-line connection and give access to the Bodiam Castle traffic. He considered that only this way would enough money be made to purchase the line and added that 'Felix' would withdraw his backing if the opposite course of action was taken.

When Capt. Manisty opened the meeting to general discussion the question was asked as to whether there was to be a weekday service. Peter B-A replied by quoting from the Policy Statement that the extent of the service would be 'dependent on public demand' but that the Committee was not authorized to pour money down the drain. Ron Cann said he was pleased to learn that the whole line was still to be purchased. The money in the RVR Trust Fund was for that purpose and not for the purchase of a shorter section, Arthur Penny adding that the Trustees must be satisfied the funds were to be used for the purpose for which they were deposited before parting with them.

Ron Cann then confirmed to the meeting that he was 'Felix' and that if the line was to be truncated then his money would certainly not be forthcoming. The service to be provided was entirely up to the Association as long as it paid. Len Heath Humphrys spoke in favour of Robertsbridge–Bodiam in order to get the railway running across the A21 before the road was widened, but was followed by Alan Dixon who said the new policy, which was backed by a large proportion of the membership, was necessary because the old policy had been rejected by the Ministry of Transport. He was backed in this by Peter B-A, who stated a realistic approach was needed to create confidence outside the Association. In addition, Tenterden–Rolvenden would require considerably less work and expense.

The meeting concluded with members agreeing to resolutions from the floor approving the Policy Statement and indicating their confidence in the Committee.

All this, for the moment, left open the question of the relationship with the Rother Valley Railway Company and the RVR Trust (the Trustees were all Directors of the RVR Company) but it did set matters on the course the Committee wanted. It could, however, be argued that this had been the most dangerous moment in the history of the K&ESR. Through the bankruptcy of the old Company in 1932, final closure in 1961 and the refusal of the Light Railway Transfer Order, the railway had survived because of the people who cared about it. The Special General Meeting of 1969 had threatened to split the ranks of the K&ESR's closest supporters. If the Association had hopelessly divided at that point that would truly have been the end. Blame can be distributed in all directions, the management for complacency in assuming everyone was following them (and perhaps for not creating an atmosphere in which those with doubts felt they could be critical of the Policy Statement), the 'Fifty' for having pressed their case so hard and the volunteers for having taken the bait and formed a counterfaction. Neither will I loftily exempt myself. Neutrality and absence were not particularly honourable attitudes in the circumstances.

From a positive point of view, many preservation groups have experienced this sort of internecine bickering before emerging stronger on the other side. I know of only one person who may have been influenced by these events to leave the volunteer force, but even the evidence for that is rather doubtful. Robin Doust was, of course, unable to return, but even this departure was not for ever. It is related, by those who were there, that even at the height of this episode, no friendships were actually broken, which says much for the spirit of determination which had been so correctly identified by Alan Dixon and the comradeship which has often been referred to.

As to the basic issue of which section to re-open first, both sides could, and did, bring valid arguments to the debate. History is, of course, written by the winners. In this case it was made by them as well. Tenterden–Rolvenden not only carried the day but proved to be a viable proposition. It is now known that Robertsbridge–Bodiam would have again run foul of road proposals. The economic viability of that section remains an open and unanswerable question, although the moves begun in the early 1990s to restore the line to Robertsbridge may provide clue to the truth of the matter.

XVIII

While arguments had been under way about the future course of the scheme, various moves had been taking place which looked towards the eventual operation of passenger services. Company records show that on 10 May an Operating Sub-Committee had met for the first time, while on the 16th of the same month the efforts to persuade the local authorities to back the project began to pay off when Kent County Council wrote expressing its support for the project, although again with some reservations about the level crossings.

During May negotiations had also started with the steel manufacturer Stewart and Lloyd for two of its 0–6–0 saddle tanks, *Jupiter* and *Gunby*. This reflected the locomotive policy suggested by Peter Davis, *Jupiter* being a Hunslet-designed Austerity built by Robert Stephenson and Hawthorns in 1950. *Gunby* was a very similar locomotive, built in 1941 by Hunslet, but to the immediate predecessor design of the famous Austerity type. By November it had been decided not to proceed with the purchase of either locomotive (the boiler reports were not very satisfactory), but the idea of using this type had taken hold.

The BR ban on movement remained very much in force, but the existing motive power was not being allowed to remain cold and lifeless. There was no actual prohibition on steaming locomotives, and during the summer of 1969 steam and coal smoke again rose over Rolvenden on successive Sundays, with the result that even this limited and frustrating degree of operation succeeded in providing a considerable and much-needed boost to morale.

The locomotives involved in this upturn were *Bodiam, Marcia, Arthur* and *Maunsell*. The last-mentioned USA had successfully passed hydraulic and steam tests in May and been officially steamed for the first time at Whitsun. A new coal bunker was being constructed to replace the corroded original, but

Ex-GWR railcar No. 20 at Rolvenden (Dennis Ovenden)

only limited work was possible on No. 21 *Wainwright*, as it was unsafe to lift the locomotive where it stood. *Marcia* was also receiving a new bunker to replace the original and inadequate coal storage space inside the cab. This new bunker was of a hopper design which appeared both to owe something to, and be an improvement on, the bunkers of USAs and BR Standard tanks!

Work on the Manning Wardle, *Arthur*, had progressed well, thus allowing this 0–6–0ST to be steamed, but *Charwelton*, despite receiving three new boiler tubes and a new main steam pipe, was found to be short of a rivet head in the firebox. Closer inspection was to follow. *Arthur* had, incidentally, been repainted in K&ESR apple green, a reversal of the earlier decision to paint ex-industrial types blue. Neither were the Terriers forgotten, *Bodiam* having passed its annual inspection and *Sutton* having received a replacement dome. This item had been cast locally, an example of the kind of self-help that was to become commonplace on steam railways with the disappearance of spares and much, if not all, suitable help from BR.

The Farmers' Line for July carried an interesting note that a 'good friend' from the Keighley and Worth Valley Railway had started repainting the ex-SE&CR brake van. This refers to occasional exchanges between the two railways around the end of the 1960s, when volunteers took to spending holidays on each other's lines. The K&WVR was very much the railway of the moment, having defiantly re-opened shortly before BR steam came to an end. The Worth Valley line was not without particular interest to K&ESR members, being both home to the Westerham coaches and the owner of

Manning Wardle L class 0–6–0 saddle tank Arthur under restoration at Rolvenden in 1969. The dumb buffers were later replaced and vacuum brakes fitted (Dennis Ovenden)

another USA. The K&ESR men had gone north expecting to be regarded as pampered Southerners by the gritty, ale-loving Yorkshire folk, only to find that the Worth Valley mess coach was somewhat less rugged than their own accommodation. As Terry Heaslip once remarked, 'They even go behind the curtain to take their socks off!'

The Civil Engineering Department was continuing work on the new steelwork for bridge 2330 (although it was not, of course, able to place it in position), the components of the structure having been treated with bright orange protective paint. Clearance work and fishplate-greasing on Tenterden Bank continued and work had recommenced at Northiam at Whitsun (with assistance from the King's Wimbledon group and the local Brickwall School). Particular attention was given to hedge-trimming and weedkilling, the long interval since maintenance had been undertaken on that section having done nothing to improve matters. Northiam station building was to be repainted and receive routine repairs.

Despite the renewed weed and tree growth along much of the line, the S&T section was fighting a valiant battle to keep the telephone system intact. As the trees fouled the line, breaks became more frequent, while the rapidly growing weeds made access to some of the remoter sections very difficult. The efforts which Chris Lowry made to keep the system in operation were much appreciated at the time, and, believe it or not, he is still doing the same work today. The Signalling Group had meanwhile acquired a Saxby & Farmer 18-lever frame from Hailsham, 1,200 ft of channel-section point rodding and a

Terriers No. 3 and No. 10 looking very smart in May 1969 (Dennis Ovenden)

number of Midland Railway three-position block instruments. The best of these were to be overhauled for service on the K&ESR and it was intended to resell the remainder via the Pullman sales counter. The Signalling Group now had an increasingly large volume of equipment and had, accordingly, taken over the former museum room at Tenterden from the Public Relations Group. Even the parcels office/museum/signals workshop did not provide enough room and the lean-to shed at the end of the station building was also in use as storage accommodation.

Before turning once again to strategic and management matters, record must be made of what *The Farmers' Line* described as a 'new phenomenon' – Gordon Laming and his gang. This may not sound much in itself, even allowing for the fact that Gordon was a professional railwayman. The 'gang' was, however, very worthy of comment for, on a steam railway project which in its early years had always had decidedly youthful personnel, this group was very young indeed. They were all about twelve years of age! Every three weeks or so this group of young people was entrusted to Gordon's care. Aided by a good selection of technical equipment, including gauges, levels and superelevation templates, the Laming gang quickly re-aligned and packed the platform road at Tenterden, improved track drainage in the station area, trimmed undergrowth and replaced a number of sleepers between Rolvenden and Tenterden. They were even known to work well after dark with the aid of Tilley lamps. All this accorded very well with the developing notions of a

Youth Adventure Project. The Laming gang soon became known as the Plebs, in part because of their capacity for vast amounts of (plebeian) manual work and partly because the south-east Londoners among the volunteers soon spotted a particular irony in the situation. Without exception the Plebs came from the well-heeled and influential (patrician) families of Blackheath! Gordon was a man with a social conscience and some of the lads, although from affluent backgrounds, were also from 'broken home situations'.

The July magazine had carried the first of a series of articles by Peter Davis entitled 'The Problems We Face'. The initial subject tackled was the thorny matter of roads and level crossings. After an introduction, which included one of the first public admissions that the refusal of the LRTO might have more to do with credibility than holding up the traffic, Peter detailed the situation road by road, foreseeing relatively little problem from Tenterden to Bodiam, but with the need to provide either gates or lifting barriers. Much difficulty was envisaged between Bodiam and Robertsbridge. At that time the Ministry and the County Council proposed a new road linking the A21 and the A229 (known, of course, as Junction Road on the K&ESR), while the Robertsbridge bypass which eventually emerged was seen as an unlikely alternative. The timescale for a start to construction was fifteen years and it was known that the railway would be required to contribute at least a proportion of the cost of a bridge over the line. The RVR Trust Fund was suggested as a means of raising the money.

A number of developments which resulted from recent proposals and events were considered by the Committee on 3 August. On the less positive side, BR had refused to sell Rolvenden yard on its own and had also said that no further locomotives were to be allowed onto the site. Despite this, the K&ESR was seeking to buy the Hodson's Mill P class which was up for sale following the cessation of rail freight deliveries to Robertsbridge. The Bluebell Railway had also announced its interest in the locomotive; it already owned two of the surviving members of the class and was about to buy the Bowaters example. Mr S.J. Benge-Abbott negotiated with Hodson's Mill and offered £1,000 against the Bluebell's £900.

Ron Cann had now withdrawn his offer to provide security for a bank loan (he felt that the Association's aims had now departed too far from its original intentions), thus bringing to an end that possible source of finance. As a separate, but obviously linked, item it was agreed to try and bring the RVR Company under the control of the Association.

The 1969 AGM was held on 29 September at Highbury Lane. Philip Shaw's Treasurer's report again showed that the Association had, of necessity, met the expenses (mainly incurred in connection with legal matters) by the Company.

Otherwise, the minutes of the event have an air of the organization continuing to 'mark time' – a point emphasized when Peter B-A reminded members that the Association's prospects had changed little since 1967. Efforts on behalf of the Association by Terence Boston MP warranted particular mention, but it was made clear to everyone that even if the court case against the Ministry was won, there was no guarantee the Association would be offered all the line, be offered it for £36,000 or that the project would not be opposed by the Ministry of Transport in any other way.

The Chairman reiterated that the Committee still aimed to re-open the entire line. If the court case was lost it would probably be necessary to call a Special General Meeting to decide the course the Association should take.

But the long hiatus in progress was nearly over, a fact brought home by Alan Dixon's editorial in the October *Farmer's Line*. 'So the crunch is finally here,' he wrote, ' – or almost; for by the time this issue . . . appears, the High Court action whereby we seek . . . to re-present our case . . . will be perhaps only a few days away, since it is certain to be heard during this law term.'

The same edition of *The Farmer's Line* brought the second of Peter Davis' articles in his series, 'The Problems We Face'. This time the subject was bridges. A basic problem with this subject was that Col. Stephens had built the Robertsbridge–Rolvenden section very cheaply and lightly. The K&ESR had, however, no really large engineering features. The largest structure on the remaining section of the line was the Rother Bridge (Southern Region No. 2353), which was known to require professional remedial work, and two others would need to be completely rebuilt. One of these was, of course, 1029 (2336) across New Mill Channel and the other was across Hexden Channel.

There were nine bridges on the line (in its 1969 Robertsbridge–Tenterden length) of under 20 ft span which could be either piped or filled in. This left twelve which the Association would be capable of repairing. Four required lesser attention and the remainder could be repaired along the lines of 2330 at Rolvenden. These smaller bridges consisted of two parallel steel girders set directly into unreinforced concrete abutments. These had been among the first applications of concrete to that type of work and its poor condition reflected the lack of knowledge of the material at the turn of the century. Inevitable movement had caused cracking, and rainwater running down the face of the abutments had severely corroded the girders where they entered the concrete. The earliest possible replacement was essential, and at the same time the opportunity would be taken to increase the axle loadings to 18 tons.

The organization of staff training courses was now being co-ordinated by Kevin Blakiston and included classes for guards, shunters, and locomotive, signalling and booking office staff. The resultant lectures were to commence during November and their starting time was to be 4.30 p.m., which seems to have been a sensible use of time as the winter evenings drew in. Not surprisingly, it was stated that those attending would be most favourably looked upon once trains actually started running!

Much of the history of the K&ESR preservation project may be mapped by reference to *The Farmers' Line* – that is, both in the contents of the magazine and by changes in its presentation. Volume 8, Number 1 was certainly such a landmark edition, appearing as a new decade dawned on a Britain, and not least its railway system, greatly changed in the years since 1960. There was now another minor change in the magazine itself. The quarterly publication date, which had been adopted in 1969, was further reduced to three times a year, on the winter-spring-autumn pattern which was to be inherited by the *Tenterden Terrier*.

Alan Dixon had caught the mood of the moment with another of his apt editorials which were proving worthy successors to those penned in Preservation Society days by Robin Doust:

'To be or not to be', that is a question which remains unanswered as we go to press, for with the judgement deferred in our High Court action against the Ministry of Transport, the K&ESR is still left in a vacuum. Meanwhile, British Rail have made it clear that the only alternative available to us in the event of our losing the case, is a goods yard site.

The thought of our equipment on static display, and abandonment of the line is anathema, and it is quite clear we must fight for our operational railway to the bitter end.

Tenacity and singleness of purpose have brought us thus far, to a point where, in contesting an action which we could so easily have lost, we have survived to fight another day – this time in the Appeal Court if the High Court decision is ultimately against us.

All that has been achieved, all the money that has been committed so far, will be worthless, however, if we are forced to appeal, unless there is sufficient additional money with which to finance this further litigation, for the Association's existing reserves are fully allocated to the purchase of the railway.

The new fighting fund, set up for the purpose with a target figure of £2,000, would require a subscription of £2 from every member of the Association. Think about this: but not for too long, because 31st March 1970 is the deadline. £2 represents the price of a packet of cigarettes saved for each week in the interim, and it may mean the difference between re-opening and oblivion for *The Farmers' Line*. 'To be or not to be, that is the question', and the answer is up to you.

Further on in the magazine, and as usual, the Progress Report brought members up to date with all the current developments, even if the Civil Engineering Department summed up the mood of the time by noting a reluctance to spend money on permanent works. Bodiam was even temporarily out of use by the Association – a contractor had taken it over in connection with the conversion to North Sea gas which was then taking place. A positive advantage resulting from this was that the whole station had been reglazed and repainted.

Philip Shaw had acquired an ex-SE&CR Birdcage brake from the Longmoor Military Railway and it was hoped to bring the vehicle to join the collection still waiting in Robertsbridge yard. The LMR was also the source of two further goods brake vans, a standard Southern Railway 25 ton type with extended end platforms and another 25 ton brake with a platform at one end. This latter vehicle was, at the time, thought to be of L&SWR origin but this was later amended to London and North Western. The exact history of this brake van remains a mystery. But the best news of all was that the Hodson's Mill P class had been purchased by the K&ESR, although she would have to remain at Robertsbridge until movement on the line could resume. There was a certain amount of glee at having beaten the Bluebell Railway to this purchase; the old enmity was beginning to decline but it had far from disappeared. Much credit was due to the monthly draw for having raised the money for *Pride of Sussex*.

The arrival of the P class brought forth a 'letter to the editor'. This was reminiscent of the disgruntled opinions held by some members a few years earlier, but balanced matters by including some positive views similar to the opinions of Peter Davis. It began by pointing out that the locomotive was already sixty years old, that spare parts must have been non-existent and that it would be no joy trying to depend on it twenty years later.

Having visited the Worth Valley Railway, however, the writer of the letter had seen their 1954 built ex-Stewarts and Lloyds 0–6–0st No. 63 in operation, which, although recognized by its owners as an ugly brute, was modern and powerful. He contended that this was the sort of locomotive the K&ESR should be going after to operate the summer service in the 1990s. There were plenty of late model Austerities around, and if action was not quickly taken it would be too late. In general terms, this proved to be a totally accurate prediction.

The third of Peter Davis' 'Problems' articles was on the subject of track. It provided a glimpse of the railway in early 1970, some eight years after the Preservation Society arrived and two years after efforts to maintain the lower section had substantially ceased. The article is, in fact, of such interest that it is here reproduced in full.

Kent is reputed to be the 'Garden of England'; well, like all gardens it has a phenomenal capacity for growing weeds. This, of course, is reflected in the overgrown state of our railway. All but a few hundred yards of the 13½ miles are very badly weedgrown indeed. Additionally, in wooded areas there are substantial saplings growing between the rails. These have seeded from neighbouring trees, and in the two years since we abandoned comprehensive maintenance work, the rate of growth has to be seen to be believed.

What effect will this have on our chances of success? The main detriment is to the sleepers and keys; the fact that they have lain under wet grass for several years has meant the rot has been accelerated and at least seven miles of sleepers will need total replacement before public traffic can be run on them. It is true that good second-hand sleepers can be obtained from various sources, but wooden keys present a problem because the sections requiring them are all laid in 91¼ lb rail – an obsolete type for which keys are no longer available.

So the very first thing we must do after receiving the go-ahead is to remove all unwanted vegetation. This must necessarily take place in two stages; first the entire formation will be chemically weedkilled to halt the deterioration of the track materials. Secondly, the loading gauge will be cleared of more substantial growth as the line is re-opened section by section. During the past summer we have experimented with a liquid weedkiller developed by the Chipman Chemical Company for British Rail, and the results have been mixed, it's effectiveness naturally depending on the type of ballast and the maturity of the weeds. In terms of hard cash it is going to cost at least £30 per mile and application will probably take about 3-4 days using a high-pressure spray boom mounted on a Wickham trolley. In the light of our experience, we will be able to build up a suitable apparatus cheaply and quickly. Choosing the right time is most important and we believe that with our system, weedkilling application in late March, just as the new growth begins will render the formation suitably barren.

The more substantial growth is a different proposition and this is where the hard graft begins. As you know, our stalwart forestry gang, under the supervision of Norton Brown, has spent the last 18 months attacking the considerable overgrowth between Tenterden and Rolvenden. Now this section had not been attended to for many years, and it was almost impossible to penetrate the thicket in some places. Today it looks as good as it did in days of passenger traffic, and it is indeed a tribute to Norton's enthusiasm, as, let's face it, there has not been much to encourage our efforts of late. The forestry gang has averaged five volunteers every Sunday during last summer, and between March and November they have collectively worked 1261 man hours, or six months' work for one man, or £500 worth of labour.

During this period the gang was active on 35 days and cleared approximately ¾ mile of formation, a further ¾ mile having been cleared in a similar period before it was decided to record the man hours involved. The lesson learnt from this is that a gang of ten men, working one day a week, will progress at a rate of two miles per annum. As it is desirable that they work ahead of the track laying gang, suitable adjustments will be made to ensure this, either by reducing the standard of clearance, if acceleration is thought necessary, or reducing the size of the gang if progress outstrips the calculated requirements. Whatever the argument, we will need ten men every weekend for this section of the project, so please give thought to this, perhaps one of the most agreeable tasks we can offer. We are, incidentally, devising various mechanical aids for scrub clearance and it may well be we can do better in this field than at first thought. [One of these mechanical aids, of typically K&ESR ingenuity, involved attaching a rotary lawn mower to either side of the front of a Wickham trolley. This arrangement was apparently quite effective.]

The track itself needs carefully consideration. The initial one and a half miles from Tenterden is laid with 95 lb bullhead rail on ash ballast and partly on Meldon dust. It is in relatively good condition and needs only about 50 new sleepers and a certain amount of packing and re-aligning. Six weeks' hard work should see this section in good enough fettle to satisfy the Ministry of Transport.

Half a mile outside Rolvenden the picture is very different, for the 95 lb rail gives way to $91\frac{1}{4}$ lb material on ash ballast. This was reclaimed from the Elham Valley line and laid here during the early fifties, it stretches almost to Bodiam and although the rail is in excellent condition, the sleepers and keys will need renewal, a monumental task as there are 7-8 miles involved. This work is difficult to programme at this stage, as we have no experience in track renewal. However, a few deductions will bear out that about 30 men will be tied up for four years, working weekends only. This is by far the most demanding aspect of the restoration and our volunteer labour force must not lose its enthusiasm or sense of purpose if schedules are to be met. Apart from the morale aspect there will be expenditure of some £1,000 per mile on sleepers and packing materials, and the problem of producing thousands of nonstandard wooden keys. Again we have ideas for the mechanization of all these tasks, and we are confident that trial and error will result in an acceptable system. The remaining section consists of heavier section rail and substantial sections are laid with steel sleepers. These are laid in ash ballast and it is thought that the track may tend to 'weave' under heavier locomotives, such as the USAs with their very heavy front ends. This is something we may have to rectify by ballasting with granular material, which will afford better stability for these sleepers.

This brief summary has shown that a truly heroic effort is necessary to prepare the permanent way that is so vital to our scheme. Let us hope that our members will rise to the occasion, as they have done to so many challenges in the past.

On Monday 23 February, and while the magazine was being prepared, Mr Justice Megarry heard the case against the Ministry of Transport in the High Court. His judgement was in favour of the RVR Company although the judge himself thought it might prove 'a Pyrrhic victory'. The following Statement of Position as at 24 February was included with the winter edition of *The Farmers' Line*:

As many members will know, we won our High Court Action against the Ministry of Transport on Monday 23 February.

It is emphasized that this is purely one major battle in our campaign to re-open the line and that many difficulties remain to be overcome.

The most immediate difficulty is the likelihood that the Ministry of Transport will appeal against [the] decision and we must be in a position to resist any such appeal.

Further progress, therefore, will involve considerable cost, particularly for legal expenses and if you have not already contributed to the Second Fighting Fund, please now do so. Up to last weekend just under a third of the Association's members had contributed, raising a figure of just over £700. Much more money will be needed before we can be certain that the line is safe.

In due course a further appeal will be made to members for financial support towards purchasing the line, thus avoiding the heavy costs of present-day interest charges on borrowed capital.

The Committee's proposals in this respect will be outlined at a Special General Meeting which will be held on Sunday 5th April at the Youth Club Hall, Tenterden at 3 p.m.

Please do your best to attend and please also do your best to strengthen the finances of the Association at this most heartening point in our history.

The satisfying pleasure of receiving this news, even if tempered by the possibility of an appeal, remains a clear memory more than two decades later. In the latter part of March the Society issued a list of all those who had contributed to the fighting fund up until the 7th of the month. It was another interesting collection of individuals, ranging from venerable and respected enthusiasts of the pre-war years, through the regular and tenacious members of the volunteer force, to, once again, names of people who would become prominent in years that were to follow. As evidence that the rift of the previous year was healing, it was also possible to find names which had been among the 'Fifty', as well as those who had been part of the group who had signed the letter in opposition to them. By 17 March the Second Fighting Fund had reached £1,100. It is pleasing to report that among those who had contributed were Ron Cann and Robin Doust. Ron Cann was also still active in the Association in the role of Purchases Officer, a post he continued to hold until the early days of the Tenterden Railway Company. Although not actively involved in later years, he has continued to live near the line and to be a respected member of the Company.

The covering letter to the mailing which informed members of all this included a 'stop press'. The Ministry of Transport had decided to appeal against Mr Justice Megarry's decision.

0–4–0WT King and the Ford diesel in Robertsbridge yard on 20 July 1969 (Dennis Ovenden)

XIX

The phase which began in the spring of 1970 was, to say the least, characterized by a marked increase in the pace of developments.

Most heartening of all, although for perhaps the least substantial reasons, was the return of not just locos in steam but actual stock movement! Machines of most sorts dislike inactivity, the Association had grown concerned at the effects on the rolling stock, and BR was approached with a view to getting the prohibition lifted. After what was described as 'fairly lengthy' negotiations, BR relented, on condition that the movements should be for maintenance purposes only, that they should be confined to the limits of Rolvenden yard and that all liability and insurance should be borne by the Association.

This welcome crack in the ice was exactly what the Association and the morale of the volunteer force needed. The news was received shortly before Easter (which that year ran from Friday 27 March to Monday 30) and it was immediately decided to take advantage of this happy coincidence. The first movements would be that weekend. A great deal of water had flowed under the Rother Bridge since the Granada TV train had travelled the line and much needed to be organized. Quite apart from the insurance, coal had to be purchased and steam oil obtained from the NCB at Snowdown Colliery. By

Volunteer party leaving Rolvenden by trolley in 1971. The figure second from the left on the trolley is Peter Carey. Peter was at the inaugural meeting in 1961 and was still working as a volunteer in the Carriage and Wagon Department in 1993 (Author)

pure chance it was the same weekend that only a few miles away, the narrow gauge Sittingbourne and Kemsley Light Railway re-opened.

This is also a good point to pay tribute to Malcolm Knight, a professional railwayman brought in to enhance the K&ESR's expertise. He organized the training of the footplatemen at Rolvenden and played no small part in winning the confidence of the authorities. In later years he became associated with Scotrail's notable steam initiatives north of the border.

There was no time to tell the membership what was happening. I, for instance, only found out because I had gone to Challock during the Saturday afternoon to book some lessons with the Kent Gliding Club, and drove on to Tenterden afterwards. The atmosphere around the station was vibrant and almost tangible; it was as if the long pent-up will of the railway to run again had suddenly burst its restraints.

The Loco Department had been tempted to steam the USA No. 22, but, on the insistence of Peter Davis, had decided against the understandable wish to try out its most powerful type – she was still only in undercoat. Despite the new rival attraction in the north of the county, the public were expected in sizable numbers and it was decided to use *Sutton*, the best prepared of the locomotives at that time. Sunday and Monday were to be the main operating days, but a small fire was lit in *Sutton* on the Saturday to warm up a too-long cold boiler. Other vehicles were greased up and, most symbolically, the single-line staff, which carried the point-lock keys, was collected from Robertsbridge signal-box. (BR had locked the points during the ban on movement – the necessary mechanisms were, of course, already fitted.)

At 11.00 a.m. on Sunday 29 March, steam was lightly blowing from *Sutton*'s safety valves and there was that expectant air which only live steam can produce. Charlie Kentsley was in charge of the footplate crews and Terry Heaslip of the movements in the yard. The public had also found out what was happening – the enthusiasts' 'grapevine' had obviously been at work – and Rolvenden yard began to fill up with visitors.

At midday the Terrier's whistle briefly sounded and she moved slowly forward to test the air brake system which had received some modifications. The next step was to propel No. 3 to the limit of shunt, which was about 300 yds in the Wittersham direction. Great care was taken, as *Bodiam* had been fitted with new big ends which needed to be run in, and a start was then made to shunting the yard. This involved a quite complicated set of manoeuvres, some involving substantial loads, the object being to bring the best stock into public view while the less attractive vehicles were placed in less prominent positions. In particular, the wagons were moved from the back siding and unloaded, as it was anticipated they would be needed for reconstruction work if the K&ESR Light Railway Transfer Order was forthcoming. The opportunity was also taken to run the railcar under its own power.

Sunday evening also seemed to see a positive return to earlier times, the volunteers being in a celebratory mood so reminiscent of that Whitsun weekend six years earlier. As on that earlier occasion the mess coach was crowded, and it was a reflection of the floating population that has always made up any volunteer force to see how many familiar faces could be seen among the newcomers who had been attracted to the K&ESR.

On the Monday morning the public arrived at Rolvenden in even larger numbers. Both *Sutton* and No. 3 were steamed and, whatever the future might have held once the appeal to the High Court's decision was heard, it was inspiring to see two green Terriers at work in Rolvenden yard. *Bodiam* began running in her new bearings and the task of re-arranging the stock was completed. Later in the day the railcar was again moved under its own power on one engine, the opportunity being taken to commence the diesel crew training course. Taken overall, Easter weekend was a great success, running very smoothly and raising £300, which more than covered running expenses.

It was also at this point that Peter B–A, after piloting the organization through the difficult two-and-a-half year transitional period, resigned from the post of Chairman for family and business reasons. Fortunately, this did not produce a leadership crisis, as Peter Davis was well able to take over the role. His predecessor remained a Committee member until the autumn and S.J. Benge-Abbott took over the role of Vice-Chairman which was particularly useful as his contract painting business caused him to have many relevant contacts in the various official bodies involved. In the spring edition of *The Farmers' Line*, the editorial column wished Peter Davis well. Many echoed this but few would have dared to hope that this new era would actually culminate in success. In recognition of his service, the Committee presented Peter B–A with a silver salver with an inscription which read, 'Presented to Peter Benge-Abbott by the members of the Committee in appreciation of his outstanding service as Chairman of the K&ESR Association.'

Members of the RVR Company Board still retained hopes of pursuing at least some of the project's original objectives. An Association Special General Meeting on 5 April had re-affirmed its support both for the new aims and the Company coming under the control of the Association. One of Peter Davis' first tasks was to continue delicate negotiations which were under way with the RVR Board. These concluded with the voluntary resignation of most of the Directors and Ron Cann from the post of Chairman. The Board was reconstituted at a meeting held at Tenterden Town station on Sunday 26 April, with the result that control of the Company passed into the hands of the Association. In connection with this, debts due from the RVR Company were exchanged for an issue of ordinary shares and the Association became controlling shareholder.

The make-up of the new Board was well balanced, with Peter Davis himself in the post of Chairman and Philip Shaw adding the role of Company Secretary to his existing post of Association Treasurer. The redoubtable Arthur Penny continued as a Director, thus providing continuity with the original Board, while new members from the K&ESRA Committee were Derek Dunlavey and Peter Goddard.

Elsewhere in the organization, David Kitton had had to resign, also for personal reasons, from his post of Exhibition Organizer. Rather than pass the vast amount of work to another individual, an Exhibition Group was formed under the co-ordination of Richard Halton, with each member of the Public Relations Group as an area leader for their particular locality.

Rolling stock developments were also continuing to move forward purposefully, with the acquisition of a second ex-Longmoor Birdcage brake and, significantly, the success of a bid to buy one of the LMR's Austerity tanks, No. 196 *Errol Lonsdale*. BR at first refused to deliver the the Birdcage because of a worn wheelset. Fortunately, Longmoor provided and fitted a spare free of charge and the coach soon joined its sister vehicle, plus the ex-LMR brake vans, in Tonbridge yard. BR was no longer running regular freight services on the Hastings line, and while arrangements were made for the vehicles to be transferred to Robertsbridge, the Association had to pay storage charges to BR. Thoughts had focused on the Longmoor Austerities following a casual visit to the LMR by Peter Davis. To his horror, Peter found the first of a row of Austerities being demolished by a contractor. To make matters worse, the locomotives had evidently had little use and were in almost new condition.

Peter had discussed these sad facts with Dick Beckett shortly afterwards, and from there matters quickly developed. No. 196 was also known to be in excellent condition, having been retubed not long before. The locomotive was required at Longmoor until the end of May, and it was at first hoped that delivery to Robertsbridge could be made by rail. In the event, this did not prove to be possible and *Errol Lonsdale* arrived at Rolvenden, by road, on 20 June, the first of a type which was to become almost as associated with the K&ESR as the Terriers – even if that wasn't going to please everybody.

Important though these developments were, it was in the area of overall strategy and negotiations that events suddenly started to move at a furious pace. The Ministry's appeal was heard by Justices Salmon, Phillimore and Buckley on 16 July. They upheld the appeal and the RVR Company had lost. In the judgement the opinion was expressed that although some public benefit would result from the re-opening of the railway, it was not considered sufficient to justify the inconvenience caused to the public by the seven level crossings. No appeal was made to the House of Lords.

Before the news and implications of the judgement could again plunge morale backwards some 'very rapid thinking' was done by the Association officers. Fortunately the groundwork had already been undertaken as, in the period between the two court hearings, Peter Davis and Peter B-A had been able to arrange the first meeting with the Ministry of Transport in over two years. Despite all the Association's efforts, news of the revised aims had not penetrated the august portals of St Christopher House. The Chairman and Vice-Chairman made it quite clear that changes had taken place and it was reported that the Ministry was suitably impressed.

In the aftermath of the appeal, the Association was able to capitalize on this, and Bill Deedes gave the railway another valuable service when he arranged a further meeting between the Ministry and the K&ESR. It is a matter of record, but one which needs to be repeated, that the Association was deeply grateful to him for his counsel and his assistance at that critical moment. Once again, much of the credit for what followed in the remaining months of 1970 must go to Peter Davis as well as to Peter B-A and his father. All three put in considerable behind-the-scenes effort in their negotiations with the various government and railway authorities. Similarly, due credit must go to Roger Crawford who, as Secretary, did much to revive support in Tenterden and the surrounding area. Roger, who was running a High Street business at the time, was well placed to maintain the railway's credibility among his peers as well as, sometimes quite literally, by knocking on doors to spread the word.

This immensely critical meeting with the Under Secretary of State for Railways was held on 31 July, and during the discussion the Association was unofficially informed that there were no fundamental objections to the Tenterden–Bodiam section being re-opened. According to Peter Davis the conversation went something like this:

'Can we run from Tenterden to Rolvenden?'
'Yes.'
'To Wittersham Road?'
'Yes.'
'Northiam?'
'Yes.'
'Bodiam?'
'Um, yes.'
'Junction Road?'
'No!'

The Association was asked to submit a new application for a Light Railway Transfer Order, with a broad outline of proposals, by the end of August. At that stage, only two weeks after the appeal hearing, none of the level crossings were excluded from the discussions. As a gesture of compromise, the Association suggested that the line and crossings west of Bodiam should be retained on a care and maintenance basis and only used for occasional empty-stock movements. However, under no circumstances would the K&ESR be allowed to operate a regular service to Robertsbridge.

Peter Davis wrote to the Ministry of Transport on 24 August enclosing outline proposals for a new LRTO and trusting that these would completely answer the objections to the original application. The proposals commenced with a brief statement of the new aims and the abandonment of any idea of operating beyond Bodiam. Much of the remainder was concerned with road access and car parking, and developments which have taken place were accurately foreseen. It was, for example, anticipated that Rolvenden would be unusable by car-borne passengers, and that such traffic would be better dealt with at Tenterden. Similarly, it was realized that intermediate stations such as Wittersham Road would act as temporary railheads as the line was re-opened in sections.

The schedule for re-opening was, and is now recognized to have been, wildly optimistic. It was:

Tenterden–Rolvenden 6 months
Rolvenden–Wittersham Road 18 months
Wittersham–Northiam 18 months
Northiam–Bodiam 24 months

More realistically, it was stated that a new contract would have to be negotiated with BR and that all road crossings would have to be gated.

Track maintenance party near Cranbrook Road on 30 August 1970 (Chris Lowry)

Interestingly, it was at that stage proposed to use lightweight steel gates; barriers had been abandoned entirely on the advice of the Railway Inspectorate, which considered them too complex for the K&ESR to maintain.

In typical Whitehall manner, the Ministry then lost the Association's letter. This does not appear to have come to light until Peter Davis wrote again on 18 September. The resulting bout of 'hunt the missing correspondence' which probably followed would be easily imagined by anyone who has ever worked in the public sector! The Ministry's response of 30 September fortunately continued to be positive and asked for a further copy of the first letter, at the same time suggesting that the Association consult the two county councils. The Ministry enclosed a standard questionnaire (regarding civil and mechanical engineering, proposed operation and finance) to be completed and returned to Maj. Olver at the Railway Inspectorate and suggested another meeting to discuss the K&ESR's proposals in detail. Most hearteningly, the Ministry had informed BR that it was taking the revised plans for re-opening seriously and was prepared to give them serious consideration.

The counties were contacted during the autumn of 1970. Kent readily agreed to support the Association's plans but East Sussex, in the shape of its Roads and Bridges Committee, had reservations. Negotiations around this went on into 1971, but are best summarized at this point. The County Surveyor had raised the possibility of the various road developments in the area (of which, of course, only the Robertsbridge bypass was actually built) and there was also a suggestion that Bodiam station should be moved to the east side of the level crossing. To overcome these obstacles the Association had to abandon any intention of purchasing the line west of Bodiam. In a letter to East Sussex dated 12 October, Roger Crawford wrote:

> For the Association to purchase the railway beyond Bodiam . . . is now almost completely out of the question, and we therefore withdraw our proposal so to do. I write in the hope that this news may remove any reservations which you hold concerning our aims, and that as a result the Roads and Bridges Committee might be able to recommend your Council to approve our proposals . . .

The matter was finally resolved the following August when East Sussex County Council wrote stating that the Roads and Bridges Committee had agreed to Bodiam station staying west of county road C19 and that gates should be provided at Bodiam and Northiam.

The decision to finally give up on Bodiam–Robertsbridge was not well received by everyone. Some saw the resulting isolation as an unacceptable compromise, as well as the abandonment of a section on which so much effort had been expended in earlier years. But it was the only possible compromise and there were other people who, after all the years of struggle, were happy to settle for the ten miles it would be possible to save. A deciding factor which tipped the balance for many members was BR's re-evaluation of the line at £70,000. A shorter length would obviously involve a saving on capital expenditure and £60,000 was the figure agreed on in the end.

Locomotive matters were not idle either, a second Austerity, Army No. 95 (Hunslet 3800 of 1953) which had worked at Shoeburyness, having been secured. Road transport arrangements remained to be made. In September another Peckett had been delivered to Rolvenden, but one that was a far cry from *Marcia* and much more like the products usually associated with the erstwhile Bristol company. This locomotive was the 0–6–0 saddle tank *Westminster* which had been bought for the Fovant Military Railway in 1914. She had spent her latter years with APCM near Oxford, and it was from there that she was purchased by Peter Davis and Duncan MacGregor.

The Area Groups, which were to be such a feature of the K&ESR over the twenty years which followed – albeit in varying locations – began to emerge at this stage. These groups had two interesting features: they grew around existing activities and were intended to be semi-self-supporting organizations rather than 'noggin-and-natter' gatherings. The first three areas were south-east London (Gordon Laming's group), Tunbridge Wells (Norton Brown's forestry gang) and Guildford (Richard Halton's exhibition team).

The AGM, which was to be the Association's last in its then form, was upbeat, optimistic and seemingly free of major excitements. Peter Davis opened the meeting by outlining the events of the 'momentous year' just ending, the proposals for meeting the Association's aims and the highly optimistic timescale for re-opening. (The optimism of this was actually admitted to the members present at the meeting.) Philip Shaw presented the Treasurer's report and reminded everyone of the triple-nature of the organization (Association, Trust and Company), and that the Association was seeking charitable status. If that status were achieved the Association would probably be wound up and the successor organization given a new name.

The subject of the RVR Trust Fund then came up, with a question as to whether or not it was still possible to make contributions. Once Philip Shaw had replied that this was indeed the case, Arthur Penny suggested that contributors be asked whether or not they wished to transfer their money to the new organization. The Treasurer replied that, legally, they would have to be asked what they wanted done with their monies and that it was pointless doing this until definite proposals could be put to them.

The future of the funds in the Trust were, however, a very valid point, and the following letter was circulated as soon after the AGM as 18 October.

> Dear Contributor
>
> I expect you know that the Deed under which the Trust was originally constituted came to the end of its life last February. You will also know that steps are being taken to form a Charitable Trust company which it is hoped will ultimately assume ownership of the whole or such portion of the line that we may be able to purchase, responsibility for fund-raising activities and, with your approval, absorb the funds currently invested in the Rother Valley Railway Trust Fund.
>
> The new Trust Company is not yet in being but draft memorandum and articles of Association are in the course of preparation and further details will be announced shortly. As a temporary measure, we are asking for further deposits to be made to the Rother Valley Railway Trust in order to raise the balance of the purchase price.

The letter went on to state that, as this finance was to be invested in the project in its early stages, contributors were asked if they would invest their money in the railway for a minimum period of three years from 1 January 1971. Such investment could be with or without 5 per cent interest and Philip Shaw subsequently wound the Trust up (Counsel's opinion had been taken on the matter). The written consent of everyone involved was obtained – no mean feat in itself – and most people allowed their money to be transferred over. Some even regarded it as a donation rather than a loan.

The new company was to be called the Tenterden Railway Company, a title taken from an alternative name for the South Kent Railway which was proposed in 1895 and which later partially emerged as the Headcorn extension. The company was to be 'Limited by guarantee', that is, not having a share capital, each member being required to pay an annual subscription, full members in return receiving a vote at general meetings. In the event of the winding up of the company, a member's liability would be limited to the amount of his or her subscription.

Philip Shaw wrote during this period:

> The advantage of a Guarantee Company such as this, is a merger of interests in one organization, thereby obviating the need for disparate bodies; one to acquire and operate the line, and the other to support it through a members Association. As far as is known, only one other railway company is operated on this basis, the Welshpool and Llanfair, and

Arrival of Errol Lonsdale, *the first of the K&ESR Austerities, at Rolvenden (Chris Lowry)*

in this case the company does not have a charitable status. The Bluebell, Dart Valley, Keighley, Festiniog and Talyllyn railways all have conventional limited companies with share capitals which are supported by separate member bodies, although in the case of the Festiniog, the supporters' association is also an incorporated body. The Dart Valley is primarily a commercial undertaking with some voluntary assistance.

The K&ESR scheme was the first instance of charitable status being sought by an organization which proposed to operate a working railway. The Dinting Railway Centre had charitable status but did not operate a railway as such. The advantages of charitable status were exemption from corporation tax, capital gains tax, selective employment tax (a now forgotten innovation of the Wilson government) and rates relief. Charitable status would also make it possible for people to donate money under deed of covenant with the appropriate tax relief. At that stage, it was still thought that this would be the principal route by which the capital would be raised to purchase the railway.

The long hours of hard work and the professional expertise contributed by Philip Shaw, both in reaching the objectives of establishing the company and achieving charitable status, cannot be overestimated.

Errol Lonsdale *looking resplendent in Rolvenden yard on 23 March 1971 (Dennis Ovenden)*

On 7 and 8 November a grand volunteering effort was organized by Roger Crawford under the title Operation 'Ice Breaker'. The objective was to clear as much as possible of the weed growth which stubbornly persisted on Tenterden Bank. An obvious, albeit beautifully effective, selling point was to remind everyone that a sudden influx of fifty people would achieve in one weekend what would take one volunteer a whole year. The pleasures of Saturday night in Tenterden were not overlooked, a social evening plus railway film show being organized at the Vine Inn at the top of Station Road. (The Vine was at that time becoming the favoured watering hole of the volunteer force following a change of landlord at the Eight Bells.) Entertainment was provided by the folk band the Cray Folk. 'Ice Breaker' proved to be highly successful and a large number of the normally armchair-bound actually turned up and worked. As a result, the section of the bank below Cranbrook Road looked much tidier.

Work continued at its normal, rather less hectic, pace through the winter, with its romantically white Christmas and heavy snow at New Year 1971. Down at Northiam scrub clearance was under way, while, beyond Rolvenden Norton Brown's gang had cleared the undergrowth back to the loading gauge as far as Wittersham Road, and were repeating the process across the full width between the boundary fences. The early part of 1971 saw the delivery by road of Austerity No. 95 and the P class. The P was somewhat the worse for wear after standing for more than a year, but her move to Rolvenden at least enabled work on her to be given a high priority. The Austerity, as befitted its relative newness, was in excellent condition and only required the fitting of vacuum brake equipment. A vacuum ejector and combined steam

The P class (now No. 11) departs Robertsbridge for Rolvenden by road in 1971 (Chris Lowry)

brake attachment from a 'West Country' class was used as part of this modification.

The success of Operation 'Ice Breaker' led to a repeat performance on 6 and 7 March called 'Spring Fever', also organized by Roger Crawford. Unfortunately, the weather was anything but spring-like, with freezing cold snow showers, while the protracted postal strike then in progress had made it difficult for the organizers to notify potential volunteers at all. But volunteers there were, and both newcomers and regulars were again treated to the Cray Folk at the Vine plus a second band, Vulcan's Hammer. Sunday proved to be warmer and work productive, a particular feature being the recovery of 10 to 12 tons of ballast from the section of the Headcorn extension trackbed immediately north of Tenterden Town.

Also early in the year, the railway received an informal visit from the Railway Inspectorate, which by that stage had become part of the Department of the Environment. In Peter Davis' opinion, this was one of the important turning points in K&ESR history. The original plan had been for Maj. Olver to

No. 14 Charwelton *in K&ESR Oxford blue livery in March 1971 (Dennis Ovenden)*

visit the line on a Monday when there would be no volunteers about, and be met by Peter Davis in his role as Chairman. As things turned out, Maj. Olver was required elsewhere and he delegated the job to Maj. Charles ('Freddy') Rose. During his visit, the Major was able to see the work which had been carried out on the track and the rolling stock, and was also able to tour the top section of the line both by trolley and on foot. Over lunch he was able to discuss matters arising from the technical questionnaire which the Association had returned to the Ministry some time earlier. Maj. Rose was positive and helpful throughout, and the Committee members present found him most encouraging. He in turn reported that he was 'favourably impressed with the outlook of the Committee members which seemed sensible and realistic'.

As a direct result, BR was again able to allow rolling stock movements, for engineering and training purposes, between Rolvenden level crossing and bridge 2329, with motor trolleys being allowed as far as Wittersham Road.

On Sunday 23 May 1971 members again gathered for a Special General Meeting, initially planned to be held at the Town Hall but switched at a late stage to Highbury Lane Youth Centre. Details of the new Limited Company were to be considered and resolutions were to be proposed concerning the winding up of the Association. Peter Davis was in the chair and explained the details of what was involved, this including the incorporation of the RVR Company and the RVR Trust Fund in the new organization. By the end of that afternoon the K&ESR Association had voted itself out of existence and its former members were immediately invited to join the Tenterden Railway Company Limited.

It's March 1971 and the splendid condition of Maunsell *epitomizes the K&ESR's confidence that it* will *succeed (Dennis Ovenden)*

XX

The detailed history of the Tenterden Railway Company must wait for another book and quite probably another writer. The present account would, nonetheless, be incomplete without some reference to the story since 23 May 1971, and it is the purpose of this chapter to outline the principal events and, in particular, the years up to 1974.

The objectives of the Company were:

> To preserve, restore, and operate any part or parts of the railway extending from Robertsbridge in Sussex to Tenterden in Kent, as a public exhibition and museum for the advancement of technical, historical and general education, and for the permanent preservation, display and demonstration of steam and other railway locomotives, rolling stock, equipment and relics of historical, operational and general interest and educational value.

The historical importance of the railway and the rolling stock was deemed, by the Inland Revenue and the Charity Commissioners, to be sufficient to allow the Company to be granted its desired charitable status.

The formation of the TRC provided more than just a further boost to morale. Indeed, part of the intention had been to give the battle-weary scheme (and not least its volunteers) a 'new start'. Such was the success of this that the impression has sometimes been given of the TRC coming out of nowhere, possibly with new people, and taking over a totally derelict railway and a

Derek Dunlavey (left) in discussion with Malcolm Webb at Rolvenden in 1971 (Author)

moribund project. The requirement, because of a legal technicality, for everyone to rejoin rather than transfer their membership perhaps added weight to this idea. As has been shown, this was far from the case. The TRC was one step, albeit a very significant step, in the evolution of the preservation venture. For the most part, the same people were involved. Projects begun under the Association, or even the Preservation Society, were continued by the Company.

Not that anyone should underestimate the amount of work, administrative and physical, which was required of the TRC. The efforts involved were at least equal to those demanded of the predecessor organizations and the less detailed narration here should not be taken to imply otherwise.

Even at this stage, final success could not be guaranteed and one vividly recalls Peter Davis emphasizing this point at the 23 May meeting. Negotiations for the purchase of the line dragged on through 1971 but by the end of the summer the Company had got BR's price down to the £60,000 mentioned earlier – £47,000 for the track (including the Bodiam–Junction Road stretch) and the remainder for the Tenterden–Bodiam freehold. This was all very well, but the TRC had nowhere near this capital sum.

It will be recalled that years previously a request had been made to BR for the sort of credit facility which had been extended to the Keighley and Worth Valley Railway. Hopes for such an arrangement had revived in the early 1970s as, although the TRC was not totally broke, its total liquid assets (inherited from the RVR Trust Fund and the K&ESRA) amounted to around £20,000.

Peckett 0–6–0ST Westminster *at Rolvenden in August 1971 (Dennis Ovenden)*

The problem largely solved itself, when at the end of October the BR Property Board did indeed agree to the sale on the basis of £20,000 down and a £40,000 mortgage payable over twenty-five years with interest. Naturally, the TRC accepted!

By December a draft contract had been received and had been passed to the Company's solicitor. Once again, the contract was subject to the Company obtaining a Light Railway Transfer Order.

Severance of the K&ESR from the main line had been threatened in June 1971, but the TRC had succeeded in getting a stay of execution in order to arrange for the removal of its stock from Robertsbridge yard. BR and the contractors (Thomas Ward) were co-operative but took until a snowy weekend in early 1972 to make the necessary arrangements, which at least gave time for the jungle beyond Bodiam to be adequately cleared. The actual final movement over the Robertsbridge–Bodiam section was hauled by the BTH Ford diesel in an operation reminiscent of the legendary 'flight of the rolling stock', which had taken place between Newport and Haven Street, on the Isle of Wight, some months earlier.

By the autumn Peter Davis had signed the sale contract with BR and the conveyancing process had got as far as exchange of contracts. The K&ESR was at this point able to take maximum publicity advantage from an event long awaited by Southern enthusiasts – the centenary of the Brighton Terriers. Honours were evenly, and fraternally, shared with the Bluebell Railway,

Final clearance train from Robertsbridge at Northiam in January 1972 (Chris Lowry)

owners of the other 'oldest' Terrier, No. 36 *Fenchurch*. The old debate about whether No. 36 was actually older than *Bodiam*, or vice versa, got an airing in the national railway press, and it was, of course, proved that *Fenchurch* was the first in service. The K&ESR celebrations of this event were held during the afternoon of Saturday 4 November 1972.

The ceremony began at 2.30 p.m., when No. 3 herself steamed into the newly rebuilt platform at Rolvenden with a two-coach train. She was welcomed by the Mayor of Tenterden, Alderman R.J. Collison, and Peter Davis in his role as Chairman. Ron Wheele was, naturally, present together with his brother Vic, while on the footplate were Charlie Kentsley and Jack Hoad. Jack was an interesting acquisition by the TRC. He was one of the youngest, and one of the last surviving, drivers of the original K&ESR Company. In 1972 he was still working as a driver on the Southern Region. Also in steam were the USA *Maunsell*, Austerity No. 196 and the then recently acquired Norwegian Mogul. Traction engines, other vintage vehicles and a miniature railway (supplied by the Tunbridge Wells group) were present, as were representatives from the Romney, Hythe and Dymchurch and Bluebell railways. It would be the Bluebell's turn to take up the Terrier celebrations the following day. All three lines, together with the Sittingbourne and Kemsley, were soon to go into publicity partnership as 'Steam Lines South-east', a far cry from the earlier years of defection and rivalry.

The crowd which gathered on that November afternoon was satisfactorily large, so large in fact that the field hired for use as a car park rapidly filled up and a second had to be hired at short notice. Apart from those already

Work on Tenterden Town platform, ready for re-opening in 1971. Today the public can walk through the gap being dug to get to the station buffet (built much later, where the car is standing). Note the Mess coach in the background (Chris Lowry)

mentioned, many of the line's long-term supporters were present. At the Special General Meeting Mr Cannon-Rogers had made an impassioned plea, that with the creation of the new Company the K&ESR heal some of its self-inflicted wounds and welcome back those who were estranged from it. In particular, he mentioned Robin Doust and the great efforts he had made in earlier years. It was pleasing to find that Robin was present at the Terrier centenary. He was able to join the TRC and subsequently worked as a volunteer on the railway until he emigrated in 1975. He has, however, remained a member, in contact with many of his old friends, and returns to England annually.

Overall, 4 November was a great, particularly financial, success. It was said at the time to have been the railway's first 'real' event. It was a valuable preview of the future.

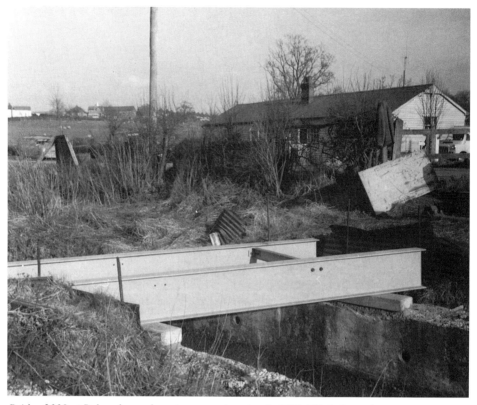

Bridge 2330 at Rolvenden undergoing reconstruction in 1971 (Chris Lowry)

In December application was made for the Light Railway Transfer Order. The Department of the Environment returned the application for minor amendment. There then started a period of negotiations with the Kent River Authority, which was still concerned about possible obstruction of the watercourses. Matters now had a feeling of *déjà vu* about them, as the contract was conditional on the granting of the LRTO by April and the deadline was approaching. The application was finally lodged with the Department of the Environment in mid-March. Maj. Rose paid a further informal visit on the 28th of that month, the Company being grateful for his very much valued advice.

Much of the preceding news was reported in the spring edition of the magazine which now appeared as Volume 1, Number 1 of the *Tenterden Terrier*. It was, in fact, almost *The Farmers' Line* format with a new front cover (the adverts on the back page were the same ones that had been appearing for years). The new-style *Tenterden Terrier* that went on to become a leader among steam railway house magazines emerged in the summer of 1974, a rather neat illustration that, like many things in life, the history of preservation on the K&ESR has had few sharp breaks, rather a series of gradual developments. The one-sheet newsletters being produced at that

A later stage in the rebuilding of bridge 2330 (Chris Lowry)

period, which carried the latest information, also survived, became *The Rooter*, and carried on bringing up-to-date news to Company members through the 1980s and into the 1990s.

The statutory notices regarding the LRTO, published in the *London Gazette* and the local papers, brought forth a small number of objections and the Company, its solicitors and the parliamentary agents set about achieving the withdrawal of these. As during the first LRTO application, events then started overrunning the deadline and, as on that earlier occasion, BR agreed to an extension. Peter Davis, with the assistance of Peter Barrett (a Board member and solicitor), was responsible for negotiating the K&ESR out of this critical situation and initially the contract was extended by one month, then until 31 August and subsequently for a period beyond that.

The volunteers were chafing at the bit by this time, but the Committee adopted a policy of pursuing matters in as low a key as possible and succeeded in getting all the objections withdrawn. This led to protective clauses (such as those safeguarding the interests of the Kent River Authority) being written into the order which as a result became a Transfer and Amendment Order.

Summer turned into autumn, the possibility of operating during the 1973 season disappeared and it was not until late in the year that matters reached a head. Then, it actually happened. On 8 November the Department of the Environment made The BR Board (K&ESR) Light Railway (Transfer and Amendment) Order 1973, this statutory instrument taking effect eleven days later. The £20,000 balance of the deposit having been paid, powers to operate the K&ESR between Tenterden and Bodiam passed to the TRC on Monday 19 November 1973. This may be regarded as the actual moment of independence, although the Company's solicitors did not complete the purchase until later in the month. To many people, although on an admittedly emotional level, this gave legal form to something which had happened twelve years earlier. The long looked-for news was announced to

Sutton *and the Norwegian by the water crane at Tenterden in 1973 (Chris Lowry)*

the members by the then Secretary, Stephen Bennett, in a newsletter dated 3 December.

There was one final, symbolic act of severance from the national network, although by that stage the track west of Bodiam had been ripped up. The single-line staff, and with it the key to all the point locks, was collected from Robertsbridge signal-box for the last time.

Although the TRC possessed operating powers, permission to run a passenger service remained subject to a formal inspection by the Department of the Environment. Various tasks remained to be completed, including a variety of items of track work, the replacement of the crossing gates at Rolvenden, final attention to the reconstructed bridge 2330 and the tasks necessary to finish the rail fencing alongside Tenterden station loop. This fence replaced the coal staithes which had been a feature of the yard since the 1950s and which had been built for the Tenterden Trading Company on the site of the second platform. All this activity took place during the period of the infamous 'three-day week' industrial-cum-constitutional crisis and as the dark winter evenings, made darker by power cuts, set in. On Boxing Day, three 'members only' special trains were run, with *Sutton* hauling two coaches. A simple timetable was adhered to and some three hundred people were successfully carried. It was a useful prelude to what was about to happen.

Maj. Rose carried out the formal inspection on Monday 21 January and passed the K&ESR to operate through Rolvenden and up to bridge 2331, without further inspection as the track was refurbished. He also authorized the line's axle loading to be raised to 17 tons, thus allowing the USAs and the Austerities to be used. In addition, stops would not be required at Cranbrook Road and Tenterden level crossings, a most valuable concession which would allow the bank to be tackled without the risk of stalling on the steepest gradients, and propelling was permitted from Rolvenden to the limit of operation, which removed the need for a second locomotive to be always in steam.

Later in the week of 21 January, Philip Shaw phoned me about a matter left over from my days of working in the museum. After a discussion of the business in hand Philip added, almost as an aside, 'Oh, by the way we're re-opening on Sunday week.' This news was half-expected, but the recollection is, nevertheless, of a slightly stunned feeling mingling with the need for a few moments of warm, quiet reflection. It was not next year any more, it was next week.

Sunday 3 February 1974 dawned cold and bright, the sun streaming from a huge Wealden sky. The first service was scheduled for 11.30 a.m. but, despite some press publicity, it wasn't until after 11.00 that, much to everyone's relief, passengers started to turn up. This culminated in a last-minute rush and then, with a blast on its air horns, the railcar, No. 20, left on the historic journey. It seemed appropriate that an innovation for the K&ESR, actually mentioned at the inaugural meeting in 1961, should form the first train.

After going down to the limit of operation, No. 20 stopped at Rolvenden, where No. 10, *Sutton*, was attached and headed the railcar back up Tenterden

The railcar on Tenterden Bank in 1974 (Chris Lowry)

Bank. *Sutton* plus two of the Maunsell coaches worked what many people, including the press, regarded as the first 'real' train, the 12.30 p.m. This train was very crowded, and drew out to the accompaniment of much whistling by No. 10 and the crack of celebratory detonators. The footplate crew were, with great regard for historical continuity, Jack Hoad, Colin Edwards and Mike Artlett. To complete the picture, Bill Austen was also present in one of the coaches. Forty minutes later the train returned, *Sutton* making a storming ascent of the bank.

For the 2.30 p.m. train, a third of the Maunsell coaches were added, together with No. 17 *Arthur*, which was already in steam as the stand-by loco with Mike Hart and Dick Dickson on the footplate, at the uphill end of the train. John Hilton took Jack Hoad's place on No. 10 during the afternoon. There were two further trains, the 1.30 p.m. as well as an additional working at 4.30 p.m., and during the day over eight hundred passengers were carried. In a manner perhaps typical of the waywardness of the K&ESR, the public had been again invited to travel its metals while the strikes of that winter rumbled on; being a Sunday, the rest of the railway network was shut down and there was a shortage of coal. The K&ESR services were, in fact, the only trains to run in Kent that day.

During the morning, I had met Robin Doust on Tenterden Town station platform. We both expressed the feeling that after the effort-filled years and all that had happened this low-key event was something of an anticlimax. But it was somehow appropriate; a ceremonial re-opening a matter of days after the final inspection would have been intrusive. All the rolling stock used on 3 February went back to the rumbustious days of the mid-1960s (even the Woolwich coach was being moved around) and the first trains took their place in the line of early steamings that had begun the first time *Gervase* had moved under her own power in 1962. Perhaps it was during the evening, while watching ITN's coverage of the day, with its footage of the 12.30 p.m. return working at Cranbrook Road, that it sunk in that the K&ESR had re-opened.

Having seen the railway through to its moment of triumph, and been much in evidence on 3 February, Peter Davis resigned from the post of Chairman. He was succeeded by Stephen Bennett.

It was never planned as such, but, in retrospect, the unofficial opening appeared something of a swansong for the early years. The official opening, on Saturday 2 June 1974, with Bill Deedes performing the ceremony and the Cranbrook Town Band present, seemed to belong to the TRC and the years that were to follow.

The limit of operation was gradually extended south-west. Bridge 1029 was replaced after much effort – the site is now quite unrecognizable as the same spot one knew in the 1960s – and services to Wittersham Road commenced in 1977. The railway had, in the interim, received government funding via the Job Creation Programme designed to combat unemployment. The limit of operation reached Hexden Bridge in 1983. From 1981, an isolated, occasional service was run for a while between Bodiam and the new Dixter Halt (near Great Dixter House). This made some use of *Marcia* but more particularly of an ex-BR four-wheeled AC railbus.

An irony among the many ironies in this story was the absence of track between Hexden Bridge and Northiam for most of the 1980s. It had been lifted for its scrap value exactly as envisaged in the plan to re-open the line from the Robertsbridge end! Trains returned to Northiam in 1990 after further outside assistance, which, in the vastly changed economic climate, had been received not from the government but from a television company. At the time of writing, work still continues for the line to be re-opened to Bodiam.

The history of the K&ESR remains a rapidly changing story. This book has set out to tell part of that story – how, as the title states, the Preservation Society, and subsequently the Association, 'held the line' from 1961 to 1971. And what of the people who accomplished these things? Many who worked on the line would readily admit that the K&ESR left a most profound impression on them. For some, the experience led elsewhere in the steam railway movement. It was, for instance, a matter of some pride to the friends of the person concerned that, when, in April 1974, the 'Merchant Navy' class *Clan Line* left Ashford to begin the Southern contribution to the revival of main-line steam, her back-up crew included a young man who had begun to

Hail smiling morn. No. 10 at the head of the first public steam train on 3 February 1974
(Kentish Express)

learn his trade with the K&ESR Loco Department. Ex-volunteers have become managers of other lines or have been instrumental in the establishment of new schemes. Some have taken their interest and their skills to other railways when circumstances have caused them to move from south-east England – a steam line as far away as Australia has had a former K&ESR volunteer. There are railway photographers and even a few writers.

But others again have, in one way or another, remained with the K&ESR, some to become leaders of the organization, and there is now a sizable railway community in the Tenterden area. There is a saying on the K&ESR that there are those who come and who stay, those who come for a time and then go on their way and that there is also a third group – those who leave for a while but one day, sooner or later, come back. The appeal is strong, and it only need take a tune on the radio or the arrival of the *Tenterden Terrier* to send minds back down the years and across the miles.

But the final word must go to Alan Dixon who, in 1972 and after the tide had turned, wrote:

> . . . credit for the achievement must be shared by everyone involved with the project . . . those whose vision it was in the first instance, long ago in the spring of 1961; those whose unflagging practical effort has created physical progress where there would otherwise have been none; those who have come and gone, but who have nevertheless given something of themselves to the railway.

Notes

1. Mr Pickin states this passage should read, '. . . BR could not transfer a section of the railway from Robertsbridge to Rolvenden to the Association's company . . .' In the light of Mr Pickin's opinions on powers available under the Light Railways Act 1896 and the scope for misunderstanding at any general meeting, this seems plausible.

2. A then Committee member who was present at the meeting has told me that P. B–A was waiting for the Committee to say something and vice versa. Any discussion on the possible course of events had either side taken the initiative would be pointless conjecture.

3. During that weekend unusually heavy rain spread across a wide area of south-east England, causing flooding in places where it would not normally be expected. These weather conditions were a contributory factor in the government's later decision to construct the Thames Barrier.

Appendices

Appendix 1: Circulars addressed to members prior to the 1964 Annual General Meeting.

Since the circulation of the *Rother Valley Railway* No. 6 a short time ago, discussions with Mr G. Pickin, the backer referred to in the magazine and accompanying enclosures, has considerably clarified the position with regard to his intentions. Since it has not proved possible so far to raise the necessary capital in any other way, the sale of the railway along the lines indicated below is being proceeded with.

It would appear that Mr Pickin has a number of theories on how any railway should be operated to the best advantage, and he wishes to use the K&ESR as a test line on which to try these out. He has two principal intentions, which are as follows. The first is that he believes that if a sufficiently intensive service is operated, that passengers will be attracted to use it. The second is that with the gradual closure of freight depots in the area round the railway, the K&ESR could become a centralized freight delivery railhead for much of Kent and Sussex.[1]

The first of these intentions he proposes to achieve by running a service of some nine trains each way daily, using some kind of railcar. Plans for the second are not yet formulated and will depend to some extent on the pattern of freight depot closures in the area, and on the extent to which BR will co-operate in allowing freight traffic to be carried on the K&ESR.

Coupled with these main proposals are a number of lesser ones, which include the organization of displays of static and operating museum pieces, consisting of locomotives and rolling stock, and it is also Mr Pickin's intention to economize to a very great extent on staffing. He proposes to rely almost exclusively on volunteer labour for the maintenance of the track, having only a paid supervisor to train volunteers and check on their work. Footplate staff he proposes shall consist of a driver and fireman only on steam-hauled trains, and a driver on the railcars. He proposes installing lifting barriers on the level crossing on the Hastings road at Robertsbridge, and is pressing strongly to purchase outright the goods yard at Robertsbridge now that BR are no longer using this for regular traffic.

Many of these proposals are broadly in line with the Society's own declared intentions, but a number are not. The principal points of difference lie in the intensity of the proposed passenger service, which is one of Mr Pickin's basic plans. The Society has always believed that a service of four to five trains each way daily would be the maximum the line could ever support, and it is strongly felt that the operation of the railway with a service such as that proposed by Mr Pickin will only result in a very considerable loss. The Society further considers that it will become apparent when the railway commences operation, that more staff will be required than Mr Pickin considers to be necessary. However, since both these points are king pins in his plans, and it is to test them that he is financing the purchase of the railway, they represent the probable basis on which the restoration of services on the line will, in fact, be accomplished in the first instance.

Mr Pickin has stated that he would prefer the existing Society to be wound up, and for it to be incorporated in the K&ESR Company, of which he is now principal shareholder, and this proposal will be placed before the AGM. He will invite members to continue to pay an annual subscription of £1, by virtue of which they would become subscription members of the Company, and also to purchase ordinary shares in his Company, which would confer normal shareholders' rights.

This proposal has been considered in some detail by members of the Society's Committee, and for a number of reasons they advise against its acceptance. Firstly, for the reasons stated above, the Committee feels that if the line is run as outlined above, that a considerable loss on working will be made, and that investment in the Company in the form of shares would be likely to bring no return. Secondly, in view of the Committee's feeling that Mr Pickin's plans may not prove to be commercially feasible in practice, [they] feel that the Society should remain in existence as an independent but associated body to continue operation of the line by taking over the Company. With this in mind a number of possible sources of finance are still being actively investigated, and the existing Appeal Trust remains open for the time being for further offers of support, as also does the appeal for bank guarantees which was opened in the latest *Rother Valley Railway*. It is further felt that the continued existence of the Society will enable its members to continue to play a more active part in the running of the line than might be the case if the existing arrangements for organizing working parties, publicity, etc. were to be taken over by the Company's officials, who will in any case have a full-time job in running the business side of the railway.

The Society's Committee therefore feels that a more satisfactory arrangement will be for Mr Pickin to carry through the purchase of the railway himself, as he is in a position to do, and for the Society to provide as much assistance as possible in the actual running of the railway. It has, however, been suggested that members who are anxious to have a financial stake in the railway, might do this by purchasing some of the necessary rolling stock required for the operation of the railway. In this way they will still be providing financial assistance to the railway, but this will take the form that the material for which the money is used will remain their property, and in the event of any kind of calamity overtaking the railway as a whole, the material could be sold, and the money returned. Alternatively, in the event of the Society ultimately acquiring control of the railway directly, the stock will then still be available for use in the way already envisaged for the Locomotive Trust's stock, which is already on the line. In either event, it is proposed that a small but reasonable rental be charged for stock used in this way, so that there would be a guaranteed return on the capital used in its purchase, such return being far from certain on money directly invested in the railway Company controlled by Mr Pickin.

It must, however, be emphasized that the above proposals are purely tentative, and that it will be up to members to decide at the AGM in July. The only facts which are completely definite are that Mr Pickin is controlling the K&ESR Company, and that he is now continuing negotiations with BR to purchase the railway. He has said that his negotiations may still take some weeks, and now that the Society no longer has any direct say in this direction, it is difficult to forecast how long it will be before services can begin again, although he is making every effort to expedite the matter.

In the meantime we are left in the position of knowing that the railway will certainly re-open, probably but not necessarily, during the next six months. Now it is certain that trains will run again, the more extensive works of rehabilitation are being undertaken. During the next two weeks, an application of weedkiller will be made to the whole line, and an order has been placed for new telephone wire to replace that which has been stolen during the last three years. Five station platforms are being rebuilt, and heavy repair work is being undertaken by the Society. Since it is imperative that the railway be fit for use as soon as the sale arrangements have been completed, it is essential that the projects mentioned be carried through immediately. The Committee therefore earnestly hope that all members will continue to support the Society as they have done in the past, particularly as the eventual re-opening of the line is a certainty. Please renew your subscription if you have not done so already, and if you can possibly get to the line at weekends to lend a hand in restoration work, you will be most welcome. There is already a hard core of some thirty to forty volunteers who turn up regularly, and they have carried out a tremendous amount of work, as those of you who have seen the railway recently will realize. However, there remains a continuing need for further help, particularly during the next few weeks when so much has to be done.

The letter, signed by Robin Doust as Hon. Secretary, ended with thanks to those members who had already renewed their subscriptions, appealed for patience on the part of those who had written asking for specific information, and thanked members for their support over the previous twelve months. There was also the following statement as an addenda:

Since the preparation of this letter, Mr Pickin has forwarded his own details on how he envisages the purchase and running of the railway. These are reproduced exactly as received:

G. Pickin's Proposals

The Company shall be a Company limited by guarantee but having a share capital, so as to incorporate both shareholders and subscription members. Mr Pickin will have a controlling interest, by reason of owning most of the shares. If that proportion of the Society's assets which corresponds to members joining the Company is transferred, their existing subscriptions will suffice until next year, while life members will be given one share. There will be no loan capital, and members will be in two classes – shareholders and subscription members, the latter to pay £1 per year (juniors 10s). Each subscription member will have one vote. On a poll each share will probably carry 10 votes, being of the denomination of £20. The details of the constitution shall be worked out by a general meeting. There will be no restrictions on membership, subject to Mr Pickin's retaining control and to a highly democratic expulsion clause.

A highly democratic constitution is proposed, with powers for a general meeting to order the directors about by ordinary resolution and with power for 5 per cent of members to summon a general meeting and distribute circulars. There will be the most democratic form of proxy voting and postal ballots. This will be the proper method of questioning policy, and proposals which have been made for separate pressure groups to operate from Tenterden will be regarded with great disfavour. The company will organize its own supporters, to whom favour will be shown, to prevent coercion by such groups, which it is anticipated would consist of strikes to compel the employment of 7 unnecessary platelayers and the like. Members are welcome to employ additional staff and do other expensive things if they pay for them, but severe reprisals will be taken against any attempt to coerce the Company by means outside the constitution.

Mr Pickin has no desire to be a Fuehrer, and is seldom in England, but no attempt to nullify the effect of his control will be permitted and representations made by outside bodies, otherwise than under railway apartheid, will be treated as being made by the spokesman alone, which experience teaches is likely to be their sole origin.

The principle of railway apartheid is to permit other societies to have full rights in their own areas and run trains over the whole line, without having any rights in the railway as a whole, but Tenterden and Rolvenden will be reserved for the Company.

Members of the Company will be given a large say in policy, but Mr Pickin reserves the right to control matters concerning his money and service to country people.

The principle to be adopted is 'Service to the public and a good time had by all.' The railway will be both a preservation and a practical one. Its management will be on a highly economical basis, and BR standards, which are foreign to the traditions of the line, will not be adopted.

It is proposed to operate a Monday to Friday service of about nine trains a day each way. Except for mixed trains and when enthusiasts can be expected, a railcar will be used, a steam one being built if practicable.

The horse bus[2] will be reinstated and a bus service introduced to Littlestone in summer to attract narrow-gauge enthusiasts. Good road services will also be introduced. Old first-class coaches will be used for second-class passengers. Catering and camping accommodation will be provided.

Mr Pickin's economical method of operation is the answer to the Beeching plan, and particular resistance will be made to expensive methods for this reason.

Approaches to the Ministry of Transport for a reduction in price have already been made and will be continued. Obtaining any further Light Railway Order will be resisted.

Efforts will be made to make the line as attractive as possible for enthusiasts and the general public. Rules will be kept to a minimum though really important ones will be strictly enforced. A preservationist policy will be adopted, and free storage facilities will be granted to outsiders.

It is hoped to relay the track to St Michaels.

Notes

1. Mr Pickin proposed to use Junction Road for a Hastings goods service
2. Mr Pickin was referring to the K&ESR horse bus service which had, in the Col. Stephens era, operated between Tenterden Town station and Smallhythe. He was not, however, referring to the vehicle which had survived on K&ESR property to be nationalized along with the railway and was, in 1964, in Clapham Museum. That would have been too small for his intentions.

Appendix 2: Peter Davis' Report on the rolling stock of the K&ESR

INTRODUCTION

For many years we have acquired locomotives and rolling stock in a haphazard manner, mainly through the offices of the K&ESR Locomotive Trust and the generosity of certain members and industrial concerns.

There are fifteen locomotives resting on the line, of which three are capable of working trains over the whole line, three are confined to the Rolvenden–Tenterden section because of their weight and the remainder, with the exception of the BTH diesel, are virtually 'museum pieces'. This state of affairs leaves us in a weak position to face the steamless years ahead, as in my opinion the success of this enterprise will lie in its ability to provide steam traction for many years to come. However, there is no doubt that the 'museum pieces' are attractive to the public and if properly prepared and displayed will be a useful asset.

The basic problem is the predominance of 'museum pieces' and the lack of working units. This must be rectified immediately, as it is unlikely that suitable locomotives will be available after the next eighteen months and those that are may well command unrealistic prices. On this basis it would be foolish to turn down offers of any steam locomotive, even if only to swell the ranks of the museum stock.

THE CURRENT SITUATION

The following locomotives are resting on the line at present:

Category A – Suitable for use over the whole line

No.	Name	Owner	Acquisition
3	*Bodiam*	R. Wheele	Permanent loan
50	*Sutton*	L. Borough of Sutton	Loan
14	*Charwelton*	K&ESR Loco Trust	Outright purchase

Category B – Suitable for use between Rolvenden and Tenterden

No.	Name	Owner	Acquisition
	Maunsell	K&ESR	Outright purchase
	Wainwright	Loco Trust	Outright purchase
	H Class	H Class Trust	Outright purchase

Category C – Diesel Traction Units

No.	Name	Owner	Acquisition
16	BTH d/electric	K&ESRA	Presented by AEI Ltd
20	GWR railcar		Outright purchase

The remaining locomotives fall into the museum category, with the possible exception of *Arthur*, which might be useful for light duties.

No.	Name	Owner	Acquisition
10	*Gervase*	K&ESR Loco Trust	Presented by Standard Brick Co.
11	*Dom*		Presented by Standard Brick Co.
12	*Marcia*	R. Beckett	Outright purchase
15	*Hastings*	K&ESR Loco Trust	Outright purchase
	King	⎫	Outright purchase
	Minnie	⎪	Presented by Skinningrove I.S. Co.
		⎬ Industrial Loco Preservation Group	
	Met	⎪	Presented by CEGB
	Arthur	⎭	Presented by APCM Ltd

It is quite clear that more locomotives of categories A & B are essential if regular steam traction is to survive for more than five or six years. Bearing in mind that standard types stand a better chance of survival, it is fortunate that we have pairs of both Terriers and USAs, potentially our most useful types. There is a possibility of widening this scope by acquisition of one or more Terriers from Butlins and loan of the USA from the SLP Co. Additionally, it is likely that we shall have first refusal on the Bowaters P class, together with numerous spares. Consequently, it is essential to make similar arrangements regarding the P class at Hodson's Mill. I am at present negotiating for two widely differing but useful locomotives from my employers. Also, the NCB (Kent Division) and the Ford Motor Co. each have three identical locomotives which might be worth investigating.

These suggestions can be summarised as follows:

Category A

3 x AIX (Terriers) at present the property of Butlins
1 x P class at present the property of Bowaters
1 x P class at present the property of Hodson's Mill
1 x Peckett 0–6–0ST at present the property of APCM Ltd

Category B

1 x USA class at present the property of SLP Co.
3 x Avonside 0–6–0ST at present the property of NCB (Kent Division)
1 x Hudswell-Clark 0–6–0T at present the property of APCM Ltd
3 x Peckett 0–6–0ST at present the property of Ford Motor Co. Ltd

Recommendations

In order to increase the available locomotive stock and generally improve our public image, I recommend adoption of the following proposals:

1. That No. 50 is purchased from LB Sutton without delay.
2. That the SLP Co. are offered accommodation for their USA class locomotive (and other rolling stock).
3. That Butlins are approached with a view to securing one or more of their Terriers.
4. That the NCB and the Ford Motor Co. are approached regarding their 0–6–0STs.
5. That a firm arrangement is made for the eventual purchase of Hodson's P class.
6. That all 'museum' locomotives are removed from the railway's number series, eventually to be replaced by new acquisitions.
7. That the 'museum' locomotives are properly prepared and displayed as the basis of an Industrial Locomotive Museum. This would be an unique collection and could well be maintained by our younger and less skilled

collection and could well be maintained by our younger and less skilled members.

8. That owners of locomotives on the line are called together to discuss the basis of an agreement for their use, if necessary, by the operating company.

Among Peter Davis' concluding remarks was the following: '. . . this is an ambitious outlook at this stage of the proceedings but I feel that failure to adopt these or similar policies will jeopardize our future efficiency and earning capacity.'

The report included a number of suggestions which did not come to pass and did not anticipate a number of developments which did take place. It was, nevertheless, the foundation on which the Tenterden Railway Company's locomotive stud was built.

Bibliography and Sources

Books

D. L. Bradley, *The Locomotives of the London, Brighton and South Coast Railway*, RCTS, 1969.

D.L. Bradley, *Locomotives of the Southern Railway, Part 1*, RCTS, 1975.

D. Cole, *The Kent and East Sussex Railway,* Union Publications, 1963.

R. Crombleholme, *Kent and East Sussex Railway Stockbook*, Union Publications on behalf of the Southern Locomotive Preservation Company, 1965.

A.G. Dixon and A.E. Loosley, *Locomotives and Stock on the Farmers' Line*, K&ESRA, 1970.

A. Dixon and D. Wilson, *Stockbook, the Locomotives and Stock of the K&ESR*, Tenterden Railway Company.

S.R. Garrett, *The Kent and East Sussex Railway* (1st edn), Oakwood Press, 1972.

J.L. Smith, *Rails to Tenterden*, Len's of Sutton, 1967.

Periodicals

Various issues of *Railway Magazine*, *Railway World*, the *Farmer's Line*, *Rother Valley Railway*, *Tenterden Terrier*, the *Guardian, Kent and Sussex Courier*, *Kentish Express*, *Kent Messenger* and *Hansard*.

Archive Material

The archives of the Tenterden Railway Company (as successor to the K&ESR Preservation Society, the K&ESR Association and the Rother Valley Railway Company).

The personal collections (as well as the recollections) of the author and several of the individuals mentioned in the acknowledgements.

Index